VOID

Library of
Davidson College

Character & Structure in the English Novel

Robert Higbie

Character
&
Structure
in the English Novel

University Presses of Florida
University of Florida Press
Gainesville

University Presses of Florida is the central agency for scholarly publishing of the State of Florida's university system. Its offices are located at 15 NW 15th Street, Gainesville, FL 32603. Works published by University Presses of Florida are evaluated and selected for publication by a faculty editorial committee of any one of Florida's nine public universities: Florida A&M University (Tallahassee), Florida Atlantic University (Boca Raton), Florida International University (Miami), Florida State University (Tallahassee), University of Central Florida (Orlando), University of Florida (Gainesville), University of North Florida (Jacksonville), University of South Florida (Tampa), University of West Florida (Pensacola). Orders for books published by all member presses of University Presses of Florida should be addressed to University Presses of Florida, 15 NW 15th Street, Gainesville FL 32603.

Library of Congress Cataloging-in-Publication Data

Higbie, Robert.
   Character and structure in the English novel.

"A University of Florida book."
Bibliography: p.
Includes index.
   1. English fiction—History and criticism.
2. Characters and characteristics in literature.
3. Fiction—Technique. I. Title.
PR830.C47H5   1984   823'.009'27   84-3533
ISBN 0-8130-0786-0

Copyright © 1984 by the Board of Regents of the State of Florida

All rights reserved

Typography by G & S Typesetters, Austin, Texas

Printed in U.S.A. on acid-free paper

acknowledgments ~~~~~~~~~~~~~

I would like to thank the following for their help, advice, and moral support: Merritt E. Lawlis, William Burgan, Alistair M. Duckworth, Bernard J. Paris, R. Brandon Kershner, and my wife, Kate.

contents

Introduction: Developing a Syncretic Criticism   1
1. Character as a Function of a Basic Narrative Structure: The Linguistic Model   13
2. Character as a Function of Sublimation: The Psychological Model   23
3. The Novel as a Transformation of Basic Narrative Structure: The Historical Context   39
4. *Clarissa* and the Transformation of Character   60
5. The Conflict between Character Intensity and Form: Richardson, Fielding, and Austen   83
6. Austen and the Conscious Character   98
7. Dickens and the Unresolved Character   121
Epilogue: The Decline of Character Intensity   164
Notes   183
Works Cited   195
Index   203

Developing a Syncretic Criticism

introduction

*I*N the English novel of the eighteenth and nineteenth centuries one finds a special kind of characterization: writers emphasize the individuality, even the eccentricity of their characters, taking delight in those characters as ends in themselves. Although one occasionally encounters similar characterization in earlier writers—especially Shakespeare—this attitude is particularly typical of the classic English novel and reached its highest development there, exercising considerable influence over the novel's form. In this study I examine this kind of characterization, seeking an understanding of the techniques writers used in creating characters of this sort, of the ways we respond to those techniques, and of the relationship of this characterization to the other aspects of the novel.

I think we cannot fully understand complex, highly developed characterization like this unless we see it in relation to characterization in general. We need to be aware of the basic kinds of literary character out of which complex characters have evolved and of the ways complex characters are related to those predecessors. I have therefore adopted a dual approach, focusing not only on the particular, on the details of characterization in complex works, but also on the general and theoretical, on the basic question of what a literary character is. The following chapters begin with this basic consideration and proceed toward the particular, trying to develop a way of understanding complex characters in terms of the fundamental character-functions from which they seem to have developed. It is no accident, then, that almost every chapter is longer than the preceding ones it is building on.

Because I am trying to see the details of particular works in relation to narrative in general, it has seemed best to try to bring to bear several critical approaches and to synthesize them in a way that will enable me to relate the particular to the general. The main approaches I have borrowed from are the structuralist, the Freudian, and the sociological. However, I have not embraced any of these without reservations, since I wished to adapt them to each other. Literature is too complex for any one theory to explain adequately; each approach needs to accommodate others. In adapting these theories, then, I have rejected that part of each which seeks to exclude other approaches, claiming to provide a sufficient explanation on its own. I have tried to remain aware that no one approach can offer final answers, that each needs help from others to minimize its inherent uncertainty. If we limit theories in this way, I think we can combine them into one unified though complex system. Probably no critical theory can do full justice to literature, but at least we can try to develop an approach that allows for as much complexity as we can manage.

The critics who seem to me most successful in dealing with the most basic kinds of character are Northrop Frye and French structuralists such as Todorov and Greimas, building on Propp's pioneering work with fairy tales. Some recent critics, I think, have been too quick to dismiss structuralism and move on to other fashions without pausing to understand the structuralist approach thoroughly and take what it has to offer of value. Therefore I will explain what I understand by the term *structuralism* and what I think we can learn from it. The structuralism I mean (not practiced by all who call themselves structuralists) starts from the hypothesis that the mind has a basic way of structuring experience which we can relate to its innate capacity to make language. The process by which we organize what is in our minds is closely related to the process by which we make language, and so the structure underlying language should also be apparent beneath other mental activities such as story-telling. And just as language only manifests this structure through a generative process of transformations, we should expect other activities to involve analogous transformations.

This concept of basic structure is not the same as that postulated by every structuralist. What I am trying to describe is that fundamental part of the mind that makes language—and makes narrative. It may be analogous to the deep structure of sentences in Chomskyan linguistics, but it is more general and basic than that. The critic who, I think, has been most successful in describing different kinds of narrative as transformations of a sort of basic structure is not a structuralist but Northrop Frye, with his concept of narrative as a displacement of myth. I owe much to Frye; nevertheless, it seems to me that his system lacks the theoretical precision and explanatory power that the structuralists are at least attempting to offer. The underlying pattern he postulates is not very clear, nor is it clearly related to the working of the mind. Therefore I have tried to combine Frye's sense of the evolution of narrative with the structuralist concept that narrative patterns can be seen in terms of a basic mental (and linguistic) structure.

Like other generalizations about the mind, structuralism probably oversimplifies. And it can only be hypothetical; we can never be certain we know what a basic structure is, or even whether such things exist at all. But it does seem likely that the mind has some innate way of patterning experience—that, as George Steiner puts it, the unconscious is "relationally structured."[1] At the least, this is a useful hypothesis, one that can enable us to make some statements about character, and so I have used it in this study. However, I have tried to remain aware that it is only a hypothesis and therefore have tried to restrict myself to the simplest, most basic concept of structure. In my first chapter I describe what I think this structure might be like and define the basic characters found in simple narrative in terms of such a structure.

One advantage of the structuralist theory of character is that it allows us to bypass the mimetic approach. It is often attractive to think of literary characters as real people; many critics, from A. C. Bradley to W. J. Harvey and Bernard J. Paris, have preferred this approach.[2] Certainly many novelists want us to think their characters are real. But there are also many characters to which we cannot do justice if we demand that they seem real—characters like the simple plot-function characters the structuralists often analyze, but also more complex characters in romances and other kinds of fiction which are not highly mimetic. Indeed all characters must be conventional to some extent, not merely imitations of reality. Even in the case of "realistic" characters, the critic is seriously hampered if he is unable to see the character *as* a character, not a person. The feeling that a character is "real" may be an appropriate response to a given work. But the critic needs to be able to analyze his response and the textual devices that caused it, and to say that a character is "real" precludes such an analysis; it provides no terms to use and even denies that there are a text and a response to analyze. We need to understand what we feel when we feel a character is real, and what the work has done to make us feel as we do. We also need to understand how less mimetic characters are presented and how we respond to them. In addition, we need to be able to relate mimetic characters to the nonmimetic characters from which they probably evolved, an analysis that requires seeing them in terms not of reality but of narrative convention. And we need to be able to relate characters to the work of which they are part. If we see them simply as people, we cannot understand the way they function as components of the work—for example, by embodying (and arousing in us) different psychic forces acting out the process of conflict and resolution that comprises the work. Structuralist theory has the advantage of seeing characters as functions of a larger whole, defined by their relation to it as words are (at least largely) defined by their syntactic relation to sentences.

On the other hand, structuralism has its drawbacks. The most serious of these, I think, arise from the fact that structuralists wish to assert a claim to complete authority and to exclude other schools of thought. The structuralist approach seems quite useful for simple narratives like fairy tales; but as Jonathan Culler admits, structuralism is not very successful in dealing with complex works and characters.[3] I think this reflects a shortcoming in their model of the mind. Structuralists sometimes speak as if literature is not produced by a particular human mind at all but merely by some sort of abstract structure; or if a mind lies behind the literary work, it seems to be a very simple one, evidently some sort of computer. Such a model hardly seems complex enough to explain most literature. Perhaps we should conclude from this failure that it is a mistake to hypothesize that all literature is generated from a basic structure. But I do not think this conclusion is necessary. It seems likely that both simple and complex narratives are expressions of a basic story-making capacity in the mind. If this is so, we can conclude that structuralism has difficulty with complex narratives because the transformations involved in generating such narratives are so many and so complicated that it is virtually impossible to know them all. To relate a complex work like a novel to some sort of basic structure, I think we need to go beyond the extreme structuralist position that everything can be wholly explained by a basic structure. We need to remind ourselves that the structures we postulate are not impersonal, abstract absolutes but rather exist within individual minds. Literature is not produced by systems, whether structuralist or Marxist, nor Frye's archetypes; it is produced by particular writers, working in particular cultures at particular historical moments. If the individual mind were no more than the kind of universal structure invoked by structuralism, minds would have no individuality. We need to allow for other forces in the mind, for aspects of the psyche which can act upon that basic structure, affecting the generative process, and which can be acted upon by the countless external influences that make up the individual's cultural context. We can see the individual as the intersection of a basic structure with particular outer influences; but we must realize that this point of intersection is very complex and rather unpredictable, that the forces involved interact in many complicated ways.

The theory of the mind that I think deals most successfully with such an interaction is Freud's, and in my second chapter I attempt an explanation of the way the psychic impulses described by Freud could interact with the kind of basic structure postulated by the structuralists. Like the structuralists, Freud assumes the existence of innate, universal forces within the mind; but in addition, he developed the concept of an ego, which attempts to mediate between those inner forces and external influences. One advantage of Freud's theories is that they not only locate certain entities within the psyche but also see those entities as dynamic forces, interacting with each other in a dialectic way which can produce complex results. No doubt there is danger that a Freudian approach, like a structuralist one, will become reductive; but if we can allow it to mediate between a structuralist theory and a sense of historical and social context, we can take into account more complexity than any one of these theories alone would explain.

Freud's theories can be related to structuralism, I think, provided that we restrict ourselves to a concept of structure that is simple and basic enough. Freud describes a process by which basic, innate psychic forces are displaced in order to reach consciousness; it resembles the process of transformation described by structuralism, the process through which a particular utterance is generated from a basic structure. In addition, Melanie Klein and her followers have developed Freud's ideas on subject-object relations, which we can relate to the structuralist idea of the linguistic (and narrative) structuring of experience in terms of subject and object. And in my version of a basic structure, I have placed emphasis on the concept of desire, a concept with which Freud also is centrally concerned. If, as I argue in my first chapter, the fundamental structure through which we order experience is based on desire, then that structure can be acted upon in the complex, dynamic way in which Freud describes the mind acting on desire. Thus we can use Freud's ideas to explain the way that structure is transformed.

Perhaps I should make it clear here that I have restricted myself to that aspect of Freud's theory which is concerned with desire and the way the mind tries to control it, since this interaction of desire with control seems to be basic to literature. The Freudian theory I am relying upon is most clearly summed up in *The Ego and the Id.* Some of Freud's ideas, especially his concept of a death instinct, I have not used. The idea of a death instinct does not seem necessary to understand what happens in literature; nor do I find the idea wholly convincing.

In relating narrative to desire, I owe a considerable debt to Northrop Frye, who although he is no Freudian does accept Freud's terms in seeing narrative as motivated by desire, a desire which Frye often compares to the son's Oedipal attraction to the mother.[4] However, I think Frye is handicapped by his preference for a Jungian approach. He seems to see literature as the product of abstract archetypes rather than individual minds, and as a result has no terms with which to describe an interaction of psychic forces that could produce the process of narrative displacement he discusses. Another theorist who places emphasis on desire is René Girard, whose concept of a subject and object of desire is close to mine.[5] However, Girard restricts himself to ironic fiction, dismissing other kinds (such as novels with happy endings) as somehow inauthentic. He says all desire in novels is illusory because it is controlled by some sort of mediator; this may be true in the kind of novel he describes, but it is not true for all novels. I do not think the idea of a mediator deserves the fundamental status he accords it. Another recent critic, Leo Bersani, also analyzes fiction in terms of desire.[6] Here too, I agree with much of what he says, but I feel that like Girard he is limited because of a bias in favor of modernist literature, a bias which makes him unduly critical of forms of control that sublimate desire. And, as in Girard's case, his terms do not seem very clearly defined nor as basic as he wants them to be; we are never told exactly what structured or fragmented desires and characters are, nor just how character and desire are related to each other and to the mind.

Among Freudian theorists, Jacques Lacan seems to be trying to relate Freud's ideas to linguistic theory in a way somewhat similar to mine. Insofar as I can understand him, Lacan seems to equate the Freudian unconscious with the mind's basic language-making structure.[7] I suspect he overstates this, but I agree that these are closely related and that desire has a crucial influence on subject-object relationships. However, I think that, like the structuralists, Lacan is limited by an intolerance of explanations outside his own system. His obscurity seems meant to intimidate us, to deter us from making connections with other systems; it is as if he is trying to force us to accept his theory uncritically, like some religious mystery. As a result, I find him too unclear to be of much use.

Another Freudian theorist whose approach overlaps mine is Norman Holland. Especially in his recent work, Holland is concerned not with the process by which narrative may be generated but rather with our response to it. I am assuming that these processes are related: the work of literature makes manifest an interaction of linguistic embodiments of what are presumably forces within the writer's mind, and the relationships among these embodiments in turn cause an interaction of forces in the reader's mind— forces which it seems reasonable to guess resemble those in the writer's mind. I agree with much of what Holland says about the way such forces interact in the reader's mind, especially where that interaction resembles the one I describe between desire and the forces attempting to control it.[8] I think Holland is more convincing than Wolfgang Iser, for example, because by rejecting any psychological theory that would allow for unconscious feelings, Iser can see response only as cognitive, a process of formulating and judging, seeing character in relation to "norms." Iser deprives himself of any psychological vocabulary that would enable him to talk about what might go on in readers' minds, so that he can only describe their "seeing" the work from some "perspective" without explaining what they are actually doing. He is concerned with how readers become "involved" but cannot define what really happens in readers' minds.[9]

Although I think Freud's terms are highly useful for understanding the psychological process associated with narrative, there are also some disadvantages to most applications of Freud's ideas. One problem, as Frederick Crews has pointed out, is their excessive emphasis on the unconscious and the infantile.[10] Freudian critics sometimes talk as if some unconscious fantasy or impulse is the "true meaning" of a work. But if we can talk about a work's "meaning," surely we should say it lies not in whatever unconscious impulses it may arouse but rather (as Holland seems aware) in the way it deals with the forces it arouses.[11] A work of literature is an interaction among forces: our (and presumably the writer's) conscious, more or less rational minds trying to act on basic impulses—I would say, desires. Neither of these is wholly in control; each affects the other. To isolate the unconscious and assert that it is what is authentic thus seems to be a falsification, just as Iser's ignoring the unconscious is a falsification. I would prefer to describe the work of literature as a way of arousing desire but also of dealing with it, either by creating an illusion of fulfilling it or by denying it but offering some way of restraining it and accepting its denial (or by some combination of these two).

Another problem with approaches like the reader-response criticism in Holland's more recent work, I think, is that it confuses different levels of response. I would say there is a primary level at which we all respond to a work in much the same manner because we are responding in the most basic way: our desire for fulfillment is aroused and we feel opposed to whatever resists fulfillment. It is at this level that we are probably safest in assuming that our responses closely resemble the writer's own impulses; and it is this level that I am mainly concerned with here. However, there are also responses that I would call secondary, like the secondary elaboration Freud describes. These are more conscious and they vary more from reader to reader. They are our reactions to the primary response, our attempts to understand, explain, rationalize, and deal with it in other ways.[12] These reactions, which we are more likely to have on re-

reading works, are the ones critics usually concentrate on. Although Holland seems to be discussing the basic level of response, I think that when he describes readers as rather self-consciously using the work to activate their own fantasies, he is actually dealing with secondary response, reactions to the original response. The responses Iser discusses are quite different, highly rational, but they too seem to be secondary. Responses of this sort are of course important in criticism; but they are less useful to me here, since I am trying to discuss literature in terms of its relation to what is basic within the mind.

Another way my approach differs from that of most Freudian criticism is in what it focuses on. Most Freudians concern themselves with a mind—either the reader's (in Holland's recent work) or the writer's or a character's, as in the work of Bernard J. Paris.[13] I think there is another object to which we can apply Freud's ideas more fruitfully—the work itself. As long as we are engaged in literary criticism, it seems to me that our primary concern should be the literary work. I have described the work as an embodiment of a relationship among psychic forces—an embodiment lying between the mind that created it and the mind that receives it. That interaction of forces presumably has actual existence only in the writer's or reader's mind. Nevertheless, it is only the objective manifestation of that interaction—the work itself—that we can really know. Therefore I propose that the best way to discuss either the writer's or the reader's mind (or at least to hope we are discussing them, accepting the fact that we cannot be certain about them) is in terms of the work that implies their activity.[14] In other words, I prefer to examine the way impulses (primarily desires and the forces opposing them) are given form by the work and the way the work deals with those impulses. Unlike Holland, I think that all we can productively discuss is what the work makes us desire in itself—the particular object it creates to activate our desire, and thus the particular form it gives to desire. The desire it makes us feel is presumably related to other, personal desires, but it is not the same as those desires. We should not forget, as Freudians sometimes seem to, that literature is verbal. What it makes us desire is not the gratification of our own fantasies but rather some sort of verbal substitute for fulfillment. It is as if desire has been translated into an abstract form.

The work of literature embodies the relationships among psychic impulses in a configuration that resembles the structure of relationships Freud postulates in his description of the mind. This configuration is not the same as a mind but is rather a construct that we take (as a working hypothesis) to be analogous to the mind—a kind of signifier of the mind. At least it is a way for us, like Freud—and like the writer—to replace the mind with something we can know, something that is no doubt more schematic than the mind itself is, but that is perhaps the best approximation we can make to the mind's complexity. Such a construct is presumably for us, as for the writer, partly a way of dealing with the mind's complexity, which can seem overwhelming, even threatening; but it can nevertheless imply something about what the mind is like. Probably we can never talk directly about a mind; the best we can hope for is such a construct, one which involves as little simplification as possible. We can hope that such a conceptualization is related to the mind as a map is related to the world: it does not reproduce its object, but it does provide a useful schematization of the relationships (or some of them) of which that object appears to be composed. If we use such an approach to literature, we can get away from the case-history atmosphere that surrounds many Freudian analyses of writers, characters, or readers. We can keep our attention on what the work is doing to us rather than simply on ourselves. Thus we can avoid the tendency of much Freudian criticism to replace the work with another object, a so-called mind. And we can integrate our approach with one like Frye's which, because it sees the work as a structure of relationships, can compare works and discuss their development.

In addition to this sense of forces interacting within the writer as manifested by his work, we also need a sense of the historical and cultural processes which could influence individual writers and explain the way narrative has evolved. Both structuralists and Freudians tend to ignore this cultural context.[15] Northrop Frye describes the evolution of narrative as a gradual displacement of its basic wish-fulfilling function, but he does not acknowledge the presence of the social and psychological forces that presumably influence such a process. To some extent literature seems to have a dynamic of its own, as Frye implies, but surely its development is affected by cultural and social forces. To understand their influence, I think we can avail ourselves of Freud's theories, since he allows for the influence of external forces on the mind. He discusses the way the mind responds to social influences, especially parental control, by creating an internalized form of authority which seeks to control desires. From the way a given work embodies forms of control, then, we can infer the way in which the writer's mind has internalized authority. Thus we can relate the form that control takes within a work to the nature of authority in the writer's society. In my third and fourth chapters I use this theory to examine a particular example of the way changes in social authority can affect literature, trying to understand the rise of the English novel and of the treatment of character it developed by relating this phenomenon to the evolution of English society.

In this consideration of social influence, I am especially indebted to Ian Watt, whose *Rise of the Novel* remains the best description of the novel's relation to social conditions. However, I prefer to see the evolution of the novel not as the rise of realism as Watt does but rather as a displacement of romance of the kind Frye describes. I have tried to understand how the social changes described by Watt and by historians of modernization could have caused a displacement of this sort. In discussing "realism" in terms of romance, I am following not only Frye but also such other critics as Frank Kermode, Harry Levin, and George Levine. The advantage of this approach is that it enables us to relate the novel to the concept of a basic structure. Seventeenth-century romance can be seen as one way in which the basic structure underlying all narratives was transformed. This transformation was affected by the particular form in which the individual tended to internalize authority in that society, creating a different balance than before between desire and control within the individual's mind. This new relationship among psychic forces found expression in the way writers developed a new transformation of narrative structure, creating a form of fiction in which embodiments of desire and control took on a different relation. Thus we can relate the rise of the novel both to social influences on the one hand and to a basic structure on the other hand; the writer mediates between these two, creating new ways of giving expression to that basic structure in response to new cultural conditions. And such a process can enable us to understand how a new kind of characterization could develop and to relate it to the basic idea of character out of which it evolved. We can see how complex characters could be generated by complex cultural influences mediated through a complex psychological process.

In my last four chapters I use this theoretical framework to consider the nature of the complex characters typical of the classic English novel and the ways they are related to the works in which they occur. While I discuss these characters in relation to the basic character-functions from which they evidently developed, I also try to do justice to the highly complex ways in which those basic functions have been transformed. Our critical systems too often fail to allow for the richness of detail in works such as novels. It is much easier for a critic to talk about form or theme (which are mainly functions of what I have called secondary response) than to deal with the word-by-word texture of a work. Yet it is precisely in these local details that characterization obtains its effects, and discussions of character that concentrate on form and theme fail to capture what really makes characters effective. This is probably the main reason that critics usually do not deal adequately with characterization like Dickens's. It seems unfortunate that as critics we tend to undervalue our primary response, our first reading of works, that experience in which every moment has value for itself regardless of its relation to what is to follow, in which each detail has an intensity we are likely to lose sight of when we become critics instead of readers, looking at the relationships among details more than at the details themselves. On the other hand, if we concentrate only on detail, we are in danger of losing sight of the relation of character to the work as a whole and the relation of the work to its predecessors. So it seems necessary to develop a way of dealing with detail that can value that detail for itself and can also see it in relation to the work as a whole. I hope my work can satisfy this requirement, offering a way of discussing the details of characterization and yet seeing them as generated from the same basic structure out of which the whole work rises, relating them to that whole and to other works generated from the same fundamental structure.

Character as a Function of a Basic Narrative Structure: The Linguistic Model

chapter 1

THE simplest, most basic characters seem to be those Tzvetan Todorov calls "apsychological";[1] although they *are* characters, they do not seem to *have* character, in the sense of personality. We can see complex characters—those who seem to have personality—as transformations of this more basic kind of character. In order to define complex characters, then, we should first attempt a definition of these basic characters. The Russian formalist Vladimir Propp defines the simple characters in fairy tales as agents of plot, functions of plot action.[2] In other words, they are what they do: they are seekers, helpers, opposers, and so on. We can define them not semantically, in terms of their relation to reality, but syntactically, in terms of their relation to the work. It is irrelevant to look "inside" such characters and ask what motivates them—why ogres are cruel and heroes brave. The goodness or badness of such characters are givens, necessary for the plot. Their traits are given them in order to create plot conflict and to make us desire the hero's victory.

If we seek to understand more about character as a function of narrative, we need to understand narrative itself. We need to examine the mental process involved in story-telling, a process which seems closely related to some of the most fundamental characteristics of the human mind. Among the various ways of understanding the mind, the approach which has offered the most insight into the nature of simple literary characters is French structuralism. Structuralists like Todorov and A. J. Greimas have developed theories based on Propp's concept of character as function. We can learn from the structuralists to see the mind (including its story-telling) in terms of its language-making capability. They hypothesize that narrative, like language, may be generated from some sort of basic mental structure and that this structure may be analogous to (or the same as) the basic structure of language itself. If narrative is structured like language, we can compare the relation of basic characters to plot with the relation of parts of speech to the sentence. Characters are defined by their plot function as parts of speech are defined by their function in the sentence: the character is a function of his action as a noun is a function of its verb.[3]

To understand basic characters, then, we need some understanding of the way language works in the mind. This is an extremely complex subject, far beyond my competence. However, in order to understand the literary evidence I have found it necessary to make some assumptions about the mind. I have tried to take psychological and linguistic theories into account, but my main concern is what narratives themselves have to teach us. I am assuming that since story-telling resembles language-making, it arises out of the same mental process: children seem to begin telling stories as a part of the process of learning to speak, playing with words to learn how to manipulate them.[4] If language is generated from some sort of basic structuring capacity in the mind, then there should be a related structure underlying narrative. And if we develop language by learning to generate complex utterances from a basic structure, we should be able to get an idea of what that structure is like by looking at the origins of children's speech. Presumably when a child first speaks he is expressing an innate, basic structure in a fairly direct way, since he has not developed many ways of transforming it.

A child's first words are the names of objects. Underlying these utterances, we can hypothesize the deep structure of a sentence: the child is apparently saying either "I want" or "I see" the object.[5] It seems likely that these two structures are fundamental, since they express basic ways of defining the self's relation to the object-world, creating a relationship with the world in order to act on it. They correspond to Freud's pleasure and reality principles and to Piaget's duality of assimilation and accommodation. I am hypothesizing that they underlie all language, including narrative. Probably they always coexist and interact; the speaker always has some awareness of the perceptual world, but he always has some desire to act on that world too. A child naming an object sees what he wants and wants what he sees; the things he probably first picks out to perceive and name are those he wants to define as objects because he desires them in some way, since naming them is like possessing or controlling them. In literature, however, desire seems to be especially predominant, and language expressing perception seems to be used primarily to serve desire. As Northrop Frye puts it, literature tends "to return to the pattern of desire."[6] In other words, literature involves a partial regression to a childlike use of language, a use which as Piaget points out is primarily egocentric.[7] Like the child naming things, literature seeks a magical power over the object-world. Reality can never fully satisfy our desires, and although desire can probably never completely escape the constraints of the reality principle, it can use fictions to make our perception of the object-world at least partly serve the pleasure principle. That is, we can use perceptual images to create an imaginary object-world which serves (or seeks to serve) our desires. Freud suggests a mechanism out of which this process could originate: the infant may learn to call up perceptual memories of objects he desires in an attempt to gratify his desire by proxy.[8] Not all literature, of course, is wish-fulfilling, but we can see literature that denies desire as a negative transformation of literature serving desire. Denial can imply desire: when literature presents an unfulfilling "reality" it may be showing the object that desire seeks to act on, the resistance it tries to overcome. Such an object is a function of desire.

If we assume, then, that narrative exists primarily to serve desire, we can derive from the child's first utterances the following basic sentence structure out of which narrative would be generated:

Subject (I)—Verb (desire)—Object (desire's fulfillment)

Todorov postulates a somewhat similar subject-predicate model underlying narrative,[9] but this model differs from his in some important ways. For one thing, I believe that the basic subject in literature is not just any agent but a transformation of the "I," and the basic action is a function of the self, a transformation of its desires. I also believe that the verb should be separated from the object, since it seems to me that desire is primarily a function of the subject and in opposition to the object. The infant separates object from verb quite early, while the subject tends to remain implicit longer—that is, not separated from the verb. My model also differs from Todorov's in not giving fundamental status to an adjectival predicate; I prefer to see adjectives as functions of the object, ways of specifying it. This is the way they first appear in children's language; they come later than the simple name of the object, and so do not seem as basic. Furthermore, my model is optative rather than indicative. Narrative presents actions *as if* they are indicative, but what is indicative from the agent's viewpoint is optative from the narrator's. That is, the narrator wants (or does not want) what the subject does.

Since I do not give fundamental status to adjectives, I disagree with those structuralists who define character as a collection of traits. Indeed, some simple characters do not even have traits. I wish to define characters in terms of their verb instead; they are ways of doing—acting and being acted on. To see such actions as traits is to reify and label, arbitrarily and reductively. It also seems wrong to think of character traits as separable from basic character function. Rather we can see many traits as generated from these functions. For example, heroes are made attractive in various ways to induce us to invest them with our desire—to root for them; they are given certain abilities to enable them to fulfill that desire—to defeat their opponents; and they are given a "heart" so that they will desire fulfillment or suffer if it is denied. Those traits which are not generated from basic character functions may exist to name the character, making him nominal so that he can act as subject or object, allowing us to conceive of him as a being able to act.[10] A name like Little Red Riding Hood, for example, uses traits simply for the purpose of making a name. Although traits are not necessary to make a character seem a thing, they reinforce our sense of his thingness, and so they seem to function at least partly in order to provide this sense of solidity.

The characteristics I wish to concentrate on here, however, are those which seem to be generated more directly from the basic structure I have described. This subject-object structure can enable us to distinguish two fundamental kinds of character: those who are transformations of the subject and those who are transformations of the object.¹¹ We can define them as functions of the narrative's basic desire: the subject is the desirer and the object is what he desires.

The main manifestation of the basic subject is of course a story's protagonist, the character who acts for the story's main desire and thus encounters its main conflict. Because he actualizes a fundamentally different function, the protagonist seems to belong to a different order of being from object-characters; he does not seem to be governed by the same laws. The protagonist functions as a transformation of or replacement for our "I." Even when he is not a first-person protagonist, he has certain characteristics we associate with our "I." He is seen as being at the center of a world which exists in an object relation to him (that is, exists to gratify or oppose his desire) and toward which he exists in a subject relation. We do not see him from the outside, as an image. Insofar as images are associated with him, we are temporarily seeing him, at least partly, as an object. But insofar as he functions as a subject, we do not perceive him as separate from ourselves but rather experience him as we experience ourselves, as an agent or extension of our own desire. I think we conceive of him as a desire seeking action. He seems not so much a thing as a potentiality. But the fact that he is named—that he is a noun—enables us to imagine him as an entity, so that we are able to convert desire into the concept of a being that is able to function as a subject.

How do we respond to the character as subject? He exists primarily as a means of making us desire: we want him to fulfill the desires that the narrative arouses in us. We evidently recreate each sentence, or each unit with a subject-object structure, in our minds, vicariously acting through the subject on its object. The verb gives expression to our desire in the form of an action which at least partly arouses or fulfills that desire. And it is the subject that relates us to the verb, enabling us to feel that its action is analogous to an action of our own, as if we are the subject of the action ourselves. We can only conceive of desire acting on the fictional world by associating desire with an entity able to function as a subject in relation to that world. Thus to fulfill our desires we must accept the character as such a subject: he enables our desire to enter into the fictional world and act on it. By doing so, he enables us to feel we have power (the ability to act for desire), and since it is he who gives us this feeling, we attribute the power to him. In other words, we see him as a character—a being having a force of his own, able to act for desire. Since the desires we impute to him are those he activates in ourselves, we accept his subject relationship to his world as if it were our own. The more fully he seems to serve the desires the narrative induces, the more fully we accept him.

Normally we say we "identify" with such a character, but identification implies a separation from someone and an attempt to overcome that separation, neither of which seems quite like our relation to a character. The character does not seem to be a separate being, and so we need not try to take possession of him. I would rather say our response is an acceptance of the subject-object structure, of a subject relationship to the narrative object. It seems likely that we always structure experience in terms of the Self and the Other, and that we respond to characters through this structure. We can say, then, that we accept the subject-character as analogous to our own "I." The character's relation to the self seems to resemble the relation of the word "I" to the self: we accept the character as a signifier for the self as we accept the word. Like the word "I," the character provides a linguistic entity able to act as subject for the self and defined by its relation to an action and its object. Because each of us sees his own self as a subject, we are willing to accept the narrative subject as analogous to the self. Our acceptance resembles the way a child accepts the name given him as a sign to represent his self, enabling him to associate that self's desires with an entity able to act as subject for them.

However, there seems to be an ambivalence in our acceptance of subject-characters. We do not so much resemble the child accepting his own name as a signifier, but rather the child re-enacting that acceptance in play, temporarily taking on a new name in order to play a part. The child simultaneously sees this play-name as signifying his "I" and also as separate from his "I." I think we too accept the subject-character as representing our "I" and yet remain partly aware that we are separate from the character. This ambivalence resembles that discussed by D. W. Winnicott in his analysis of play: he says that in play the child sees objects as transitional, meaning they seem both part of the self and separate from the self.[12] In other words, in play we can see something as both subject and object, and we seem to take a similar attitude toward literary characters. We might also describe this ambivalence by saying that the character serves both the pleasure principle (acting for desire) and the reality principle (seen as a real being). We can allow desire to be less controlled by the reality principle than usual because we are aware that the narrative is playlike, that desire is not being expressed in direct action which would require the mediation of the reality principle. We can partly detach ourselves from the desires aroused, feeling they are merely imaginary, that they belong to characters, not to ourselves. It may be this very detachment that enables us to transfer our desires to a character; if we feel the desires are not our own, we can allow them to be aroused more fully than we could if we took them more seriously.

Narrative resembles language itself in the way it replaces actual, physical fulfillment with an abstraction which signifies fulfillment but does not actually provide it. But narrative can be more playful than most language, less closely related to its signified, to the reality it pretends to replace. This increased freedom from the signified is clearest in its use of names. Unlike ordinary words which we associate with referents, the names of characters implicitly acknowledge the arbitrariness of verbal signs. I associate the word "dog" with a referent based on remembered experience, but a name like "Mr. Micawber" has no such referent. Since it is a noun, I look for some referent; and the title "Mr." makes me want to visualize that referent as a person. But I create that referent myself; in other words, I create the sense of a character. And at the same time, I remain aware that there is no actual referent; I am prevented from associating the character with any real person. Thus I see the character as if he were real, but at the same time remain aware that he is not, that he is only a signifier cut off from any signified. This very freedom from the signified may be what makes narrative playful, allowing it to manipulate signifiers in a way that real things could not be manipulated.

The basic subject can be manifested not only through a protagonist but in other parts of narratives as well. Indeed, the subject of any sentence in a narrative is presumably generated at least partly out of the basic subject. Thus other characters (and even things) can function partly as subjects. There may be subordinate protagonists, and often characters whom we see primarily as objects also function occasionally as subjects. And when a character acts as a subject, others may function temporarily as his objects. But the most important additional manifestation of the subject is in the narrator. In complex narratives, narrator and protagonist tend to become explicitly separate, but in the simplest stories we find no such acknowledgment of their separation. In such stories the narrator is usually implicit, just as in a child's first utterances the "I" is not made explicit. This suggests that in the basic narrative structure protagonist and narrator are not differentiated; both are expressions of the "I." We can see the narrator, then, as having a subject relation to the fictional world; he too is a desirer, taking the entire fictional world as his object in order to seek fulfillment in it through his protagonist. The narrator's nature seems related to the protagonist's; for example, as the narrator becomes more important, the protagonist tends to be distanced, serving (and arousing) desire less fully.

The narrative object is manifested as the protagonist's world, whatever he seeks to act on, primarily other characters. It is in the object that most narrative complexities are generated; like the actual object-world, the narrative object takes many forms. For one thing, we can distinguish between positive and negative transformations of the object.[13] The positive object makes possible the fulfillment the subject seeks. The most basic form this function takes is a goal-character such as the princess the fairy-tale hero seeks to win; possessing this goal brings fulfillment. This character can be seen as an object more completely than any other; indeed, it can be simply a thing to acquire, not a character. The positive object usually finds additional expression in some sort of auxiliary character, a helper whose function is to assist the protagonist's fulfillment, a character like the fairy godmother in "Cinderella." Unlike the goal-character, this auxiliary character is usually active; he can function as a secondary subject, acting for the protagonist's desire in his place. Perhaps he is brought into being by the subject's desire to control the object-world, to enter into it and make it become an extension of the self, serving the self's desires. This activating of the object reenacts the process by which the self enters the subject in the first place, creating a protagonist. As the protagonist serves the story-teller's desire, the helper serves the protagonist's desire. However, the helper is also seen as an object, outside the protagonist—for example, as someone to be propitiated or to serve.

The negative object embodies what the subject does not desire. The negative transformation of the goal-character can embody a state that is the opposite of fulfillment, something to avoid possessing. It can be an agent who seeks to possess the subject-character rather than be possessed by him, something to reject or flee. The negative transformation of the helper is an agent who opposes or hinders fulfillment. The hypothesis that these agents are negative transformations is supported by the way they replace positive object-characters in many stories. The story starts out presenting a subject in relation to a positive object which then gives way to its opposite, as the wicked stepmother in fairy tales often replaces a good mother. And at the story's end this transformation is often reversed, a positive character (such as Cinderella's godmother and then her prince) replacing a negative one (such as her stepmother). Negative object-characters, like positive ones, are defined by their relation to the subject's desire; they are negative because they oppose it. We see what opposes desire as bad and what serves it as good. Desire thus tends to polarize the object-world. In fact desire seems to call the negative object into being: it is because we desire something that we resent obstacles to our desire, seeing them as negative. As Northrop Frye says, desire creates a "dialectic" between obstacles and fulfillment.[14] Though it opposes desire, the negative object serves it, since by embodying opposition in an object, narratives are able to overcome that opposition or deal with it in some way. For example, the negative object can serve as a scapegoat of the kind Frye mentions, a character whose rejection makes fulfillment possible.

Our response to object-characters seems to be a function of our response to subject-characters. We see them in terms of their relation to the subject. We see them as outside the self, to some extent therefore opposed to it, existing to be acted on by it. We see them more as if they are physical objects than in the case of subject-characters—as entities which can be dealt with as if they were actual objects, which can be possessed and manipulated, made to appear and disappear.

The manifestations of the object are more likely to come under the influence of the reality principle than the subject is, since it is in the perceptual world that desire usually seeks its objects. Agents of the object are thus usually associated with images. Nevertheless, they remain a function of desire, not merely imitations of reality. We do not see characters as objects primarily to be realistic, but rather because doing so makes it easier for desire to act on them. The more "real" the positive object seems, the more satisfying is our illusion that desire can deal with reality. And the negative object is made to seem real so that desire can act upon it more convincingly. Thus the images associated with the object are usually not merely mimetic but are influenced by their relation to desire: the desirable heroine is made beautiful and the threatening villain is made ugly.

Object-characters often act as subjects of secondary actions. However, they are not subjects in the same way the basic subject is. His actions serve the desire we associate with him; but the actions of object-characters do not seem to serve their desires. Rather their actions seem to be functions of the basic subject's desire. The auxiliary character helps the hero because the hero wants him to. And the villain exists as a reaction against the hero's desire, opposing it. Thus we can see object-characters' actions as subordinate verbs. The actions of the positive object can be generated from the structure "I want (the object) to fulfill desire"; the actions of positive object-characters fulfill the subject's desire, or help to do so. And the actions of the negative object can be generated from the negative transformation of that structure: "I don't want (the object) to prevent the fulfillment of desire"; the villain acts to prevent fulfillment. The object of these subordinate verbs can be the basic subject itself; these characters act on the protagonist. Thus we get a reflexive structure: the subject's desire generates an object which in turn makes that subject its object. In other words, the self calls the fictional world into being in order for that world to act on it.

A basic structure of this sort can, I think, underlie any literary utterance. The lyric, for example, typically concentrates on a positive or negative object alone, describing it; but in doing this it at least implies a subject desiring a positive object. One way we can distinguish the narrative from the lyric is that the narrative keeps both the positive and negative objects and creates an agent of the subject (a character) who interacts with these objects. This generates a conflict and an action seeking to resolve that conflict. But the same structure seems basic to both genres, and probably to all literature.

Character as a Function of Sublimation: The Psychological Model

chapter 2

THERE are so many kinds of narrative, and they are often so complex, that generalizing about them is difficult. Even if we accept the hypothesis of a basic narrative structure, there still remains the problem of how to generate complex narratives from such a simple basis.[1] Nevertheless, I think it is possible to conceive of such a process, provided we remember that it takes place in complex individual minds shaped by particular cultures. The basic structure is only an abstraction, something that never occurs in a "pure" form; all we can really know is the particular narrative utterance. We can only guess at some process capable of generating that utterance. As in the generation of linguistic utterances, we can assume that the basic elements can be transformed in various ways—for example, deleted, combined, inverted, emphasized, diminished, reduplicated. But the rather mechanical transformations of linguistic models do not seem adequate to explain why a particular writer generates particular narrative complexities. We need to allow for psychological forces within the writer's mind and for cultural forces acting on his mind.

Cultural and psychological influences are not independent, since the individual psychology is largely influenced by culture, while at the same time cultural influences only exist for the mind as they are internalized and transformed by the individual psyche. However, it will be useful here to discuss the two separately. We can begin with the psychological level of transformation, since this seems more fundamental, acted on in different ways by different cultures. The point at which we can connect the underlying structure I have described with psychological forces is the verb "desire." Through desire the psyche can exert strong, often irrational pressures on the narrative utterance. In different kinds of narrative, desire takes different forms. For example, in children's stories[2] the desire seems to be mainly just a wish to create a subject-object relationship—to act on various objects simply for the pleasure of acting on them, of making things happen. And in stories such as rogue tales the desire seems to be a wish to escape control. But I would like to restrict myself here to the dominant form of narrative in our culture, the kind found (in different forms) in romance and the novel. Despite that limitation, this chapter will remain on quite a general level, describing a broad range of narratives, quite varied yet all related to one basic psychological process.

In romance, and still largely in the novel, desire is seen from a perspective based on or resembling that of Christianity: it is seen as fundamentally guilty and therefore in need of control. One way of defining such desire is to say that it is Oedipal. If this is indeed the nature of desire in romance and the novel, we can best understand it by using the ideas of Freudian psychology.[3] Freud relates desire to a primal force which he sees as so demanding that the ego cannot fully accept it but rather, under the importunity of the superego, reacts against it, displacing it in various ways. This process of displacement suggests a mechanism of narrative transformation; if the basic structure includes such a desire, the ego must transform that structure before it can allow it (and the desire in it) to become conscious. Thus desire seems to insert into the structure a force which is at least partly opposed to that structure, an irritant which prevents equilibrium, forcing the structure to modify itself in an attempt to give expression to something it can never fully express. To transform desire into an entity able to fulfill itself, narrative must verbalize it through a subject and verb. Yet this transformation into language evidently brings with it a partial denial of desire, since there is more desire than can be verbalized. If I understand Jacques Lacan, he sees language as a way of displacing desire, translating it into an abstract form in an attempt to avoid the Oedipal guilt it arouses.[4] By replacing desire's original object with a verbal object, we partly disavow the primal nature of desire, giving up its real, forbidden object. The desire in narrative frequently remains associated with erotic desire (a desire that to some extent seems guilty), presumably because narrative desire is generated from desire that has a strong erotic component. But narrative desire seems to be something which, like subject and object, we can best define syntactically, not in terms of any referent outside the story. It is a desire for the completion of the story, for the subject to act on the object. It is not really an erotic desire, only a verbal replacement for erotic desire. Yet although desire must be displaced in this way in order to enter narrative, I think the displacement is incomplete. In the kind of narrative I shall be discussing here, desire seems to retain enough of its forbidden nature to affect the narrative in various ways.

In narrative where desire is seen as guilty, there is an attempt to overcome that guilt by sublimating desire, binding it to some form of control which at least partly desexualizes it, so that this control is seen as virtuous. Probably any narrative involves some sublimation of desire; but in romance and the novel the sublimation is more explicit, dealt with through the narrative structure. The narrative tries to act out a process of sublimation. Evidently the mere act of story-telling is not felt to provide adequate sublimation, perhaps because in our culture desire arouses considerable anxiety and so must be dealt with in a more direct way. The work seems to be trying to create belief in some control able to sublimate desire; it does this by creating an embodiment of that control and acting out a process of submitting to that control and being accepted by it. When I refer to sublimating narratives, then, I mean narratives in which the fulfillment sought involves reconciling desire with control. The particular process we find in narratives of this sort seems to parallel the process Freud describes through which the individual learns to deal with Oedipal guilt by internalizing parental control, converting that external control into a self-control that tries to prevent Oedipal desires from arousing anxiety.[5]

The sublimating nature of most literary narratives in our culture becomes clearer if we contrast them with other kinds of narrative. In the stories of young children, for example, desire seems relatively unsublimated, not under much control and so quite aggressive. Children's stories do not usually offer resolutions in which desire is reconciled with control. They simply express desire without managing it very much, presumably because children have not yet learned to control their own desires. Similarly, rogue tales and jokes usually express rather aggressive desires and do not seem much concerned with controlling them.

In sublimating narrative the basic narrative structure is transformed by the attempt to control desire. Probably no narrative sublimates desire perfectly, and so any particular narrative would only approximate the structure I shall describe. The more complete the sublimation, the more fully the story will conform to this structure. The most highly sublimating stories are probably what Northrop Frye calls naïve romances, and such stories do follow this structure quite closely. But even in less fully sublimated works like novels the structure persists, though in modified forms.

In order to seek sublimation, narratives begin by polarizing desire into positive and negative aspects, an idealized desire which submits to proper control and a guilty desire which rebels against that control. This polarization resembles the Christian polarity between God and devil, virtue and sin. Plot conflict begins with the expression of a negative desire, a desire needing control. Thus, although the story seeks to move toward control, it begins with a rejection of that control. And although the rebellious aspect of desire is seen as negative, it exercises an attraction. Perhaps making a desire forbidden automatically makes it attractive. This attraction may be the impulse that motivates the story-telling. Even though the story ostensibly exists to impose control, it may have originally come into being to serve another, covert purpose—to allow expression of desires which oppose that control, to indulge in the excitement of rebellion. If the story pays the price of eventually rejecting those desires, it can get away with expressing them. This initial rebellion resembles a regression, an attempt to return to a childlike state in which desire is fairly free and control has not yet been internalized.

But if the sublimating narrative begins with an impulse to escape restraint, it takes its shape from a reaction against that impulse, an attempt to re-establish the control it has called into question. It rejects control in order to reverse that rejection in the end. This process of rejection and then acceptance resembles the process described by Kleinian psychologists whereby the psyche projects outward aspects of the self in order to deal with them and then introject them in a more controlled form.[6]

The main way narratives work out this process is through characters. They use characters to isolate and define the various psychic forces they seek to deal with, embodying those forces in objects so a subject can act on them.[7] Then they use the interaction among characters to work out a relationship among those forces—or at least to provide the satisfying illusion that such a relationship has been worked out. Perhaps it is only through some process like narration that these psychic forces can be conceived of at all, that we can feel we have defined them. Narrative can translate what is within the psyche into creatures able to fight, die, marry, even be reborn, giving us the sense of ordering, relating, accepting, or disposing of them. It can convert desire and control into forms that can be reconciled, defining desire as submissive and control as tolerant of desire. Thus characters are used as interrelated parts of a structure which seeks to work out a sublimating reconciliation of the forces for which those characters act. As a result, the nature of a story's characters is affected by the degree of sublimation the story provides.

It is in the object-characters that we can most clearly see the way narrative separates out aspects of the self in order to bring about sublimation. A child's first object relation is normally with his parents, so it seems reasonable to follow Melanie Klein in seeing object relations in general as based on the parent-child relationship. If we deal with Oedipal desire by internalizing parental control, it seems possible that narrative uses object-characters in an attempt to reverse that process of internalization. If narrative involves a partial regression, rejecting control, it can reject control by taking it out of the mind which has introjected it, projecting control back outside the mind again, locating it where it was before the child internalized it. If self-control originates in parental control, we can reject it by returning it to our parents. That is, we can create parentlike object-characters (though disguised, and resembling not so much real parents as a child's view of them) and make those characters embody control. Thus we can see control as an object, separate from the self. Doing this helps us work out a more satisfying relationship between the self and the control it internalizes, since we can use the narrative to transform control into a form we are willing to accept.

If object-characters are based on the child's image of its parents, we can relate the divisions that sublimating narrative makes in the narrative object to the different ways a child perceives its parents. One way narrative tends to divide the object is by separating motherlike and fatherlike object-characters. This division facilitates the separation of desire from control. For a male, the motherlike object-character is primarily associated with desire, the fatherlike character with control. The reverse seems true for a female, although the father may also be associated with control here.

Melanie Klein describes another division in the way the child perceives the object-world. The child polarizes the way he sees his parents; he idealizes them, seeing them as fulfilling his desires, and yet he also sees them as hostile, opposing his desires.[8] This split seems analogous to the way narrative creates positive and negative objects. Sublimating narrative places considerable emphasis on this polarity, using a pattern resembling the way a child polarizes his view of his parents. The stronger the desire, the stronger the reaction against it; and since Oedipal desire is quite strong, opposing control, the aspect of the object embodying control reacts strongly against that desire, becoming quite negative. Thus when sublimating narrative begins by rejecting control, it calls into being a negative object strongly opposed to sublimation.

In sublimating narrative, then, we can distinguish four kinds of object-character: there are positive and negative characters, and among each there are characters associated with control and others associated with desire. Let us begin with the positive characters. The character associated with desire is the goal-character. The goal-character seems to embody an idealized image of the self, what the subject seeks to become like. Freud says that in sublimation the ego creates an idealized image of the self (replacing the mother) and offers it to desire as a love-object.[9] Similarly, in narrative this ideal self resembles a child's idealized version of his mother (I use a male protagonist for the purpose of this discussion). Like the ideal mother, the goal-character is seen as desirable yet pure and virtually unattainable, above the protagonist morally or socially. The religious analogue to such a character is the Virgin Mary.

Although the goal-character is primarily associated with desire, she also tends to represent the control necessary for sublimation. If she is motherlike, desire for her is likely to arouse Oedipal guilt, and the narrative defends against that possibility not only by idealizing her, seeing her as at least partly desexualized, but also by making her act partly for the parentlike authority which opposes desire. Thus the goal-character may act against the protagonist's desire until he learns to restrain it; that is, she may represent the parentlike control he must learn to internalize. In doing this, she not only acts as a goal to be possessed but also embodies a goal state—the virtuous self-control the protagonist must acquire in order to achieve sublimation. For example, Agnes Wickfield embodies the discipline David Copperfield must teach his heart; Sophia Western represents a similar state Tom Jones must acquire; and Mr. Knightly embodies the restraint Emma must learn. Winning the hand of such goal-characters thus acts out the attainment of sublimation, the reconciliation of desire with control which is reproduced in the reconciliation of the protagonist with the goal-character.

Secondary object-characters can have a similar function; they can function as helpers by embodying a state of mind which the protagonist can learn to emulate. They can embody the state needed in order to attain sublimation, as Annie Strong embodies the disciplined heart David Copperfield must acquire. Or, in fiction that offers less sublimation, they can embody a way of dealing with one's failure to attain sublimation, teaching the protagonist patience as Farebrother's example teaches Lydgate. Such auxiliary characters seem to represent a rationalized version of the positive object, one which the writer has subordinated to a thematic function. They serve as alternative selves for the protagonist, and so they tend to become partial subject-characters themselves, secondary protagonists (like Jane Fairfax in *Emma*).

The other kind of positive object-character is the one primarily associated with parentlike control. This character seems to be a transformation of the helper. In sublimating narrative, the typical auxiliary character is one embodying the authority which the subject seeks to reconcile with desire. For males, this character resembles a child's idealized view of the father, older and wiser than the protagonist, protective and forgiving. The religious analogue to this character is God the Father. By locating authority in such a character, the story defines it as benign, as sanctioning desire. Thus the story creates a form of authority which can allow sublimation. Some of the protagonist's action or responsibility for his action is often transferred to characters of this sort. By making this transfer, the self can deal with the guilt its desires might otherwise arouse by shifting responsibility away from itself. If an agent representing authority acts in place of the protagonist, the desire that agent serves is sanctioned by authority and therefore guiltless. This transfer resembles the process Freud describes by which the ego deals with

Oedipal guilt by creating an ego ideal to which it can transfer the control of desire.

Among the good parent-figures in novels, one of the clearest examples is Squire Allworthy. Tom Jones's reconciliation with Allworthy acts out the reconciliation of desire with the prudent control Allworthy embodies (especially at the end of *Tom Jones*), a reconciliation which enables Tom to receive the parentlike sanction which makes fulfillment possible. Dickens also uses characters who are like fairy godfathers, from Mr. Pickwick to Noddy Boffin. There are also characters who, though they lack parentlike power, are parentlike in embodying a principle of moral authority, often one which a protagonist learns to look up to. Examples include Farebrother and Caleb Garth in *Middlemarch* and Mr. Peggotty in *David Copperfield*. Less often, the good parent is a woman, like Aunt Betsey in *Copperfield* and Mrs. Moore in *A Passage to India*. This parentlike helper can merge with the helper I have just described who functions as an alternative protagonist; Farebrother for example is seen both as fatherlike and partly as a subordinate subject-character. And for a woman writer the good fatherlike character can be combined with the goal-character, just as for a man the goal-character can be combined with motherlike control. For example, at the end of *Pride and Prejudice* Elizabeth marries the strongest, most fatherlike character in the novel; and Jane Eyre similarly finds a master as well as a mate. It is as if the heroine converts the hero from father into goal-character.

The negative versions of these object-characters evidently come into being as a result of the rebellion against control which I have said seems to initiate the narrative. While the positive object embodies the final state toward which the story aims, a reconciliation of desire and control, the negative object embodies the initial state in which desire seeks to throw off control. The negative characters resemble the positive ones, but they are like a blasphemous parody of the positive object. Desire and control are redefined, seen not as serving sublimation but as opposing it. They are polarized: desire is rebellious, opposing control, and control is repressive, opposing desire. Each is a reaction against the other, making the other negative. And since the protagonist seeks to reconcile them in order to attain sublimation, they are opposed to him. Instead of accepting his control, each force is seen as trying to gain power for itself, to take over the subject to the exclusion of its opposite. Insofar as desire and control are opposed to the subject, they are not restrained by the conscious ego but rather take irrational, aggressive forms. They are seen as outside the self, uncontrollable by it, something it must oppose.

In sublimating narrative, then, one kind of villain embodies negative control, the other negative desire. The negative transformation of the idealized parentlike authority-figure is the repressive villain.[10] This character tends to have some parentlike traits, but he embodies parentlike authority seen as opposed to the self, hated or feared. He tries to prevent fulfillment, opposing the desire for sublimation, seeking to punish or even destroy the protagonist. In particular, he seeks to prevent the protagonist from winning the goal-character. The three of these characters typically form an Oedipal triangle, the fatherlike character seeking to keep the hero from winning the motherlike character. The negative parentlike character may help the process of sublimation by enabling the narrative to separate out the aspect of parental control which is resented; by locating that negative control in a separate character, the narrative can reject it and replace it with good control. Perhaps it is easier to create an idealized image of parental authority if one isolates those aspects of authority one dislikes, removing them from the parentlike character to his opposite number. Among repressive villains of this sort we may include Mr. Harlowe in *Clarissa* and Murdstone in *Copperfield*. For a woman, the villain can be maternal, like Mrs. Norris in *Mansfield Park* or Mrs. Reed in *Jane Eyre*.

There are also characters who are partly parentlike, functioning as extensions of repressive control, but are also a kind of negative goal-character embodying the denial of desire, the absence of fulfillment—for example, Solmes in *Clarissa*, Mr. Collins in *Pride and Prejudice*, and Casaubon in *Middlemarch*. These characters are unfulfilling not only because they threaten to repress the protagonist but because they are themselves repressed, embodying within themselves the denial of feeling they also seek to impose on the protagonist and thus failing to function as satisfying goal-characters.

We can describe the negative object-character representing desire as a lustful or rebellious villain, a character embodying a passion which opposes control.[11] The religious analogue to this character is Lucifer. Sometimes negative desire is embodied in characters who are negative transformations of the goal-character, an object of desire but of a desire which is guilty, unsublimated. This negative object functions as a tempter, like Wickham in *Pride and Prejudice* or

Rosamond Vincy in *Middlemarch*. Often, however, the rebellious villain does not merely take a passive role, like a goal-character. Instead of subordinating himself to the subject's desire he seems to react against serving as a mere object and tries to supplant the subject. Thus he resembles a negative protagonist, acting like a subject but serving negative desire. He acts as a rival, trying to replace the protagonist's virtuous desires with rebellious ones. By opposing control he seeks to prevent sublimation. One way he does this is by gaining possession of the positive object for himself. He can cut the protagonist off from the good parentlike character, as Blifil turns Allworthy against Tom Jones. Or he can seek possession of the goal-character, as Blifil hopes to win Sophia Western. But though this kind of villain seems like a negative protagonist, the self—insofar as it wishes to disavow desire in this uncontrolled form—sees him not as a subject but as an object. Indeed, he is frequently pictured as alien, even monstrous, diabolical, or animal-like. Examples of this kind of villain include Iago, Lovelace in *Clarissa,* Quilp in *The Old Curiosity Shop,* and Kurtz in *Heart of Darkness,* as well as diminished, less passionate versions like Steerforth in *Copperfield* and Arthur Donnithorne in *Adam Bede*. Characters of this kind can be rationalized to function as negative transformations of the secondary, alternative protagonist: they can be bad examples the protagonist should learn to reject, as Copperfield learns he shouldn't be like Steerforth. That is, these characters can embody an uncontrolled state of mind which makes sublimation unattainable or which prevents one from accepting one's failure to attain it.

One would expect the rebellious and repressive villains to oppose each other. But since the object is a function of the protagonist's desire their main concern seems to be opposing him rather than each other, reacting against his desire by opposing agents of sublimation. Together they function as a part of a negative structure of relationships—a state of polarization, desire opposing control—a state that is the opposite of sublimation. We can thus see repression and rebellion as functions of each other, each making the other negative: to rebelliousness, control seems repressive, and to repression, desire seems rebellious. Sublimation seeks to overcome both repression and rebellion, transforming desire and control into forms that can be reconciled. Because they function together the two kinds of villain often cooperate in opposing sublimation by creating a polarization which prevents reconciliation. For example, the Harlowes and Lovelace, though enemies, join forces to prevent Clarissa's fulfillment; the repressive Dombey and the rebellious Carker combine against Florence Dombey; and in *Mansfield Park* the repressive Mrs. Norris joins the rather rebellious Bertram sisters in opposing Fanny Price.

Locating guilty desire and the reaction against it in the negative object serves sublimation by enabling the narrative to reject this polarized state. We might be attracted to rebellion; but if it is located in a negative, unattractive character, we can accept its expression yet not feel guilty because we can disavow it, seeing it as negative. The more completely rebellion and repression are segregated in a negative object, the more the positive parts of the narrative can be kept pure. If rebelliousness is located in a villain, the protagonist can be virtuous, and by defeating that villain the protagonist can repudiate rebelliousness and prove that virtue can overcome it. For example, Richardson shifts rebelliousness from Clarissa to Lovelace (and to a lesser extent to Anna Howe), thus almost entirely absolving Clarissa of guilt even though she elopes. Jane Austen transfers uncontrolled desire (for Wickham) from Elizabeth Bennet to her sister Lydia so that Elizabeth can become critical of that desire. And George Eliot transfers selfish desire from Dorothea to Rosamond Vincy (and to a lesser extent Dorothea's sister Celia), so that Dorothea does not become another Maggie Tulliver. Rebellious villains can also be used to keep the image of the parent pure so that the protagonist will not rebel against him. Perhaps the lustful villain is normally a separate character from the fatherlike character because if the father were equated with a sexual rival the Oedipal conflict would be too direct, too explicit and painful; separating the rival from the father masks the Oedipal content. In addition, if the rebellious villain turns the parentlike character against the protagonist, as Blifil does, blame can be shifted away from the parent so that the protagonist need not resent him. In other words, that aspect of the self which opposes the parent can be separated out and disavowed.

The nature of the various object-characters affects the nature of the subject-character. In this kind of narrative, the subject serves the desire for sublimation. Since sublimation seems to require the separating out of the negative aspect of desire, the narrative uses the subject to define and embody an aspect of the self capable of attaining sublimation by separating it from negative desire. The aspect of the self that seeks sublimation is usually identified with the heart;

protagonists are described as motivated by the heart's desire for virtuous love. But although sublimation requires that rebelliousness be transferred away from the protagonist, there remain some indications that those negative desires nevertheless belong to the self even though it has tried to disown them. For one thing, the protagonist is treated as if he were guilty even if the story asserts he is innocent. Even if it is a rebellious villain like Blifil who angers the parent-like character, it is generally the protagonist whom the parentlike character punishes, as Allworthy punishes Tom Jones. Similarly in Dickens, although guilt is located in other characters, it is the virtuous protagonist like Little Nell who must suffer. The fact that it is the protagonist who suffers suggests that we can see the villain's rebelliousness as displaced from the subject. Probably all desire comes from the subject; sublimating narrative tries to transfer guilty desire from subject to object but perhaps can never do so entirely, so that the subject is still treated as if it shares the guilt. This transfer of responsibility seems related to Freud's hypothesis that rebellious desire exists in the id but that it is the ego, since it partly serves the id, which feels guilt for that desire.

Transferring rebelliousness to the villain affects the protagonist in various ways. The protagonist tends to become defensive, largely functioning to oppose desire (the villain's negative desire) rather than serve it. For example, Clarissa's main function is to fight off Lovelace. As a result, the villain often has most of the energy, since he serves desire, and the protagonist is left rather passive. Richardson and sometimes Dickens make their protagonists especially virtuous—and therefore passive—by making them female. These writers evidently associate rebellious desire with masculinity and so seek to disavow both. But the rebellious energy their protagonists lack can be found in their masculine villains, characters like Lovelace and Quilp. In other words, desire can find various forms of expression in narratives. The more it is accepted, the more fully the subject serves it; but if it is not fully allowed in the subject, it can be shifted to the object, where it is likely to occur in more uncontrolled and therefore negative forms.

Since the virtuous protagonist seeks to submit to an idealized parentlike control, he is often somewhat childlike. Insofar as the narrative separates out control and locates it in the object, the subject is childlike in that he lacks self-control and instead must find control outside himself. Protagonists often seem childlike in that they are dominated by desire, not self-restraint. And their relation to their world is often like a child's perception of his relation to his world: the world exists to fulfill or oppose their desires. In fairy tales the protagonist is often a youngest child, and in romances and novels the hero is usually youthful, is often opposed by parentlike characters, and like a child is not much bound (especially in romance) by the responsibilities and restraints of reality—for example, the need to work for a living.

Some protagonists are more submissive and thus able to attain more complete sublimation than others. Although there can be varying kinds of intermediate character, it seems possible to distinguish between what we can call positive and negative protagonists. The positive protagonist accepts control and clearly opposes the rebellious villain. An example of a strongly positive protagonist is Beowulf, who completely subordinates himself to the communal authority represented by Hrothgar and as a result completely opposes the rebelliousness against that authority embodied in Grendel. In contrast, a negative protagonist comes under the domination of rebellious desire; that desire is less completely transferred from him to a villain. He tends to merge with the rebellious villain or become like him. And his rebelliousness cuts the negative protagonist off from the positive object and the sublimation it represents. For example, Othello comes under the control of Iago, who embodies rebelliousness, and thus cuts himself off from Desdemona, who represents a virtuous, controlled desire. Even comparatively virtuous protagonists often exhibit some of this tendency to come under the villain's influence: Clarissa is attracted to Lovelace, Elizabeth Bennet to Wickham, and David Copperfield to Steerforth. In ironic fiction, particularly modern works, protagonists become partly or wholly negative, as in the case of Jonathan Wild, Becky Sharp, and Nostromo. To the degree that negative desire is allowed into the protagonist, the subject becomes divided: one part of the self stands apart from the protagonist, usually finding expression in an ironic, critical narrator.

Narratives seek to work out a process of sublimation by replacing the negative object-characters with positive ones. The narrative uses the negative object to embody polarized desire and control in forms which can be rejected and replaced by positive desire and control which accept each other and can thus allow sublimation. That is, it seeks to create the sense of a control that desire can accept and be fulfilled by, a control strong enough to counteract the forces in the negative object. The process of sublimation seems like a reaction against the story's tendency to arouse desire. Although at the start of the story desire opposes control, the story rejects control only in order to transform it, separating out the repressive aspect of control to create an idealized control which is free of that repressiveness. This positive control seems to combine the good aspects of paternal and maternal objects, the father seen as controlling and the mother seen as loving; joining these two creates an ideal of loving control. This transformation of authority earned by submission is analogous to the idea of divine grace; divine authority is transformed into loving mercy by the Christian's submission. Narrative typically acts out such a transformation through the defeat of a negative parentlike character and a transfer of power to his positive counterpart, a transfer that reflects a shift in attitude toward authority, from resentment to acceptance. Once parentlike control is accepted, desire can be freed of Oedipal guilt and thus allowed fulfillment.

The fulfillment that sublimating narrative makes us want, then, is the complete reconciliation of desire and control. The embodiments of control and desire in the object are joined together, and this controlled desire in the positive object is united with the subject. The positive object is like an idealized version of the self, idealized by identifying it with an ideal image of the parents. The narrative seems to create this ideal in order to take it into the self. This introjection reverses the process that initiated the plot conflict, the projection out of the self of those entities the story seeks to deal with. As I have mentioned, this process resembles Freud's description of the way the child deals with his Oedipus complex, by taking into himself an idealized version of parental control, transforming it into self-control. Perhaps narratives begin by rebelling against control and arousing Oedipal anxiety in order to help us get that anxiety out of our system and so put it to rest, as least momentarily.

In addition to working out a reunion with control, sublimating narrative also seeks to redeem desire. I have mentioned that desire often seems to be largely shifted from the protagonist to a villain; but once the negative object has been rejected, that negative desire can be transformed into a positive, controlled desire which can then be returned to the subject. Thus the rejection of the villain frees the protagonist to become active, serving desire by sublimating it. The protagonist can be allowed to serve desire because he has been reconciled with an embodiment of control, a control that prevents his desire from becoming guilty. Evidently narrative begins by expressing rebellious desire so it can be redeemed in this way, and thus made acceptable.

Although this narrative model is still rather simple, it has a potential for complexity in the interaction of desire and control. There can be considerable variation in the degree to which these two forces are reconciled—that is, in how much sublimation the work provides. Perfect sublimation is probably impossible. Frank Kermode argues that narrative has an inherent tendency to seek transformation, becoming more and more displaced.[12] This tendency, which I think is mainly to be found in sublimating narrative, probably results from the way that narrative first seeks to allow desire as much expression as possible but then seeks to impose control on that desire. This contradiction sets up a tension in the narrative structure. Desire seems incommensurate with control, so that there is always more desire than the narrative can quite control. Perhaps the forms of control a given culture finds for dealing with desire lose their efficacy for later generations. In any case, some desire seems to remain as a disturbing element, arousing guilt and thus impelling story-tellers to seek new forms of control, modifying their fictions to do so.

These modifications affect the relationships and natures of the various characters. Since the characters are interrelated parts of one structure, a modification of that structure produces a different configuration of character functions. For example, the stronger the protagonist's desire, the more likely the negative object is to express a repressive reaction against that desire. Beowulf seems to have no rebellious desires at all, and so there is no repressive villain opposing him; on the other hand, Clarissa feels strong desires attracting her to Lovelace despite her virtuous self-control, and so she is opposed by a highly repressive father. If a protagonist is submissive, there is likely to be a rebellious reaction against that submission expressed in the negative object, as Grendel expresses rebellion against submissiveness like Beowulf's and Quilp against Little Nell's. Object-characters tend to come in opposing pairs: a repressive villain expressing a reaction against the desire embodied in a highly desirable goal-character, or a rebellious villain expressing a reaction against a strong parentlike authority to which the protagonist submits. The more idealized the protagonist is, the more his adversary is likely to be seen as evil; and the more virtuous the protagonist is, the more the positive object can be idealized, since the protagonist can be allowed a high degree of sublimation.

These configurations seem analogous to different psychological configurations, different ways of relating desire and control within the self.[13] We can distinguish certain configurations, particular ways of transforming narrative, which are typical of particular writers or cultures. To describe a particular configuration, we can tell how completely positive and negative functions are polarized, and how fully and in what way conflicts are dealt with. The degree to which the protagonist is dominated by other characters can reflect the ego's relation to other psychological forces; like a protagonist, the ego can rebel against control, submit to it, or seek some sort of balance between these extremes. If a rebellious villain is dominant, as Lovelace is in *Clarissa,* we can infer that the writer feels uncontrolled desire to be a serious threat he must deal with. If the protagonist is submissive to a strong embodiment of authority, as Beowulf is, we can guess that the writer believes in or wishes for a strong control over desire, a submission like a Christian's submission to God. If on the other hand a writer believes in an independent, rational self-control, he is likely to shift more power to the subject, either the narrator (as in Fielding's case) or the protagonist (as in Jane Austen's case). In the following chapters we shall examine one of the forms sublimating narrative has taken—the novel—and consider the particular ways it has transformed narrative structure.

The Novel as a Transformation of Basic Narrative Structure: The Historical Context

chapter 3

To understand the particular way the novel transforms the structure of sublimating narrative, we need to understand the effect of social change on novelists and on the way they structure narrative. Here again I must venture beyond my own specialty and try to make use of nonliterary theory, in this case historical theory dealing with the evolution of modern society.

In relating literature to history, there is a danger of leaving out an intermediary process connecting the two. We must remember that cultural forces act on the minds of individual writers who react to (and against) those forces in complex ways. We can postulate that those influences change the way the mind structures its experience. If a particular way of organizing narrative reflects a particular psychological configuration in the writer, social forces can alter that configuration. That is, they can affect the way the writer defines and relates aspects of the subject and object. Subject and object seem to be analogous to forces within the psyche, so that a psychological change will be accompanied by an alteration in the subject-object structure. Those psychological forces in turn seem influenced by social factors, so that social change can cause psychological change. The main way society seems to affect the mind is by providing forms of authority which the mind internalizes. Thus the particular form authority takes in a given society and the relation of that authority to the individual's desires probably affect the way narrative embodies and relates desire and control. In this chapter, then, I shall concentrate on the way the structure of relationships among characters in the novel seems to reflect the individual's relation to authority during the period in which the novel developed.

If we follow Northrop Frye in seeing the novel as a "displacement" of romance,[1] we can understand its evolution by comparing its structure with that of romance. The novel evolved in a cultural context which provided writers with a conventional way of structuring narrative—that is, romance. They apparently could not escape that convention entirely; they work within it even while reacting against it. The particular romances they reacted against were those of the late Renaissance, old-fashioned, highly conventional and idealized works like *The Grand Cyrus*—works I would call baroque romances.[2] In these works object-characters are highly polarized: the heroine embodies pure virtue, a virtue requiring total submission to higher authority, and the villain embodies an equally extreme evil quality, a lustful passion which seems to exist simply to oppose authority by destroying the heroine's virtue. Authority is usually embodied in a fatherlike character such as a king, also idealized. And the hero is totally submissive to authority and opposed to rebelliousness, accepting the heroine's virtuous control and opposing the villain. Although the story requires that he be cut off from parentlike approval until the ending, his ostracism is seen not as his own fault but rather is blamed on a rebellious villain; and the hero acts to defend submission to authority—for example, by protecting the heroine's virtue. Thus rebellious passion is kept wholly separate from virtuous desire; there is no middle ground between them. Desire can be completely reconciled with control. In other words, it can be highly sublimated.

This narrative structure seems to reflect a particular psychological configuration, one in which rebellious passion is strongly opposed by authority, an authority evidently internalized from the writer's culture. We do not find much indication of an ego mediating between these two forces. Rather the ego, like the protagonist, seems able to submit to internalized authority (what Freud calls the superego). It can submit because that authority is evidently able to control desire adequately, making it virtuous, and yet at the same time can allow desire to be fulfilled. Since desire can be sublimated in this way, the ego need not seek to restrain it. Therefore the individual need not try to use his own ego to control desire and instead can believe in total submission to authority. This belief in authority is no doubt partly a product of Christian belief in a divine control able to sublimate desire. But it also seems to reflect the attitudes of the aristocratic audience for whom baroque romance was mainly created. Submission to social control is fulfilling if you belong to a class which society rewards. Such a class is thus likely to believe in authority—for example, absolute monarchy and the papacy. The condemnation of any opposition to authority which we find in baroque romance seems to reflect a Counter-Reformation ideology, the aristocratic reaction against the attack on the idea of feudal authority. Counter-Reformation ideology defends a status quo based on traditional authority; similarly, the romance hero defends the ideal of submission (as in rescuing the heroine), opposes those who rebel against authority, asserts the value of submission despite all temptations, and returns to the status quo at the end, winning the approval of authority. The authority to which he submits is the established social order. Yet the status quo seems more beleaguered and harder to regain than in earlier romance, and the hero and heroine seem more on the defensive. This probably reflects the increasingly defensive position of seventeenth-century conservatives. However, this defensiveness merely makes the assertion of absolute authority the more dogmatic.

The novel apparently came into being in reaction against this kind of narrative based on total submission to authority. The novel modifies the narrative form it inherits from romance by altering the subject's relation to embodiments of authority, a modification that affects other aspects of the work as well. In many ways the English novel still resembles romance, keeping the structure of sublimating narrative in which the hero seeks to reconcile his desire with control. But there are important differences. The best place in which to see the change from romance to novel taking place, I think, is in *Clarissa;* it seems to me to be the first work that successfully modifies romance in the way typical of the novel. *Clarissa* resembles baroque romance in many ways, especially in its endorsement of a high degree of submission to authority. Clarissa herself is nearly as virtuous as a romance heroine. But the object-characters in the story form a different structure from those in baroque romance. What we would expect to be the positive object has been transformed into a negative object. The figure of authority, Clarissa's father, is repressive, preventing fulfillment (even though Richardson asserts that Clarissa should submit to him). In other words, submission to authority no longer provides sublimation. As a result, Clarissa partly rejects authority. Even though Richardson largely absolves her of responsibility, he maneuvers her into a situation where she runs away from her family, and he makes us feel that her only hope for fulfillment lies in escaping their control. Furthermore, he offers no positive embodiment of authority able to enter Clarissa's world and help her. The good parentlike characters are either powerless or (in the case of Morden) absent until it is too late. Since there is no control which can be reconciled with desire, sublimation is impossible in her world (although Richardson still believes it is possible through death), and as a result Richardson also deletes the positive goal-character who would embody that sublimation. The character whom we would expect to represent fulfillment, Lovelace, is transformed instead into a lustful villain, an embodiment of desire which opposes control. It seems that authority in this world is so repressive that desire is forced to take a rebellious form.

This narrative restructuring appears to reflect an attitude toward authority quite different from that underlying baroque romance. As in the case of romance, we can relate this attitude to the writer's social class. Richardson of course is a middle-class writer, and his popularity suggests that his attitudes must have been fairly typical of his class. If so, we can conclude that he expresses a middle-class resentment of authority. We must beware of oversimplifying; he (and presumably his readers) continued to a large extent to believe in traditional forms of authority, at least consciously. But submission to authority is no longer so easy and complete as it was in baroque romance; it is no longer unquestioned. This attitude seems analogous to the Protestant questioning of the dogma of an authoritarian church and the Puritan attack on absolute monarchy.

Clarissa's example suggests that we can relate this attitude to changes in the family. Historians of the family like Philippe Ariès believe that during this period there was increased emphasis on the family and on parental control.[3] *Clarissa* provides a picture (although a sentimentally exaggerated one) of the great importance of the family in the individual's life and of the father's power over his child. One probable reason for paternal power during this period was that traditional forms of social authority had lost some of their importance. In *Clarissa* the father need share his power with no one. There no longer seem to be any outside forms of social authority able to counteract him; he is free to treat Clarissa as he wishes. In addition, middle-class fathers had gained considerable economic power, as Richardson shows. The middle-class father seemed to model his role on the entrepreneur exploiting his employees rather than the feudal lord whose power was limited by his responsibilities to his subjects. It is their concern with economic power that makes the Harlowes so domineering; they seem to seek control and possession as ends in themselves, treating Clarissa as mere property to exploit, perverting the parent-child relationship into a power relationship. Given such a family structure, the emphasis on parent-child relations of which Ariès speaks seems rather sinister: the more the parent is concerned with the child, the more likely he is to be (or seem) repressive.

This change in social control probably caused a psychological change. If authority was repressive, it would have been harder for the individual to internalize it and thus harder to believe in the very concept of authority. As I have mentioned, the child evidently internalizes control in order to deal with his Oedipal desires. If they are not restrained, the child feels guilt; but on the other hand, he does not wish to suppress them entirely. One way to avoid these extremes would be to find some substitute for parental control to internalize instead. In feudal society it might have been easier to find such a substitute, a form of control which the child was willing to internalize because it was less repressive than direct submission to a father would have been. The feudal hierarchy provided many forms of control that the individual could accept in place of his parents. Thus he could partly reject his father and yet avoid rebellion because he was submitting to some other form of authority. But with modernization, the various institutions supplementing parental control decreased in power; society no longer offered alternative forms of control that the individual could internalize. He either had to submit to his father and be quite repressed or else rebel against his father and incur Oedipal guilt. Neither alternative was very acceptable, and so the individual experienced unresolved conflict. As a result, there seems to have occurred a split in the attitude toward authority. Ideally authority restrains desire yet fulfills it, providing enough sublimation to compensate for the submission it demands.

But with modernization these two aspects of authority—controlling and fulfilling—began to seem opposed, as submission and ambition could no longer be fully reconciled. People still sought to hold onto a belief in some form of fulfilling control, but they tended to separate that concept from actual social control, which they saw as repressive. Thus people like the Puritans sought to replace social control with some form of ideal control that could offer the sublimation society no longer provided.

At the same time that society began to seem more repressive, economic forces also tended to cause increased rebellion against its authority. The rise of what Ian Watt calls economic individualism[4] would presumably make sons become concerned with economic power just as fathers were. In a class that sought to rise socially, the son would no longer simply wish to accept his father's trade but would want to attain a higher rank, thus breaking free of parental control and setting out on his own. At the same time that fathers tried to exercise greater control, then, sons (and probably daughters too) became more independent. And the father's authoritarianism was likely to make the child more rebellious, as the child's rebellion was likely to make the father stricter.

We can see a reflection of this change in the way narrative structure relates desire and control. In baroque romance the protagonist serves authority, reflecting a mental configuration in which desire can submit to and serve internalized authority, the superego. But in the kind of configuration exemplified by *Clarissa,* desire (represented by the protagonist) seems more separate from that control, seeking some independence so that it may not be denied so much. One can accept social control as long as one believes that control sublimates one's desires, providing them with a fulfilling outlet. But as the superego comes to seem repressive, desire opposes it more and so can no longer be so fully sublimated. As a result, it becomes harder for people to believe in sublimation, in reconciling their desires with a higher control like God's. They may still believe in God, but that belief seems to require greater effort and to offer less fulfillment.

This rejection of authority seems to have been a gradual process in which rebelliousness coexisted with submission, the two interacting and taking many forms. We can find many different expressions of this process in literature of the period preceding the rise of the novel. One striking example of rebelliousness is Marlowe's

Faustus, who begins the play by rejecting such conventional forms of authority as the law and religion, since those forms no longer fulfill his desires. Other Renaissance writers express a similar sense of the individual's unfulfilled—perhaps unfulfillable—aspirations: we feel a similar desire for power in Macbeth and Iago, for example, and in Milton's Satan. Renaissance writers usually see this desire as guilty, but their concern with it, the fullness with which they express it, indicates that they consider it a problem to be dealt with. In other words, submission to authority has become somewhat problematic, no longer a foregone conclusion.

In prose fiction, the clearest example of a rejection of traditional authority is probably *Don Quixote,* which like *Clarissa* presents no positive object able to provide the kind of sublimated fulfillment romance offers. There is neither a positive goal-character (a virtuous heroine) nor a fulfilling embodiment of authority for Quixote. Instead, the forms of authority Cervantes seems mainly concerned with are the conventions of romance; that is, he sees authority as merely a convention. He no longer believes it can provide sublimation. In the absence of sublimation, Quixote faces only a negative object—the whole world he lives in. Defoe also creates a world in which no sublimating control of desire is possible because there is no object-character embodying that control. Moll Flanders and Robinson Crusoe both leave home, evidently unable to accept the traditional social authority it represents. They escape society almost entirely, determining their own identities rather than accepting a social identity. As a result, they cannot return to a status quo as romance protagonists do.

In Richardson this conflict with society is more serious. He seems torn between resentment of authority and belief in submission to it, and as a result he makes society much more enclosing and harder to reject than Cervantes and Defoe do. Pamela and Clarissa both leave home too, rejecting the unfulfilling identity society tries to impose on them and asserting their right to self-determination. Thus like Defoe's protagonists they cannot return to a status quo. But their rejection of society is much more difficult than in Defoe and arouses strong conflicts. In *Clarissa* Richardson seems unable to resolve the conflict entirely: Clarissa can neither find fulfillment within society nor escape from her duty to it (except in death).

We find a similar rejection of social and parental authority in later novels as well. The subject and object don't seem to fit together as easily as in traditional narratives; the object no longer fulfills the subject's desires perfectly. That is, sublimation is only partial. Desire and authority no longer exist in forms that can be wholly reconciled. Characters embodying authority in the novel are rarely both good and strong—that is, both willing and able to serve the protagonist's desire, to help him sublimate it. Good father figures—like Squire Allworthy, Walter Shandy, Mr. Bennet in *Pride and Prejudice,* Davie Deans in *Heart of Midlothian,* Mr. Earnshaw in *Wuthering Heights,* Mr. Micawber, and Mr. Tulliver in *Mill on the Floss*—tend to lack the power to assist desire and also tend to be flawed, so that they often function partly as negative characters, hindering fulfillment. Good control can no longer be fully identified with social power, in contrast with romances where the representative of social authority, the king, is idealized.

Instead, social power is largely shifted to negative characters like Mr. Harlowe. In the novel the protagonist is typically opposed by a whole world of negative characters representing a society that opposes his desires. Because this negative function is usually divided among quite a few characters, there is often no one simple villain; even if there is one main villain, he is often not as simply evil as in romance. However, since the negative object is spread out among a whole community of characters, it seems more of an obstacle than in romance. When the negative object is seen as a whole world, it becomes more enclosing (as it does in Richardson) and harder to escape. Resistance to fulfillment becomes increasingly pervasive in the novel, and the search for fulfillment becomes an increasingly serious, difficult business. It is often harder for the protagonist to escape the negative object because he is more closely related to it than in romance, bound to negative characters by social ties which he cannot wholly reject. And when such characters are not purely evil, they become harder to reject. One can kill off an ogre, but not one's father. Characters like Mr. Harlowe, Mrs. Bennet, and Dombey are not simply villains; they are also parents whom their children (the protagonists) must come to terms with or at least try to. The protagonist of *Middlemarch* is even more closely tied to a similar character; she is actually married to Casaubon. George Eliot contrasts Casaubon with a dragon which a romance hero could defeat; Casaubon is "more unmanageable" because he has "collective society at his back" (21.241).[5] Another way the negative object includes greater resistance to desire is through the novel's greater emphasis on physical obstacles, its detailing of space and time. Already in *Clarissa* setting is used to enclose the protagonist and time is used to frustrate her.

This shift in the attitude toward control affects other parts of the novel's structure as well. As authority becomes less acceptable, rebellion against it becomes less unthinkable, and as a result rebellious villains cease to be so villainous. In baroque romance the main villain is a character embodying a rebellious desire which is seen as wholly evil so that it can be entirely rejected. But in most novels, the main opposition the protagonist seeks to deal with is a social control that opposes his desires. When the novel retains a rebellious villain, it usually treats him with more sympathy than does its predecessor. For example, Lovelace resembles the lustful villain of romance, but he is more attractive and harder to reject. Wickham in *Pride and Prejudice* also functions as a lustful villain, but he is much less lustful and villainous than in romance, so that we feel the uncontrolled desire he represents is not a very serious threat. I think this shift reflects an attraction to rebelliousness. Although Jane Austen condemns Elizabeth's rebelliousness, she also sympathizes with it to some extent: she too mocks social control. Dickens often retains the rebellious villain of romance, but in his later novels he tends to treat such characters with sympathy, as in the case of Steerforth and Richard Carstone. George Eliot shows considerable sympathy for characters (like Arthur Donnithorne and Maggie Tulliver) who cannot completely control their desires. And Emily Brontë seems so attracted to Heathcliff's rebelliousness that he ceases to be a villain and, even more than Lovelace, takes over the novel, becoming a rival protagonist.

As it becomes harder to reconcile desire with some form of authority, sublimation becomes more difficult. Until the middle of the nineteenth century, novelists continued to believe in and seek sublimation, judging by the way they embody it in an idealized goal-character who represents a union of control with desire—characters like Sophia Western, Darcy, and Agnes Wickfield. But some novelists, like Richardson in *Clarissa*, express pessimism about the possibility of sublimation by transforming the goal-character into a negative character. In *Tristram Shandy* there is no goal-character, unless the Widow Wadman is a parody of one. The Victorians seem to have difficulty believing in sublimation, a tendency betrayed by the fact that their goal-characters are often weak, perfunctory, and unconvincing. Thackeray doesn't allow us to see Amelia as wholly fulfilling. Estella in *Great Expectations* is another imperfect goal-character reflecting her creator's growing pessimism. In *Middlemarch* George Eliot creates two negative goal-characters, Rosamond and Casaubon, and weakens two other goal-characters, Fred Vincy and Will Ladislaw, so that they do not seem wholly fulfilling. And later novels offer even less fulfillment, as I hope to show in my final section.

As the negative object becomes stronger than the positive, the protagonist becomes weaker, since his world opposes him more strongly. Northrop Frye has pointed out how protagonists in "mimetic" fiction become less wish-fulfilling, less godlike and heroic[6]—that is, more restricted by social and physical opposition. Don Quixote is a good example of the way the outer world can prevent a protagonist from becoming like a romance hero. One reason novel protagonists are usually weaker than romance heroes is that they do not have the same social sanction; they do not serve a higher authority (such as a king or an ideal of virtue as represented by a heroine) which endorses them. As a result, the desire that novel protagonists serve is more opposed to authority and is partly guilty. The romance hero's submissiveness makes his desire virtuous, so that he can get away with being quite wish-fulfilling: he can kill off villains and win a highly idealized goal-character. The novel protagonist is rarely virtuous enough to be allowed this much fulfillment. At the same time, however, the novel protagonist's independence gives him a negative strength, an ability to resist control. Romance heroes often seem controlled by some higher power—for example, fortune or love (both often described as godlike forces outside the self). Thus even though the romance hero seems strong, his strength does not seem his own; it is given him by the authority he serves. In contrast, a protagonist like Clarissa, even though she lacks the power to overcome the negative object, has the strength to oppose that object. Like most novel protagonists, she can assert her independence through the individuality of her speech and action. As novel protagonists become less passive, fortune plays a smaller role than in romance, since novelists see most action as originating in the individual, not in some higher power. Nevertheless, I think the strength we feel in novel protagonists remains mainly negative, an ability to resist control more than an ability to attain sublimation.

The partial rejection of authority typical of post-Renaissance culture has far-reaching effects. Again the example of *Clarissa* can help us see how attitudes were changing. Clarissa of course does not simply rebel against authority. After she leaves her family she feels guilty and attempts to atone for her rebelliousness by rejecting Lovelace (who represents rebelliousness), thus reasserting her submissiveness. She cannot return to her father, but she can replace his control with one to which she can submit—God's control. Thus she creates a substitute for the authority she has rejected.

I think the process that takes place in Clarissa reflects that which took place in middle-class attitudes. It seems likely that as people began to question authority, they also began to feel guilty about doing so. The more they felt their desires could not be fulfilled through traditional social forms, the more those desires would seem antisocial and therefore guilty. Resentment of authority resembles Oedipal rebellion and thus causes some Oedipal guilt; and people seem to have tried to deal with this guilt as a child deals with Oedipal guilt, by creating some internalized form of control in place of the outer control he has opposed. Like Clarissa, people tried to develop ways of dealing with guilt through self-control. As social authority became harder to internalize, self-control became more self-conscious and willed, more uncertain, but all the stricter because of its insecurity. For example, the Puritans, after rejecting traditional religious authority, replaced it with a rigid control of their own, as if to atone for having rebelled. Calvin replaced the pope and Cromwell replaced the king with a control more rigid than the one they had rejected. And just as Clarissa turns inward in her attempt to recreate within herself a control to replace the external authority she has rejected, so the Puritans attempted to replace traditional, external forms of control with an internalized self-restraint, involving a self-questioning and self-criticism quite like Clarissa's.[7]

We can also see this concern with self-control in the increased emphasis the middle class placed on education and literacy. Education, and especially reading, involves a self-discipline which enables one to find out things for oneself rather than receiving them from some social authority; one can choose one's own authority, and can replace authority that directly controls the self with a more remote, abstract form of authority. Louis B. Wright has pointed out how literacy increased middle-class religious independence and offered a means of self-help.[8] In other words, it helped readers reject authority.

The shift from an external version of authority to an internalized version may have influenced the shift from drama to fiction. The drama is communal and offers a social experience; the reader of fiction substitutes a private experience for that public one. Christopher Hill holds that members of the middle class gradually replaced communal forms with private ones,[9] and the Puritan distrust of drama may be an expression of that resistance to social authority. By replacing play-going with reading, one could feel one was exercising greater self-control; instead of being shown the story, one visualized it for oneself. And for the Puritan reader, the act of reading may also have involved a rational effort which counterbalanced the feeling that literature is escapist and thus potentially immoral.

When we look at the literature of this period, we can find examples of this kind of reaction against rebelliousness. The rebellion of Faustus and other tragic heroes, for example, leads to guilt. But Renaissance tragedy does not seek to create a new form of control to deal with that guilt, apparently because most writers still believed in a traditional form of authority, a status quo to which the play can return at the end, an authority still able to counterbalance rebelliousness (though just barely). When we reach Milton the return to authority seems more typically Puritan, in that traditional authority is recreated in a personal version. Milton does not simply take God for granted; he feels he must justify God's ways to man. Evidently he needs to create anew for himself an ideal of divine control able to counterbalance satanic rebellion. This replacement of authority increases in later writers; for example, Romantic poets often try to compensate for their rebelliousness by creating some new form of divinity to replace the god they have rejected.

In prose fiction before Richardson, there does not seem to be much of this need to react against the rejection of authority. Cervantes does not offer any ideal authority with which to replace the romance conventions he rejects, at least until the work's very end; rather, he asks us to accept the absence of such an ideal. Defoe does make some attempt to compensate for his protagonists' independence by moralizing, but he is not concerned enough with authority to embody moral control in an object-character to which the protagonist can submit or to locate much guilt or self-opposition in his protagonists. His works, like rogue stories and like *Quixote*, are mainly concerned with reconciling desire to the outer world, not to self-control. Since neither writer is primarily concerned with submission to authority, both reject the romance conventions which are based on that submission.

But from Richardson on, the novel typically involves the search for some ideal form of control to replace the social control which has been rejected, so that the protagonist can avoid the guilt which his rebellion would otherwise arouse. This search gives the novel its organizing principle. We could describe the novel as an enactment of this process of seeking to replace conventional social authority with some form of control that desire can accept more fully. Earlier novels usually try to justify self-control by making it completely replace traditional authority, as David Copperfield's learning to discipline his heart enables him to attain sublimation. Later novels, unable to offer sublimation, usually try to make self-control seem valuable as an end in itself even though it is only a partial, less fulfilling substitute for sublimating control; one needs to learn restraint, as Isabel Archer does. But even when the novel offers a sublimating form of control, this control, unlike that in traditional romance, is not usually equated with social control. Rather, the novel replaces the social with some idealized form of control, just as the middle class sought new forms of authority to replace those of feudal society. For example, Esther Summerson has to leave the world of Chancery and find sublimation on some higher level of existence, replacing the old Bleak House with a purified version of it. Even in Jane Austen, where the control accepted at the end is more fully located in society, there is a removal to a higher plane and an escape from the repressive social control that has been dominant during the novel. Instead of returning to a status quo like romance, then, the novel—like the middle class itself—seeks progress, some better form of control.

This search for control finds expression in the structuring of character-functions. The protagonist seeks a positive object-character to replace the negative one embodying unacceptable control. This positive transformation of the object may be a new character or the same character, converted from bad to good. For example, Tom Jones converts Squire Allworthy by freeing him from the influence of the rebelliousness (shifted from Tom to Blifil) that made him react repressively; by doing so, Tom is also able to replace various negative goal-characters (temptresses) with Sophia. Jane Austen's heroines find strong fatherlike heroes, functioning both as goal-characters and authority figures, who replace unacceptable parents, fathers too weak to provide adequate control or motherlike characters who oppose desire. David Copperfield replaces a weak mother and a cruel father figure (Murdstone) with a series of characters offering increasingly idealized control, from Steerforth and then Micawber through Betsey Trotwood to Agnes; while Florence Dombey and Louisa Gradgrind convert their fathers from repressive to loving parents. Dorothea Brooke replaces Casaubon with Will Ladislaw but also, like Clarissa, with inner restraint, chastening her ardor, making it more unselfish. These novels thus reenact the process that gave rise to the novel itself—the individual's replacement of external forms of authority with a control that he has chosen (or created) for himself.

I suspect that this development of forms of self-control to replace external authority is a crucial feature of modern culture, the culture expressed in the novel.[10] It seems to correspond to a psychological change, which we can describe as a gradual shift from the superego—an unconscious, unquestioned internalization of parental and social control—to the ego—a more conscious self-control. Before the modern period people could evidently accept authority without having to become conscious of doing so, thus leaving self-control largely outside the conscious ego. This acceptance is mirrored by the protagonist's submission in traditional romance. Presumably such a submission was possible because sons could normally accept their father's control as the romance hero accepts control; thus they would internalize that control fairly easily and completely. But as desire became less completely controlled and sublimated, it aroused more guilt, and the psyche was impelled to face that guilty desire and try to deal with it more consciously, developing the ego to do so. However, the ego seems unable to replace the superego completely. When it tries, it incurs a sense of guilt for having challenged the superego's authority, like a son trying to replace his father. As the ego loses the superego's sanction, it becomes less able to sublimate desire, to offer a control that can purify yet fulfill desire. Instead the ego increasingly attempts to control desire in negative, unsublimating ways, through awareness and self-criticism. It tries to be rational, divided between a sense of duty toward the conscience and a wish to serve desire, uncertain and defensive—more like a politician than an absolute monarch, since it lacks the power to sublimate desire completely.

There are various cultural indications of the development of an increasingly conscious ego—for example, the rise of science and rationalism. In the novel, we can see an expression of ego awareness in an increased concern with the protagonist's interaction with his world. In baroque romance there is little sense of the self's relation to its world; the heroine is almost the only object that affects the hero, who remains impervious to everything but love. And there is little sense of the effort necessary to deal with the object-world, of the means necessary to accomplish an end. The novel shows more consciousness of the way reality resists desire, a consciousness that Freud describes as the ego's function. In addition, the novel locates more consciousness within protagonists; like the ego, they deal with desire by becoming aware of it and criticizing it as Clarissa does.

However, the main manifestation of ego control I want to concentrate on here is the ego's tendency to create compromise formations. Because the ego seems unable to replace the superego entirely and to repress irrational impulses completely, it typically works out a compromise with those impulses. It seems to lack the power to separate itself completely from those forces in the psyche, to reject them. Instead it allows them some expression: to some extent it accepts rebellious desires, but it tries to find a way of expressing them which is acceptable to the conscience, the superego seeking to repress those desires. Since these opposing forces are in strong conflict, it can fully satisfy neither; but it keeps on trying. Here again, *Clarissa* provides a good example of the psychological configuration I am describing. Clarissa finds herself caught between rebellious desire (Lovelace) and repressive control (her father), and like the ego she attempts to reconcile their demands. She cannot do so, but Richardson does allow her to work out a kind of compromise between the rebellious and submissive sides of herself: by replacing her father with God she both rejects her father and remains submissive.

If we look at historical changes during this period we can see some evidence of this tendency to seek compromises. In the period following Cromwell, people seem to have reacted against both rebellious and authoritarian extremes and to have sought some middle ground between them, attempting to balance king and Parliament, individual freedom and social control. Perhaps we can parallel this with the Deist attempt to find a compromise between religious faith and rational doubt. And individuals generally seem to have sought to balance some independence with an acceptance of traditional values.

This concern with compromise may be related to the development noted by Ariès of the concept of an intermediate phase between infancy and adulthood.[11] In the Middle Ages there seems to have been little middle ground between child and adult, just as there seems to have been little middle ground between a childlike freedom from restraint and the submission to social control expected of an adult. Perhaps it was because it became more difficult for people to internalize parental authority that an in-between stage evolved, a state in which the individual sought to combine some independence with some submission. By doing so the individual could attempt to satisfy some of his own desires yet placate both his parents and his conscience. And it may be that people have increasingly retained some of this intermediate stage in later life, remaining partly adolescent.

If we compare the novel to traditional romance, we find a greater tendency toward compromise in the novel. In medieval literature in general there does not seem to be much need to find a compromise between private desires and social control; the two are allowed to exist side by side, like Chaucer's virtuous knight and rebellious miller. The ideal of authority seems secure enough so that contradictions do not threaten it and can be accepted. And in romance good and evil are highly polarized; no compromise between them is possible. In contrast, the novel balances desire and control, rebellion and submission, pleasure and reality principles in many ways. In fact we can see the novel itself (and realism) as a compromise formation,[12] an attempt to offer sublimation as romance does, yet allow desire more uncontrolled expression than in romance. As members of the English middle class reached an accommodation with traditional values, so the English novel remained tolerant of romance. In this we can contrast the English with the French, who rejected romance more completely just as they rebelled more decisively against monarchic authority. Especially in the English novel, there remains a search for sublimation like that in romance; the narrative structure includes embodiments of desire and control which the work seeks to reconcile with each other. But at the same time sublimation is diminished in various ways, the opposing forces not so fully reconciled as in traditional romance.

Probably all literature involves some degree of compromise, but the novel seems more directly, consciously concerned with working out a compromise. It apparently does so because it contains more unresolved tension which it must try to deal with in some way. Since it cannot fully sublimate desire, reconciling it with control, more rebellious desire remains and conflicts cannot be completely resolved. Yet despite this conflict, the classic English novel typically seeks sublimation. Thus the novel becomes a search for a romancelike ideal, but a search that must take into account greater resistance than in traditional romance. Sublimation cannot be completely attained, but it remains desirable. In other words, the novel seeks to work out a compromise between belief (that one can attain sublimation) and doubt (a sense of the difficulty of attaining it). It is as if the writer is trying to regain religious certainty, to recreate belief in an ideal authority. This process of deflecting fulfillment, replacing sublimation with less perfect substitutes, resembles the development of narrative that Frank Kermode describes in *The Sense of an Ending;* writers try not to give up the ideal they seek, but they are constrained to make the process of seeking it more and more difficult and complex.

We can see this combination of romance with opposition to it in *Clarissa*. Clarissa resembles a romance heroine, but she lives in an antiromance world. Like a romance heroine, she believes in and seeks an ideal of virtuous submission to authority. But she must seek that ideal not in a wish-fulfilling land, an imaginary Persia or Arcadia, but within a restrictive social world. In other words, her world is dominated by the negative object. The less sublimation a work offers, the more rebellious desire it contains, and the more repressiveness opposing that rebelliousness. These polarized impulses find expression in the negative object. Clarissa's search for sublimation thus takes place within a world that prevents total sublimation. The imperfect sublimation she does finally attain—in dying—involves a compromise with Richardson's awareness of the difficulty of attaining an ideal. He believes in the ideal (perfect sublimation), but he can't fully believe that it is possible in reality; so he compromises by locating it in heaven, in effect saying that the ideal does exist but not in reality. In other words, there is a conflict between his wish to believe in an ideal and his doubt about actually attaining it.

This heightened conflict in the novel between the individual's desires and outer opposition probably reflects middle-class attitudes. Romance sublimation evidently came to seem too easy and wish-fulfilling to middle-class readers because it was not so easy for them to reconcile their own desires with social constraints. An aristocratic reader of romance could feel that the existing social order automatically provided fulfillment, since he could accept his rank. But middle-class readers who had to work and overcome social obstacles to get ahead would feel that fulfillment was something that should be earned, that required effort. Though they still wanted fiction to provide a romancelike happy ending, they also wanted it to make that ending more convincing by dealing with resistance to it.

We can see this sense of the way the world opposes the individual's desires not only in Richardson but in Cervantes and Defoe. Richardson differs from them, however, in staying closer to romance, compromising with it more. Just as he is more concerned with accepting authority, though also redeeming it, he also retains more of the romance framework based on belief in authority, though also modifying that framework. Cervantes offers no compromise between Quixote's desire for romance wish-fulfillment and his world's negation of that desire. But Richardson has more sympathy with his protagonist, presumably because he believes in her search for an ideal. As a result, he makes her a character who (unlike Quixote) has the ability to serve the desire for sublimation convincingly and with some success: she can interact with reality, taking it into account and adapting to it to some extent. Richardson is also unlike Defoe in valuing the search for sublimation. Moll and Crusoe largely accept the fact that they must live in an unromancelike world; Defoe expresses little desire for anything better. Richardson represents a compromise between romance and Defoe: he is willing to accommodate desire to reality more than romance does, yet unlike Defoe he does not surrender to reality entirely but keeps the search for an ideal. His belief in sublimation enables him to retain a romancelike narrative structure. Where Cervantes and Defoe create worlds which merely present the absence of romancelike sublimation, Richardson creates a world which, like that in romance, contains embodiments of the desire and control he seeks to reconcile. This probably reflects the strength of his desire for sublimation. He cannot simply accept the absence of that ideal; instead he sees its absence as an active denial. That is, he sees the world which prevents sublimation as actively villainous rather than simply neutral. As a result he keeps the romance structure but transforms it negatively, creating characters (Lovelace and Mr. Harlowe) who are negative transformations of the idealized goal-character and the idealized parent figure. We do not find such romancelike characters, either idealized or villainous, in Cervantes and Defoe.

By using this romance structure, Richardson is able to organize his fiction in a more controlled way than Cervantes and Defoe. Instead of writing in episodes, he uses a form that offers a linear progression from an initial to a final state. Defoe is episodic because his protagonists content themselves with desires that are quickly satisfied; but Clarissa desires an ideal that she must keep seeking. And Cervantes is episodic because Quixote's desires are easily shown to be wrong and are totally defeated; there is no fulfillment toward which he can progress. In contrast, Clarissa's desires are too important to Richardson for him to block them like this. Instead Clarissa is only partially frustrated, so that each narrative section leaves an opening for further searching instead of coming to a full stop. Furthermore, because Clarissa's world contains forces that she must reconcile if she is to attain sublimation, the novel's form becomes a protracted attempt to come to terms with the object-characters embodying these forces. This too prevents Richardson from writing in episodes, since Clarissa cannot simply leave behind one set of characters but must continue trying to deal with them until she works out some resolution of their conflict.

This gradual working out of a resolution is itself a compromise formation, an attempt to find some way of accommodating desire with resistance. It is the fact that it involves a compromise which makes it take so long; neither force can be denied but rather both must be taken into account as fully as possible. In other words, compromise formations make possible a progressive form. In baroque romance even more than in Cervantes and Defoe the opposing forces are too polarized for compromise; thus each episode must end either in the complete victory or the complete destruction or subjugation of rebelliousness. In contrast, *Clarissa* can progress because the narrative sections can have partial closure, a compromise that allows both opposing forces to continue existing. Thus each section can progress to a new balance between those forces; in each section desire and control can be slightly altered and thus somewhat more reconciled with each other.[13]

Later novels resemble *Clarissa* in working out a compromise between romance structure and the novelist's sense of the forces opposing romancelike sublimation. When we say the novel is more "realistic" than romance, we evidently mean that it includes more resistance to sublimation. This seems realistic, I think, because it offers a balance between desire and control like that we feel in ourselves. We feel we have learned to restrain our desires in order to allow for reality, and novels that accept a similar restraint seem "realistic." As Harry Levin points out, "realism" is negative; by itself it offers no positive goal that can provide an organizing principle.[14] Rather it exists as a way of modifying romance, decreasing sublimation. It is a means, not an end, existing to satisfy our doubts about the possibility of sublimation enough so that we can accept the romancelike elements in a work. But it is those elements that provide what E. M. Forster calls the "backbone" on which the story is built, since they give the novelist access to the basic narrative structure he is modifying.[15]

The novel, then, still seeks a romancelike happy ending, but this final sublimation becomes increasingly deflected; only partial sublimation is offered. For example, in many novels the villain is not simply killed off; rather, we must settle for some limited victory. In Fielding and Jane Austen we partly reject some villainlike characters by seeing through them and laughing at them; in George Eliot we learn to pity such characters and thus not feel threatened by them. We cannot wholly escape them and the negative forces they represent, and so those forces cannot be wholly sublimated. Perhaps the clearest example of the way the novel retains yet limits romancelike fulfillment is the end of *Middlemarch,* where George Eliot explicitly diminishes Dorothea's fulfillment, telling us Dorothea's life is not "ideally beautiful" but rather is "mixed"—a compromise between "noble impulse" and an "imperfect social state" (epilogue, p. 896). Thus the novel typically offers a compromise between desire and the awareness of forces (especially social forces) opposing desire. It is because the typical novel ending involves a compromise that it cannot simply be a return to a status quo but rather must involve finding some substitute for the authority that the protagonist originally rejected. Finding a substitute for repressive social control involves a compromise, since the protagonist simultaneously rebels against that control and submits to some more acceptable, though usually imperfect, form of authority.

Working out a compromise of this sort seems rather difficult. In *Clarissa* the compromise is not entirely satisfying. The opposing forces remain polarized; Richardson kills off Lovelace and Mr. Harlowe instead of reconciling them with Clarissa. The ego here seems to lack the strength to mediate fully between desire and control, perhaps because it can only sublimate desire imperfectly. As a result, some unsublimated desire remains present (primarily expressed through Lovelace), and that rebellious force threatens the ego control which seeks to work out a compromise. In later novelists, especially Jane Austen, we find a more successful balance between individual desire and authority, but perhaps these two can never be totally reconciled. It may be that the compromise upon which the novel is based is inherently unstable, that the union of romance and antiromance is always somewhat uneasy. In my epilogue I will discuss the effect of this instability on later fiction; but in the following chapters I want to concentrate on the English novel from Richardson through the mid-nineteenth century. It was in this period that I think the novel's compromise was most successful, and I want to examine ways in which it influenced the development of characterization.

Clarissa & the Transformation of Character

chapter 4

THE concept of the compromise formation provides the crucial link between a basic narrative structure and the complexity of detail typical of the novel. The same process that transformed the structure of the novel in the way I have been describing, combining desire and control in compromise formations, also transformed the texture of the novel, particularly the way it presents characters. In the preceding chapter I concentrated on the way the novel transforms the narrative object; but changes in the object bring with them changes in the subject. In this chapter, then, we shall examine the effect of the novel's structural changes on the protagonist, especially on the details by which he is characterized. Here again we can use the example of *Clarissa* to illustrate the nature of this effect and then relate it to the later development of the novel.

Even though Clarissa remains rather like a romance protagonist, she differs from her predecessors in exhibiting inner conflict. Structurally we can describe her as serving two opposing desires: on the one hand, she seeks to escape her father's control and love Lovelace, but on the other hand, she seeks to escape Lovelace's control and regain her father's approval. We can call these two functions those of the negative and positive subjects. The negative subject can be seen as a transformation of the positive because it reverses its relation to the object, taking the positive object as negative and vice versa. The positive subject—Clarissa seeking to submit to her father or to God—seeks sublimation and thus accepts control, seeing it as positive. But the negative subject—Clarissa when she is attracted to Lovelace—sees that control as negative and rebels against it. In this role Clarissa resembles Lovelace; she seems to be taken over by the rebelliousness he embodies. In other words, the negative subject serves the negative object as the positive one serves the positive object; it resembles the subject-like component of the negative object, the rebellious villain.

In romance the villain's rebelliousness is seen as wholly alien to the subject and the character embodying rebellion is seen as simply a villain. But in Richardson the separation of the positive and negative aspects of desire is no longer so complete, and so rebellious desire can no longer be kept entirely out of the subject. We can see Richardson's inability to reject that desire fully in the way he makes Lovelace into something of a protagonist (though a negative one) instead of simply seeing him as an object-character. Richardson's attraction to Lovelace, like Clarissa's, implies an attraction to rebellious desire. Because of this attraction he allows rebelliousness to find expression through Clarissa too. As a result, she takes on a second function. She is like a romance heroine; but she also is like a romance villain, rebelling against the control she seeks.

As this example suggests, then, the novel differs from romance in allowing conflict in the narrative subject. We can relate this conflict to the tendencies I discussed in the previous chapter. Traditional romance can reject rebellious desire entirely because it accepts authority completely. But as writers become unable to submit to authority so completely, they are no longer able to reject rebelliousness entirely either. Rebellious desire can no longer be seen as wholly alien to the self. There is apparently too much unsublimated desire to be restricted to the negative object; so that desire finds expression in other areas, which thus become like the negative object, as Clarissa becomes partly like Lovelace. At the same time, the self (like Clarissa) reacts guiltily against that desire and seeks to regain control over it. The same reaction against desire we have seen in the novel's world thus finds expression within the protagonist. As a result, he becomes a compromise formation, expressing both some rebellious desire and this reaction against it. We can see the kind of character typical of the novel—the character with inner conflict—as a transformation, then, of a basic narrative function: the simple subject-character is transformed by combining it with functions normally located in the negative object.

This new concept of character as a locus of conflict seems to be the accepted view by the time we come to Hazlitt, who describes "character" as a thing "of striking contrast."[1] Although this kind of character is typical of the novel, we find it already in Shakespeare, who here as in so many ways seems an exception to the rules; and no doubt it was partly Shakespeare's example that taught Richardson. However, it is not until Richardson that this kind of characterization becomes established in fiction. Many later protagonists resemble Clarissa in combining positive and negative functions. Some Jane Austen characters, for example, resemble domesticated versions of Clarissa, attracted to negative characters who resemble diminished Lovelaces; I shall discuss one such example in my chapter on *Pride and Prejudice*. In *Wuthering Heights,* both Catherines manifest conflicting desires, wanting both the submission to a fulfilling, parentlike control that Thrushcross seems to offer and also the natural freedom and passion that Wuthering Heights represents, even though Emily Brontë tries to avoid showing either as negative and seeks to allow both. Maggie Tulliver is another character with a clear dual function, the rebellious side of her desiring to run off with Stephen Guest and the positive side desiring the parentlike approval of her brother Tom and Philip Wakem. In *Great Expectations* Pip is divided between his attraction to Estella and his filial piety toward Joe. And in many later novels protagonists tend to become increasingly negative, as I shall show in my final section.

This increased conflict in the subject can cause it to split. Sometimes, instead of combining positive and negative functions in one protagonist, writers allow conflict into the subject by dividing the protagonist in two. For example, Cervantes locates uncontrolled desire in Quixote and rational awareness, which seeks to control that desire, in Sancho. By thus separating desire and control he weakens each, making them unable to join and achieve sublimation. Later writers sometimes supplement their main subject-character, the one serving desire most fully, with a secondary subject representing another attitude towards that desire. For example, in *Middlemarch* Dorothea serves a desire able to submit to control and thus attain at least partial sublimation, whereas Lydgate serves a less controlled desire which thus cannot be sublimated. Dickens often uses multiple subjects, supplementing his virtuous central characters with diminished, comic secondary subjects who represent a less controlled form of the central subject's desire.

When positive characters acquire a negative function, they become less like idealized romance characters. Sometimes novelists explicitly give us a sense of a character's conflict by telling of aspects of the character that oppose a romance function. For instance, Thackeray deliberately makes the protagonist of *Vanity Fair* unlike a romance hero, as the novel's subtitle tells us; he splits the protagonist into characters who are either good (Amelia) or strong (Becky) but not both. One especially clear example of the way a novelist defines characters by contrasting them with romance characters is in Austen. In *Northanger Abbey* she talks about the way her characters differ from those in romancelike novels:

> Charming as were all Mrs. Radcliffe's works . . . , it was not in them perhaps that human nature, at least in the midland counties of England, was to be looked for. . . . in the central part of England there was surely some security . . . in the laws of the land, and the manners of the age . . . . Among the Alps and Pyrenees, perhaps, there were no mixed characters. There, such as were not spotless as an angel, might have the dispositions of a fiend. But . . . among the English, . . . in their hearts and habits, there was a general though unequal mixture of good and bad.[2]

Austen gives her characters this "mixed" quality by reacting against their romancelike function, adding other characteristics that contrast with romancelike traits. Like the romance writer she believes in "good and bad," but unlike him she locates these within the same character. In this particular passage, she relates her characters' mixed nature to the fact that they are social beings. Desire (in either its positive, wish-fulfilling form or its negative, guilty form) cannot be simply expressed through her characters because she also locates in those characters a social control that to some extent restrains desire. Outer restrictions ("laws") are internalized as restraints ("manners") so that characters contain a balance of natural and social qualities—both "hearts and habits." Social control no longer exists in a form that can fully allow desire, and so it is perceived as separate from and opposed to desire. Consequently, desire is seen as at least partly opposed to control and therefore separate from the social—in other words, as something natural instead of social. Because desire cannot be wholly reconciled with social control, the character cannot become wholly virtuous; thus he is unlike a romance character.

The way of looking at character exemplified by Austen seems to reflect a cultural change in the whole concept of what personality is. Austen is assuming that in addition to the social self there is something else, what she calls in *Pride and Prejudice* the "real character" (2.12.200). Though Austen values social control enough to feel that it can improve character by teaching the individual to restrain certain tendencies in his innate disposition, she nevertheless seems to share the modern idea that beneath the social self there is a separate level of personality which is more basic, more authentic—more "real."

In contrast, in premodern society identity was generally equated with social role. If one inherits one's social position, as in a feudal society, then society does largely define one's identity, as a master "gives a character" (meaning a character reference) to a servant, defining that servant in terms of his ability to meet his social obligations. One can still see this attitude toward character in baroque romance, where the protagonist ultimately regains his rightful title, thus receiving an identity from social authority. His character is his virtue, which means his acceptance of authority. Similarly the word *courtly* equates personal qualities with social role; the courtly man behaves as a member of the court should.

In "What a Character Is," Sir Thomas Overbury points out that the word *character* originally meant a letter in a word,[3] and he seems to retain a concept of character based on that original meaning. Like a letter, the individual's character is seen as public, and as with a letter, outward appearance communicates meaning: a person is what he appears to be. He is defined by his public self; public forms (like language) are adequate to express private meaning. But if premodern culture sees character as a sign identical with what it signifies, in modern culture that concept seems to be replaced by the idea of character as something concealed, not directly represented by the appearance that supposedly communicates it but rather existing in opposition to that apparent identity.

Probably the main reason people stopped equating identity

with social role was that they no longer were content to follow in their parents' footsteps. As members of the middle class set out to improve their social status, they presumably felt that their identity was something they should determine for themselves. And as predetermined social roles became less clear and dominant, people had to try to define themselves more. This self-definition is probably mainly a negative process, a rejection of social roles like that which takes place at the beginning of *Doctor Faustus*. We have seen Defoe's and Richardson's protagonists also rejecting their social identities. As a result of such self-individuation, people became more conscious of character as an entity to be defined, an end in itself. As desire became less fulfilled through social forms, people became more aware of it as an inner force, and this self-awareness probably contributed to a consciousness of inner character. We can see this kind of self-awareness in the way Clarissa keeps trying to define and understand the forces in her mind, apparently because her rebelliousness arouses guilt, expressed through her reaction against her desires. One sign of this increased self-consciousness is the proliferation of words to describe personality, almost all of them of modern coinage—words like *consciousness, individual, mentality, sentiment*.[4] Such language suggests that people were becoming aware of character as something individual, discrete, even peculiar—something within the mind, not on the surface. Perhaps the clearest expression of this new concern with what is within the self can be found in Locke.[5] Locke defines the individual through his consciousness of the outer world, thus expressing a sense of the individual's separation from that world. And by emphasizing how the individual is formed by his experience, Locke frees the individual of a socially determined identity or of other external, absolute, general determinants of character (such as the four humors).

We can see this changed attitude toward personality in the new way the novel treats character. In earlier fiction, characters are often determined by external considerations. Sometimes these are social; a character can be made the way he is to represent a social type. Identity is thus seen as social, rather than opposed to the social as in the novel. The traits of the Overburian characters, for example, seem to be chosen to place the character in a category, showing him to be a typical representative of a general kind. Our interest lies in seeing how the traits fit the type so that the character reaffirms the validity of the general system that determines his nature. In addition, there are moral type-characters. These too seem to be used to illustrate the validity of a system, one which seems analogous to the social hierarchy. As the example of the Canterbury pilgrims shows, a sense of social control tends to be equated with a sense of moral order. Thus type-characters often represent the validity not just of social categories but of moral categories as well. Chaucer's knight represents a social class but also a moral class; by being what a knight should be, he represents virtuous acceptance of control. Other pilgrims represent negative types; they show what a friar or a woman should *not* be like. Thus their moral meaning is also a function of their relation to social control. As with the social type, the moral character's traits are largely chosen to illustrate a larger, abstract concept of order, an order the writer probably accepts because he also accepts the idea of social order.

But as social control came to seem less acceptable, it was not so closely equated with moral order. Thus the novel no longer tends to see character as externally determined by a didactic purpose any more than by social role. Novel characters can still be put to thematic uses, of course, but they aren't wholly determined by their moral function as are characters in, for example, *Pilgrim's Progress.* Clarissa is partly made the way she is, like a romance heroine, to exemplify a moral ideal; but there is another side of her character which is not determined by this moral purpose—which instead expresses a reaction against that moral control. Thus, like such later protagonists as Elizabeth Bennet and Dorothea Brooke, she doesn't simply represent an ideal; rather she must gradually attain it. We might say that instead of seeing character in terms of a moral system, the novelist sees morality in terms of character. Morality is conceived of as existing within character, not above it; controlled by it, not controlling it.

Novelists also show their sense of the increased independence of character in the way they free characters to some extent from plot control. Although the novel retains (in modified form) the romance way of structuring plot to bring about sublimation, it partly frees characters from their function as agents of that sublimation. Thus, for example, Clarissa and Lovelace are given secondary functions in conflict with their primary functions as seeker and opponent of sublimation. And by the time we reach Dickens there are some characters who seem quite independent of their structural function. A character like Mrs. Gamp has many traits which are unrelated to her plot role, indeed opposed to it, making her (like Lovelace) function as a secondary subject instead of playing the villainous role we would expect. This resistance to plot control seems to result from a sense of the value of character in itself, and a sense that character is an entity which—rather than being defined by social control, as before—exists through its opposition to control. To be a character means to be eccentric, independent, uncontrolled. We can describe this tendency by saying that in the novel character becomes an end in itself.[6] In other words, characters are more likely to function partly as subjects. We can see this tendency in *Clarissa;* because of the epistolary form, each character who narrates becomes temporarily a subject, a central "I." And Dickens asks our sympathy for many minor characters whom previous novelists would only ask us to laugh at; he asks us to laugh *with* them as well.

The example of *Clarissa* can help us understand the means novelists use to shift our attention to character. We respond to plot because it creates a conflict between desire and the opposition to desire, a conflict acted out by the narrative agents. Richardson makes us respond in a similar way to characters by creating a similar conflict within them. By giving Clarissa a second, negative function, he sets up a subject-object conflict in her. There is an aspect of her that we feel is opposed to her desire; thus we see that aspect partly as an object, something for desire to act on, to overcome. We can see Clarissa trying to treat herself as an object by detaching herself from and opposing her own negative desires. Probably we take each aspect of her character partly as a subject, accepting its desires, and as we do so seeing the other aspect as partly a negative object opposing our wishes.[7] It is as if she alternately plays the role of heroine and villain, trying to overcome her own desires just as she tries to overcome Lovelace, and trying to overcome her own self-control just as Lovelace tries to overcome her. Thus character has taken over some of the conflict hitherto found in plot. The novelist uses character (like plot) as a way of relating desire and control.

This kind of character conflict increases the intensity of our response. It makes us focus *on* the character rather than through him on the plot conflict, since the conflict is located in the character. As a result we gain a stronger sense of the character's presence. I think the character creates this effect by causing a tension within us.[8] If we take a character as an extension of our desire, when that character opposes the desire he has aroused in us it is as if a part of ourselves has disobeyed us, making us do or want something against our will. This frustration creates a tension in us. For example, Clarissa both makes us want sublimation and arouses rebellious impulses in us which oppose that desire. Because it is through our acceptance of the character as an extension of our desire that we feel tension, we attribute the tension (like the desire) to the character: we feel it as a conflict in the character. Thus we feel the character has a personality. Because the character opposes the desire he arouses in us, he seems independent of us, as actual people are, and so he seems "real." We infer the presence in him of something we call "character," a force that enables him to be independent. And when a character creates tension in us, we naturally look to him to deal with the tension in some way. This too makes us focus more on the character.

This tension may be created by the way the narrative utterance deviates from the basic structure it transforms. If our minds tend to structure narrative in a basic way, they will respond to the way a particular utterance distorts that basic structure, trying to deal with that gap in some way and feeling a tension between structure and transformation. If the structure I have postulated earlier is the kind of structure we want in narrative, then we want the subject to control the object. But if the object is not separate from the subject, the subject cannot fully control it; by entering into the subject, the object is partly controlling it instead. This reversal of the basic structure makes us feel tension.

Richardson himself seems to have been aware that he was using character to create an intense response. He evidently rejects the kind of detachment toward character that is taken for granted in earlier fiction and in the drama. Instead of detachment, he seeks to arouse emotional sympathy. He describes himself as becoming "absorbed in" a character so that he is not "any-where,"[9] as if he has somehow escaped his sense of self. He values getting at the depths of the heart, as Clarissa gets at hers, discovering the "inwardest mind."[10] To do this, he evidently feels the need to escape rational self-restraint. In his letters he describes letter-writers as "regarding not the head" but rather letting "whatever comes uppermost" freely "flow" from "undesigning hearts" which the act of letter-writing has "unlockt"[11]—much like what Clarissa and Anna do. Partly this unlocking of the heart seems to involve an escape from social restraint, since as he points out the letter-writer is in her closet, taking refuge from the public world. But the writer also escapes "the head," by which he evidently means the kind of prudent self-control that society makes necessary, a restraint that usually denies the heart expression. Here again we find a sense that the real self (in the heart) has become separated from the social self. For Richardson the function of fiction seems to be to get at that sense of inner self, not only in his characters but, through them, in his and his readers' hearts. That is, character has become a device to make us feel. It does this by inducing us partly to suspend our self-restraint, like Richardson's letter-writer.

We can compare the suspension of self-control that Richardson asks of the reader with what Clarissa herself does. Richardson apparently sees social control as repressive, judging by the embodiment of it he creates in Mr. Harlowe. Thus it seems desirable to free the heart from social control within the self, as Clarissa (embodying the heart's desire for sublimation) seeks to free herself from her father's control. Clarissa retreats into herself, closing herself in her room and turning inward, finally escaping her home altogether. Similarly, Richardson invites us to escape our self-control—in Freud's terms, partly to suspend the ego's allegiance to the superego. But when Clarissa leaves home, she feels guilty and seeks to find another control to which she can submit. Similarly, Richardson has a moral purpose which conflicts with his emotional one. Although he seems to value emotion as an end in itself, even though it brings inner conflict with it, he also seeks to teach virtuous submission. He apparently believes that the heart is basically virtuous, so that if one can free it from repressive control, it will accept an ideal control instead. But during most of *Clarissa,* he offers us suspension of restraint and indulgence in sentiment, a self-indulgence apparently made acceptable by the moral purpose that he believes it will ultimately serve. This use of fiction to arouse emotion seems to me different from what we find in traditional literature, where the emotional response is more clearly subservient to the moral purpose and the reader is asked to accept stronger restraints.

Richardson's suspension of restraint seems to be part of a larger cultural trend, one that found expression not only in the novel but in other literature as well, such as Romantic poetry. For example, what Richardson does is something like Coleridge's suspension of disbelief; both attempt to escape a rational part of the mind which is seen as opposing emotion. And Richardson's ability to make this suspension and enter into his characters also resembles Keats's negative capability, which seems to be another description of a suspension of rational control in order to achieve greater intensity.[12] Shelley's image of himself as an Aeolian lyre seems to describe such a suspension too, a state in which the mind passively accepts impulses rising out of the heart's depths. The closest parallel to Richardson's attitude toward characters is probably Wordsworth's statement, in the preface to the *Lyrical Ballads,* that the poet wishes "to bring his feeling near to those of the persons whose feeling he describes, nay, for short spaces of time perhaps, to let himself slip into an entire delusion, and even confound and identify his feelings with theirs." Perhaps we can also draw a parallel between the increase of emotional intensity in character and the increased importance that the Romantic period placed on melody in music, since melody seems to be used like character as a way of arousing an intense localized response, a response more emotional than the kind of controlled response we feel to a work where overall structure is more important.

By partly suspending control, Richardson allows the presence of more uncontrolled desire within the self. Just as he allows that desire expression in the protagonist, he seems to be asking us (through our response to his characters) to accept the same impulses in ourselves. Presumably he allows expression to the unsublimated desires which self-control normally tries to suppress because for him (and for many of his readers) private feelings could no longer be fully reconciled with the demands of the social self. Thus those feelings sought some less controlled, more antisocial form of expression. The strain of trying to reconcile desire with control had evidently become so great that it came as a relief simply to stop trying to reconcile the two. Of course Richardson was much too moral to countenance any serious repudiation of self-restraint. But in the safety of the imagination (like the letter-writer in his closet) he could get away with some limited suspension of restraint, especially since he took care to counteract his emotional release with plentiful doses of morality.

We can see this suspension of control in Richardson's treatment of the narrator. He does not provide a central embodiment of the subject, a narrator speaking for the kind of rational, detached, public self we find in traditional narratives. Instead he gives us conflicting subjects, primarily Lovelace and Clarissa. That is, he introduces conflict into the subject, just as he allows conflict within his subject-characters. Like the novel as a whole, Clarissa lacks a single "I" and instead combines conflicting selves. It is as if a unified ego has become impossible for Richardson, apparently because the ego can no longer fully accept authority and so is torn between rebellion and submission.

The suspension of restraint causes Richardson to place increased emphasis on character. As he allows conflict into the subject, the subject becomes manifested as characters rather than as a narrator. This shift in emphasis seems to reflect his attitude toward authority. A narrator in traditional narrative represents authority, controlling the characters and us, and Richardson no longer seems able to believe fully in that kind of control. Characters, on the other hand, can serve desire and thus oppose control, as Lovelace especially does. As the novel allows more rebellious energy, then, it is likely to shift its focus more from narrator to character and to make character more opposed to control like a narrator's.

Although Richardson's is rather an extreme case, I think later novelists resemble him in their emphasizing of character in order to create tension. Dickens is perhaps the best example of a novelist who uses character to suspend self-restraint and express uncontrolled desire. But even a fairly restrained writer like Austen largely allows characters to replace a detached narrator, using characters to arouse tension (though in her case she creates tension in order to resolve it).

The novel not only allows greater conflict in character but also develops a new way to express that conflict. In traditional romance, uncontrolled desire is segregated from the subject and located in discrete narrative units. As I have mentioned, in romance each larger unit has fairly complete closure, ending with a reassertion of the necessity of submission and a complete rejection of rebelliousness. Thus each new unit presents a restatement of the same polarization. Within those units, the conflict takes place between separate polarized entities (such as characters), each utterance being positive or negative. In the novel, however, conflict is often located *within* the small units of the work, so that the units are less opposed. The novelist partly depolarizes desire and control, allowing them to enter into the same utterance—that is, to create compromise formations. Thus not only are the novel as a whole and its larger units compromise formations, but many of the small units within the work (even individual sentences) become compromise formations as well, containing unresolved conflict.

Combining opposed forces in compromise formations alters the nature of those forces. When forces are polarized, they are strongly opposed. For example, in baroque romance the only alternative to virtuous submission like the hero's is total rebelliousness like the villain's. But in the novel, since these forces are partly combined, rebelliousness need not be totally bad nor submissiveness totally good. At the same time that the ego allows rebelliousness some expression, it moderates that expression, compromising with the opposition to it. Insofar as the conscious mind controls the expression of irrational forces, those forces become less irrational and uncontrollable. They are diminished and modified by being combined with opposing impulses.

Because of the diffusion of compromise formations throughout the details of the novel, character conflict is expressed in a new way, implied through the details of the character's speech and action. This new kind of characterization probably explains the increased emphasis on particularity in characters. The particular details of characterization took on increased importance because they were compromise formations, used to imply character tension. The concept of the compromise formation enables us to explain the particular details of a complex work in terms of a basic narrative structure: complexity can be generated from that structure through compromise formations.

To understand what is distinctive about this way of expressing character conflict, we can contrast it with the way characters normally express conflict in traditional romance. As I have mentioned, in such works conflicting forces are not usually implied within one character; but even when they are, they are still separated. First of all, conflict is usually segregated by being located in a long set speech, usually a soliloquy about choosing a course of action—a speech that is not related to the character's plot action. The action stops while he speaks, then the story resumes, and the conflict expressed in the speech is not shown in the action, in which the character (having made his choice) remains purely virtuous or wicked. In addition, the formal rhetoric that characters normally use prevents us from feeling the conflict the character claims to express, since formality implies a control over emotion, removing any sense that the desire expressed is really rebellious. What rebellious feeling exists does not affect the writer's rhetorical control; the writer does not modify his rhetoric to accommodate that feeling, so we don't feel the emotion really threatens control. In other words, control and rebelliousness are kept safely separate. This same separation is usually reproduced in the content of the speeches. Characters typically alternate, speaking as if in two voices, so that inner debates tend to take the form of dialogues in which the character addresses himself in the second person or apostrophizes someone or something. Characters are often like Marlowe's Faustus, who alternately asserts his rebellious desires and, addressing himself in the second person, speaks for his conscience, the Good Angel that condemns his desires. The conflict is not contained in one compromise formation but rather takes place between separate units.

We can see this tendency to segregate forces in the way the mind is described. When Sir Philip Sidney, for example, describes the mental processes of a character, he makes them a series of transactions among separate entities: ". . . when once it was enacted, not only by the commonalty of passions, but agreed unto by her most noble thoughts, and that by reason itself . . . had granted his royal assent; then friendship (a diligent officer) took care to see the statute thoroughly observed. . . ."[13] The segregation of mental entities here seems related to the belief in a strong authority of the kind Richardson no longer fully believes in. Sidney expresses a conservative belief in a social hierarchy like that in feudal society, ruled by a king. This authority has been internalized in the form of an inner monarch, reason, able to keep passions in their place. Because things are in their place, they are segregated, just as commonalty and nobles are segregated in feudal society. Submission to authority thus causes polarization.

Sidney's way of treating conflict does not make the conflict seem to be within a character. Rather it seems as if the character has been temporarily replaced as agent by a set of abstractions: passions and reason become the actors here. Like love, virtue, and fortune, these abstractions are spoken of as if they are outside the character, external controls to which he submits. Thus we seem to have an external conflict between units each of which embodies a single quality; there is no sense that conflicting forces have combined within one unit.

In contrast, the novel typically makes character the locus of conflict, and it does this by expressing character through compromise formations which allow the conflicting forces to coexist within the character. The character continues to function as an actor rather than being replaced by other entities; he can do so because the conflict is implied through the way his behavior is modified, implying there is some aspect of him partly opposed to and influencing the self as actor. And where baroque romance distances conflict by raising it to an abstract, general plane, the novel makes it more intense by particularizing it in a character, preventing us from separating our sense of conflict from our response to the character. We feel the opposing forces are inseparable and therefore are both within the character.

Again, Richardson provides a good example of this new way of presenting character. He was aware that he was using details of characterization in this way, expressing "passion" in "The minute particulars of events." As he says in a letter, "in the minutiae lie often the unfoldings of the story, as well as of the heart."[14] Although to some extent he probably learned this technique from Shakespeare, he is able to make his characters' voices even more expressive because they are not using the comparatively formal, controlled language of verse drama, a language that is often as rhetorical as that in baroque romance. Perhaps because Richardson could not rely on actors to make his language expressive, he tries to put expressiveness into the language itself. And by using colloquial language he can give fuller expression to the private self, to the individual's rejection of the formal language of a public role. He makes us infer some force within his characters able to overcome conventionality and create an idiosyncratic language. Thus, as Richardson says, the "Styles" of letters "are indicative, generally beyond the power of disguise, of the mind of the writer." It is not merely what characters say but "their *manner* of saying" it that expresses "character."[15] Thus he sees style as serving characterization, in contrast to baroque romance, where the display of rhetoric seems an end in itself and speeches do not function to give us a sense of character.

We can examine this use of language in his presentation of Clarissa. Anna Howe says there is "a latent, unowned inclination . . . balancing, or *preponderating* rather" in Clarissa's mind (1.451) — that is, Clarissa's attraction to Lovelace. This way of describing Clarissa's inner conflict shows how the two forces are mixed together. If Clarissa's desire is "unowned," it is not conscious and cannot be separated out and expressed through the kind of formal statement we would find in a romance speech. And if it is unowned, the conscious mind apparently wishes to repudiate it; thus the very fact that the desire is expressed indirectly implies that there is another part of the mind opposing it—that there is a conflict in the character. Yet despite conscious opposition, the desire is able to preponderate—to overcome conscious restraint, but not entirely—so that the opposing impulses are mixed, interacting so that each is expressed in a form that implies the force opposing it. In other words, they are expressed through compromise formations. Richardson continually gives Clarissa's language this mixed nature. The more rational side of her tries to understand, rationalize, and deal with her irrational desires, to reconcile them with the dictates of her conscience; but often those irrational impulses partly resist her control, unable to accept the demands of her conscience as she herself is unable to accept her father's demands. Thus her desires remain partly uncontrolled, causing her to keep on vacillating and justifying herself.

We can see Richardson's use of language to imply this conflict in a letter in which Clarissa argues with Anna about her attraction to Lovelace:

> 'Tis true I have owned more than once, that I could have liked Mr. Lovelace above all men. I remember the debates you and I used to have on this subject.... You used to say... that men of his cast are the men that our sex do not *naturally* dislike: while I held that such were not (however *that* might be) the men we *ought* to like. But what with my relations precipitating of me, on the one hand, and what with his unhappy character, and embarrassing ways, on the other, I had no more leisure than inclination to examine my own heart in this particular. And this reminds me of a passage in one of your former letters .... And should we not endeavour, as much as we can, as much as human frailty and partiality will permit (where we are not attached by *natural* ties), to like and dislike as reason bids us, and according to the merit or demerit of the object? If love, as it is called, is allowed to be an excuse for our most unreasonable follies, and to lay level all the fences that a careful education has surrounded us by, what is meant by the doctrine of subduing our passions? But, O my dearest friend, am I not guilty of a punishable fault, were I to love this man of errors? And has not my own heart deceived me, when I thought I did

not? And what must be that, love that has not some degree of purity for its object? I am afraid of recollecting some passages in my Cousin Morden's letter. And yet why fly I from subjects that, duly considered, might correct and purify my heart? I have carried, I doubt, my notions on this head too high, not for practice, but for *my* practice. Yet think me not guilty of prudery neither; for had I found out as much of myself before, or, rather, had he given me heart's ease enough before to find it out, you should have had my confession sooner.

Nevertheless let me tell you (what I hope I may justly tell you) that . . . I hope my reason will gather strength enough from his imperfections to enable me to keep my passions under. What can we do more than govern ourselves by the temporary lights lent us?

You will not wonder that I am grave on this detection— *detection*, must I call it? What can I call it?

Dissatisfied with myself, I am afraid to look back upon what I have written: and yet know not how to have done writing. I never was in such an odd frame of mind. I know not how to describe it. (2.438–39)

Clarissa's language here beautifully captures her inner conflict. I think it is possible to relate these details of language to the way the entire novel transforms narrative structure, so that we can see the work's specific complexities as generated by the same process, the same way of transforming the subject-object structure, that I have been describing as underlying the work as a whole. Here as elsewhere, we can find a conflict between two aspects of the self, a positive subject (like Clarissa's dominant function) seeking to "examine," to "govern" and thus to "purify" the heart's desires, "subduing" the "passions"; and a negative subject (like Lovelace) attracted to those passions, to "human frailty and partiality," and opposed to the way reason seeks to control them, seeing that control as mere "prudery." The negative subject seems to correspond to that aspect of the ego which serves the id, trying to gratify desire; the positive subject seems to correspond to that aspect of the ego which tries to serve the superego, opposing desire, trying to make desire acceptable to the superego or else reject it. These two functions, like two characters, argue with each other. Since Anna functions here primarily as an extension of Clarissa's rebellious side, speaking to and for Clarissa's desire to resist her family's control, the argument with Anna externalizes Clarissa's debate with her own desires. But in addition to arguing with Anna, Clarissa argues with herself, questioning herself, defending herself against imagined accusations, trying to excuse herself and then condemning herself, wandering from one side of the argument to the other. She says there are things in herself she is afraid to look at, yet she keeps talking of them, as if fascinated by her passions despite herself. It is as if she is two contradictory selves.

But in addition to this debate, the two opposing sides of Clarissa also speak together in various compromise formations. For example, she begins by saying "'Tis true I have owned more than once, that I could have liked Mr. Lovelace above all men." We can see this as a transformation of "I desire Lovelace." That is presumably what Clarissa would say if she were merely a negative subject. But she is also a positive subject, seeking to deal with her desire for Lovelace; and the two functions combine here to produce a statement that both expresses her desire and seeks to distance, even disavow it. The statement of desire is enclosed in another statement, which implies opposition to desire by the way it turns the statement of attraction into a rather grudging concession ("'Tis true I have owned"), making us feel she doesn't want to admit her desire. We can see the first "I," the one who reluctantly "owns" this statement, as the positive subject, separated from the second "I" (the one who "could have liked" Lovelace), opposing and trying to control that negative subject. But even within the subordinate clause which admits desire, the opposition to desire finds expression, transforming "like" into "could have liked," disavowing desire even while admitting it. Thus desire and restraint seem inseparably interrelated, parts of one complex character rather than separate narrative units.

Further on, Clarissa asks: "should we not endeavour, as much as we can, as much as human frailty and partiality will permit (where we are not attached by *natural* ties), to like and dislike as reason bids us, and according to the merit or demerit of the object?" We can see this sentence too as an utterance she transforms by combining it with an opposing utterance. In this case it seems best to describe the statement as an utterance of the positive subject (asserting that reason should control desire—"partiality"), an utterance that has been displaced by the negative subject's resistance to control. It is as if the statement has been modified to try to deal with the negative subject's objections. The statement has been subjected to several transformations, all of which dilute it, implying an unwillingness to accept what it says. For one thing, "I" has become "we," as if Clarissa wishes to disown her statement, not accepting it as expressing what her "I" wants. She also makes the statement negative ("should we not"); thus at the same time that she says she should endeavor to like rationally, she also says that she should *not* do so. And she transforms the statement into a question; this implies the sense of an opposition against which she needs to argue, so that we feel she is not wholly certain, that part of her disagrees. The contingent form of the question allows her to express her negative desire while simultaneously opposing it. In addition, she adds various qualifiers which give us the sense that she is trying to overcome an opposing argument and not wholly succeeding: "as much as we can" implies that she cannot wholly control her desires, as does her use of "endeavour." And her statement that frailty "will permit" only so much control makes desire (even though she tries to reduce it to mere frailty), not control, the dominant force. Thus we find imbedded in an ostensibly positive statement an opposing, negative utterance. Clarissa distances this negative statement, transforming her own desire into "human frailty," making it general and abstract and condemning it. But the statement she is transforming, trying to negate, seems to be "I will not permit reason to bid me like"—that is, to control my desires. The conflict between the positive and negative attitudes can explain the indirectness and contortion of this sentence.

Near the end of this passage, Clarissa says, "I am afraid to look back upon what I have written." This statement seems to me an especially clear example of the division of the subject. The first "I" is afraid to look at what the second "I" has written, implying that the two are opposed. Apparently the positive "I" is afraid to admit the existence of the guilty desires that the negative "I" has betrayed. Once more the statement of those desires is imbedded within a statement by the positive subject which attempts to deal with those desires, attempting to control them by the very act of enclosing them within another sentence. But here the inability of the positive subject to overcome the negative is clear; it cannot control those desires, only look at them—and it is afraid even to do that. This sentence shows the way the positive subject seems opposed to and unable to control its own predicate. In sentences like this, as in the novel as a whole, the positive subject seeks a positive, sublimating object, but the only object it can find is negative, an embodiment of unfulfilling desire, just as all Clarissa finds is Lovelace. And in the structure of such sentences as this, the object she finds is an aspect of herself. That is, her object is a statement of which the negative "I" is subject. She can only treat uncontrolled desire as a negative object; she cannot join it to the positive subject by sublimating it. Similarly in the novel as a whole, the negative object she finds—Lovelace—can be seen as an aspect of herself, an embodiment of the same rebellious desires she opposes in herself. Because desire cannot be fulfilled, it cannot attain any external object this side of death; it can only continually encounter and oppose itself.

The unfulfilling nature of the positive subject, cut off from desire, relegates it to a role like a narrator's. The positive subject in these sentences acts like a narrator, standing back from the negative subject (the one which, like a character, serves desire), criticizing and analyzing it. While the negative "I" has access to desire, can express it, the positive is separated from desire, restricted to introductory clauses such as "I have owned that" and "I am afraid of recollecting." This separation resembles a narrator's separation from the protagonist. Like a narrator, the positive subject in Clarissa cannot serve desire through action, since desire is seen as guilty, and so the positive subject remains separate from the action, observing it. Of course the two subjects interact much more than narrator and protagonist, since they are combined within Clarissa. Yet it is rather as if she is doomed to play Sancho to her own Quixote.

Richardson uses quite a few other devices in this passage to imply the conflict in Clarissa. She sometimes shifts the negative subject to Anna, disowning responsibility for it: she says Anna "used to say" Lovelace was likable, which we can take as a way of saying she herself likes Lovelace while at the same time trying to deny it. She also distances desire by transforming "like" into "do not dislike," negating it even while admitting it. She separates herself from Anna's attitude, thus trying to separate positive from negative subject; but negative desire reenters in parenthetic phrases like "(however *that* might be)." Her use of parentheses, like her use of questions, implies inner division; it is as if one part of herself interrupts the other, as if she has two voices. Her use of italics also makes her sound as if she is arguing, as if she has to emphasize her points in order to overcome some opposition. She also distances passion by using an "if" clause to enclose and make contingent a statement of negative desire (to excuse "follies").

In addition, the way Clarissa tries to deal with her desires is a compromise formation. She doesn't simply repress them but rather tries to understand and rationalize them, and such an activity combines a partial rejection of desire with a partial acceptance of it, admitting its presence. Letters help create this interaction, since they are a way of distancing and criticizing the desire they express, talking about it instead of directly acting for it, more like a narrator analyzing it than a character serving it.

This analysis, then, shows how we can relate particular details of language to a basic narrative structure. Assuming that structure to have a sentencelike form, we can examine the individual sentences of a work and discover how their way of relating subject to object is analogous to the particular transformation of the basic subject-object relationship in the work as a whole. In other words, the stylistic details of the work can be seen as generated by the same way of transforming structure that produces the set of function-relationships on which the work is based. And the conflict implied in a particular detail can be seen as a transformation of the basic conflict underlying the whole work.[16]

By creating this complex interplay of attitudes in Clarissa, Richardson gives us the sense of a character with a deep inner life. His willingness to do this indicates that his moral attitude is more complex than the morality he preaches, especially toward the novel's end. He implies that although the individual must strive for virtue, she cannot escape her frailty or the external forces that push and pull even the most virtuous person into mistakes, as Lovelace and the Harlowes push and pull Clarissa. Yet Richardson doesn't allow these factors to excuse failures. He is aware that the heart alone is not enough; it can deceive, as Clarissa says here. And as she also points out, reason is imperfect, not always in control, not always able to face and understand the heart's depths. But even though virtue is thus quite difficult, it must be attempted. Furthermore, Clarissa not only asserts in this passage that one should govern one's passions; she also practices what she preaches. The passage captures her attempts to understand and thus control the impulses within her, and its very complexity reproduces the difficulty of achieving that control.

Other characters in *Clarissa* also imply their inner conflicts through their particular ways of using language. Each character is distinctive, yet I think we can see each character as a function of the basic conflict in the novel as a whole. The language of each character structures the forces in that conflict; in different characters the balance between desire and control differs. But though they combine in different ways, throughout the novel desire is potentially quite rebellious, control quite repressive. Clarissa manages to distance passion and remain critically conscious of it, even if not wholly in control. Anna Howe is more rebellious, but she can use irony to prevent her rebelliousness from becoming more than playful, to help her not take it too seriously. In Lovelace rebelliousness is in control and his attempts to overcome it and become virtuous not only fail but are themselves too passionate. His lack of self-restraint is reproduced in his frequent use of exclamation marks and italics and in his continual hyperbole.

The technique Richardson uses to make these characters distinctive seems to me to be fundamentally the technique used by later novelists, at least in the classic English novel. Of course different characters express different conflicts, but most novelists rely primarily on compromise formations like those I have been describing here to make us feel there is conflict in their characters. The negative function of a character can distort or deflect the speech or action or appearance of his positive function in many ways, as well as vice versa. Characters can oppose their basic function by contradicting themselves, for example, or by failing to function as we desire them to.

The main advantage of this way of presenting character is probably that it increases the intensity of our response. To appreciate this kind of characterization, we need to focus on those local details, compromise formations, which create moments of intensity. Not all details arouse this kind of complex response, but in the greatest of the classic English novels a great many details do so. They create in us not just a conflict between alternating forces but a tension between two simultaneous forces. Whereas our response to plot conflict is spread out over the time required to present separate, conflicting units, our response to character tension can be virtually instantaneous, and constantly renewed. Probably our response is also stronger because the tension is only partly resolved. Our desire is both partly satisfied and partly frustrated. The frustration arouses our desire, and the more we desire the greater our frustration. The more unresolved conflict the novelist includes, the more we must react to it ourselves instead of letting the work resolve it for us. The wider the gap between our desires and the form in which the character expresses them, the more tension we feel and the more we must try to deal with it.

In Clarissa's case, I think our primary response is to share the rebellious desires of that side of her I have called negative. Insofar as we do, we are frustrated by the restraints her positive function imposes on those desires. We want her to say not that she could have liked Lovelace but that she does like him. But at the same time, we are prevented from separating ourselves from that positive side of her, from seeing it as an object as we would if it were located in another character. We also share its desire for control, and so we are forced to oppose our desire that she love Lovelace, to some extent seeing that desire as an object—as alien to the self Clarissa should have. Thus Clarissa causes tension in us, making us oppose our own desires. We respond to this by inferring that there is some force in her that opposes her desires as it opposes our desires.

Combining desire with opposition to it may make desire more acceptable to the reader. If ungoverned desire arouses anxiety, then we will feel more willing to allow our desires to be aroused by a work that provides a way of managing—or at least disguising and deflecting—that desire. As Norman Holland has suggested, we can see character as a way of defending against impulses.[17] By opposing the desire he arouses, a character can provide us with a defense against the anxiety the desire might cause. Thus he compensates us for the frustration he causes. If he restrains desire for us, we need not restrain it; we can release the energy normally needed for self-restraint. The characters who give us most pleasure, then, are probably those who both cause tension in us and help us deal with that tension.

In the following chapters I want to examine characters of this sort more closely, first considering their relation to the novel's form and then looking at the way two of the greatest masters of this kind of characterization put its techniques to their own uses.

The Conflict between Character Intensity & Form: Richardson, Fielding, & Austen

chapter 5

THE new emphasis we find in *Clarissa* on character as an end in itself altered the relationship between character and other elements in the novel. Novelists worked out new fictional forms appropriate to their new treatment of character, forms that enabled them to present character tension effectively yet relate it to other elements.

Richardson's example suggests that the change in characterization may have preceded and generated many of the other changes that produced the novel. Richardson evidently allowed his concern with expressing character conflict to determine much of what he wrote. Making character predominant seems to be one of the results of the way he partly suspended self-control in writing. In his letters he tells us that his characters rise upon him, that he does not write "by plan." He says he writes with the heart not the head, letting one letter lead to the next and writing what is necessary for his characters.[1] In *Clarissa* the characters let their ideas "run" (1.187), and Richardson too seems to have allowed himself to be carried away by the act of writing, using his characters as a kind of disguise behind which he could explore the heart's depths, getting at its conflicts. To a large extent he evidently let this process of discovery determine what should come next in the novel. Though the basic outline of the plot was presumably in his head from the start, the details seem to have come to him as he went deeper and deeper into Clarissa's inner conflict. He seems to have largely allowed himself to be carried along by the uncontrolled forces within him, rather as Clarissa is carried off by Lovelace.

But if Richardson is partly passive like Clarissa, he also resembles her in opposing the forces whose expression he has allowed. He uses Clarissa to do this; her search for self-comprehension and self-control becomes the way the novel deals with the uncontrolled desires it has expressed. Thus Richardson not only uses character to create conflict but also to deal with that conflict. Because the conflict is largely within the character, its resolution can be in the character also. Instead of defeating Lovelace through plot action, then, Clarissa defeats her own desire for him. If Richardson had placed his primary emphasis on plot, he would probably have used plot to reject Lovelace in some way—for example, by allowing Morden (a simple helper character who serves plot) to kill Lovelace earlier in the story. But since Richardson wishes to work through character tension, he works out a gradual transformation within Lovelace, a reflection of Clarissa's own rejection of her rebelliousness. It is not until Lovelace has learned to condemn his own rebellious desires, and thus condemn himself, that he dies. Thus he seems to seek his own death, to expiate his guilt. As with Clarissa, his conflict and its resolution take place through characterization rather than being imposed by plot from outside (for example, by fortune).

In Richardson, then, form exists primarily to arouse and deal with character tension, whereas in most earlier fiction character exists mainly to serve formal controls. Here again, I think Richardson resembles later novelists. Where most earlier narrative seems to start with a plot idea, often using a traditional story, novelists usually seem to start with character tension and work out a form to deal with it.[2] Austen and George Eliot, for example, base their form on a learning process in which the protagonist confronts and resolves his inner conflict. James uses a similar form, and in his preface to *The Portrait of a Lady* he tells us that that novel originated in his idea of its protagonist. Even novelists like Fielding and Dickens, who give plot more importance, expand form to allow for the display of character tension. Until the late nineteenth century, the English novel almost always frees characters to seek self-expression and fulfillment commensurate with their inner tension, and allows this interaction with their tension largely to determine form.

This new kind of characterization affects the novel in many ways. For one thing, as characters acquire greater inner conflict, the plot relating them to each other is altered. As desire and control become less polarized, they are no longer separated out in simple characters. When the desire for fulfillment can no longer find a pure, unopposed expression in a hero, it seeks partial, indirect outlets not only through an imperfect protagonist but through other characters as well. Thus those characters tend to function partly as subjects, as Lovelace and Anna do in *Clarissa*. But that desire brings conflict with it, so that secondary subjects tend to acquire inner tension like protagonists.

Another result of the depolarization of desire and control is that the sublimation which the plot seeks can no longer be so complete. If uncontrolled desire is not located in a villain but is partly found in the subject and positive object, the subject cannot wholly reject it or attain a goal which is wholly free of it. A villain is outside the self and can be rejected, even destroyed; but inner opposition is harder to overcome. And if a protagonist is partly negative, he is likely to be weakened in his conflict with the villain, since one part of him is on the villain's side. He must spend some of his energy on his inner conflict instead of devoting it all to defeating the villain.

Thus as characters become more complex, they interact in more complex ways. Instead of simply defeating a villain, the protagonist must often reach some compromise with what opposes him; instead of wholly rejecting negative desire, he seeks some way of dealing with that uncontrolled desire, in himself and in other characters as well. If there is negative desire in the protagonist, he can be transformed. He (like other characters) can be transformed because he is a complex character; two functions are implied in him, and so he can change by making the positive rather than the negative one dominant. It is usually this change in the protagonist on which the novel concentrates. This change can be reflected in the transformation of the positive object, serving the subject's positive function. If the positive object is imperfect, the work may transform or replace it—a process that is more difficult than merely returning to the same ideal object with which the story began, as in baroque romance.

In addition, Richardson—and later novelists—alter the novel's form in various ways to allow for the display of character tension. For example, the novel uses summary less than earlier narratives and relies more on dramatic scenes. I have shown how Richardson uses his characters' language to imply their inner tension; dramatic dialogue helps him do this. When a novelist replaces summary with dialogue, he is making character more important and deemphasizing the narrator. While the character is speaking, he entirely takes over the narrative "I." As a result, the desire he serves is less distanced and controlled and we have a more direct subject relation to it, reflecting the way desire becomes more dominant and uncontrolled in the novel. In addition, as characters become more complex their interaction becomes complex, and dramatic dialogue helps show that interaction. Simple characters can interact in simple ways; a hero can fight and defeat a villain—an event that lends itself to summary. But if protagonist and antagonist are complex, their interaction becomes more diffused and indirect, not a simple matter of victory or defeat. If characters who are interacting with each other have both positive and negative functions, dialogue can enable them to interact in complex ways since dialogue can include compromise formations which express both their functions. Speeches offer more complicated, indirect ways for characters to relate to each other than physical action does; they can oppose each other yet partly accommodate each other. For example, Richardson uses dialogue to show Clarissa simultaneously resisting her family—but not too directly—and expressing some subservience to their control. When characters interact in such ways, their conflicts become harder to resolve and take up more space, a tendency that reaches an extreme in *Clarissa*. When a hero defeats a villain, the fight can be described in a fairly short episode; but when a character with a complex inner conflict gradually resolves that conflict, both conflict and resolution require long, detailed expression through compromise formations, typically dialogue.

But although the novel partly replaces plot conflict with character tension, it of course keeps some plot conflict. The two kinds of conflict are usually related, so that we can see character tension as a transformation of plot conflict. That is, the same kind of desire and the same force reacting against it seem to occur throughout a novel, finding expression (in varied proportions) in all the conflicts, both within and among characters; thus all these conflicts are interrelated. For example, the two sides of Clarissa, rebellious and submissive, correspond to Lovelace on the one hand and her family on the other. Her inner conflict thus echoes the Lovelace-Harlowe conflict. Even if a character has an inner conflict, he normally has a dominant plot function corresponding to whichever side of his inner conflict is dominant. For example, in Lovelace rebelliousness is clearly dominant, even though he also feels guilty; in the plot he therefore functions as an embodiment of rebelliousness, attracting Clarissa toward rebellion. A character's plot function, then, can coexist with his function of inducing in us a sense of his inner tension. Characters can be given their plot functions because they represent different ways of dealing with inner tension. Lovelace is a villain because he fails to control rebellious desire, and Clarissa a heroine because she can control it. In other words, the protagonist is the protagonist because she offers the most fulfilling way of dealing with inner tension; and the villain is the villain because he represents an unsatisfactory solution to the same problem, too rebellious or (like Mr. Harlowe) too repressive.

The forces in the protagonist are reflected by the object-characters, so that when a protagonist is dominated by negative desires his object-characters are likely to be mainly negative. Clarissa's rebellious desire, for example, is reflected by the fact that she can only find a negative goal-character, Lovelace, since her negative desire cannot be allowed the fulfillment a positive goal-character would represent. And the object-characters embodying control (the Harlowes) are also negative, acting repressive in reaction against her negative desire. When a protagonist changes, there is likely to be a corresponding change in the object-characters, or at least in his (and our) relation to them, making them seem different. For instance, when Pamela is able to accept her desire for Mr. B., Mr. B. himself changes from a negative to a positive goal-character. Similarly, when Clarissa finally masters her own desires completely, her father and brother cease to function as villains and she can replace Lovelace with a positive object (God), an object that represents the suppression of her earthly desires.

Making character so dominant, however, creates a formal conflict in the novel. Once again we can use Richardson as an example of this tendency. He uses his characters to suspend self-restraint and allow expression to relatively uncontrolled desire; but to impose a form on a story requires control. In sublimating narrative, the plot seeks to reconcile desire with control, creating some moral authority the characters can accept. But if all Richardson did were to explore his characters' hearts, there would be no plot at all. If he merely suspended restraint, Lovelace and the uncontrolled desire he represents would take over the novel entirely and there would be no final submission to control—no sublimating ending. Clearly, however, Richardson wishes to find a way of controlling the impulses that his acceptance of character tension leads him to express. The act of writing *Clarissa,* then, seems to have become a dialectic between two impulses, one seeking imaginative release and the other seeking moral control. These two work out their conflict as Lovelace, desiring release, and Clarissa, seeking control, work out their conflict. But the conflict between the two remains imperfectly resolved; to find an acceptable form of control, Clarissa must go beyond the novel's world. And judging by the length of time it takes him to work out this resolution, to reject rebelliousness and sublimate Clarissa's desire, it was difficult for Richardson to reconcile character intensity with formal control.

Although *Clarissa* is an extreme case, I think the conflict it reveals between character and form is one that persists in the novel.[3] We can see this conflict, for example, when a novelist like Dickens gives his characters room in which to display themselves; he does so by partly freeing them from formal controls, so that they often no longer serve plot much. A character like Sairy Gamp hardly has a plot function; she mainly exists just to make us respond to her. As characters become mixed, they become less plot-determined, since the opposing force in them opposes their plot function; for example, Lovelace ceases to seem simply a villain, since there is another side to his character which attracts us. The more we are attracted to the display of tension in a character like Lovelace, the less we wish to submit to the moral (and formal) control Clarissa seeks, as Lovelace resists Clarissa's control. Perhaps the extreme case of the tendency of character to resist plot controls is in *Tristram Shandy.* In that novel character breaks free of plot almost entirely. The work seems to exist simply to display tensions inherent in the unstable human psyche, sacrificing plot to that concern. The search for a plot resolution to those tensions survives only in parodic vestiges.

Form works by making us aware of other things than what we are reading about at a particular moment; we relate a particular passage to other parts of the work. For example, we can make comparisons of a character's behavior with other events in the work, seeing he has contradicted himself or seeing he is inferior to some other character. But in doing this we partly detach ourselves from our response to the particular passage we are reading. Character intensity arises from our concentration on the particular moment. We respond intensely to a passage of characterization when it arouses strong desires in us; but the detachment that form can induce makes us critical of such desires, aware of elements in the work that oppose them. The more form induces awareness, the less character arouses tension. Thus form and characterization are opposed.

To some extent the novel does manage to resolve this conflict. It does so because it is a compromise formation, modifying the form through which it controls desire in order to allow that desire more freedom. As a result, formal elements are no longer so taken for granted, so conventional. Instead, the novel seeks a new form. Just as the protagonist seeks a new form of authority that will allow him greater independence, the novelist seeks to replace traditional narrative forms with a new kind of control which he works out for himself. Most novelists, beginning with Richardson, use the protagonist's search for control as the basis for this form. In other words, the form becomes a search for form. Thus, as Georg Lukács and José Ortega y Gasset both have pointed out, the novel's form becomes a process.[4]

Nevertheless, as I have mentioned, the compromise seems somewhat unstable. The unsublimated desire that finds expression in the novel (mainly through character) cannot be completely dealt with; it creates a disequilibrium which is a source of the novel's dynamism, impelling it to seek newness. But the tension between desire and control persists. Desire remains imperfectly sublimated, finding expression through character tension. One result of this tension is a tendency for the novel to split into two different kinds. There are works of the kind Scholes and Kellogg call "fictional," which emphasize plot, and works they call "empirical," which concentrate on character.[5] We can see this divergence already in Richardson and Fielding. Whereas Richardson concentrates on the conflict within characters, Fielding concentrates on plot conflicts between the protagonist and his world. Thus in Fielding the object-characters making up the protagonist's world take on greater importance than in Richardson, and most of the character tension occurs in them—a tension between their social masks and their private selfishness. Evidently Fielding believes in exercising a stronger control over desire, not allowing much uncontrolled desire into the subject but rather keeping it in the negative object so that the subject (especially the narrator) can distance and criticize it. It is not that he is less sympathetic to desire than Richardson is. Richardson is attracted to desire but finds it frightening; Fielding seems able to accept desire because he feels able to control it. He evidently does not feel very threatened by rebellious impulses and so need not take uncontrolled desire as seriously as Richardson does. Fielding's protagonists do not exhibit much rebelliousness; they can accept control, including the plot control through which Fielding leads them to submit to fatherlike authority. Because they have less uncontrolled desire, they usually seem controlled by plot rather than generating plot action out of their inner conflict as Richardson's characters do. In Fielding, most plot action is initiated by the negative object-characters, so that conflict remains on the level of plot, the interaction of subject and object-characters.

Each of these ways of modifying romance has disadvantages as well as advantages. Fielding partly sacrifices character intensity and Richardson partly sacrifices formal control over his work. Thus it seems that character and control cannot be fully reconciled.

In order to create intense characterization, Richardson allows considerable rebellious desire to enter the narrative subject. But to do so he must partly suspend control, weakening the positive aspect of the subject which seeks to deal with desire. For instance, he provides no central narrator able to detach himself from the work, judging and controlling it. The only embodiment of control is within characters, mainly the protagonist. But the protagonist lacks a narrator's ability to detach herself from desire; desire and control remain inextricably locked in conflict within her. Thus she has difficulty dealing with desire and reaching any final sublimation. Because control is weakened in this way the negative object becomes quite uncontrolled. The absence of a detached narrator makes it difficult for Richardson to deal with object-characters. He cannot keep them in their place; each character in turn takes over point of view, demanding our sympathy even where Richardson apparently wants us to be critical (as his footnotes criticizing Lovelace tell us). As a result, even a villain like Lovelace tends to become a subject-character, although Richardson needs to treat him as a villain to resolve the plot conflict. The object-world not only contains much rebellious desire but also forces reacting repressively against that desire, making the world nightmarish and claustrophobic. The world becomes so polarized that not much middle ground is left for rationality and it is difficult for the relatively rational protagonist to act in it. In other words, plot action is limited.

In contrast, Fielding's fiction opposes desire not with a repressive control demanding submission as in Richardson but with rational self-restraint like that Tom Jones learns. This control is more rational because it is more fully located within a strong positive subject and thus segregated from the uncontrolled forces in the narrative object. We can see Fielding's emphasis on control in his strong narrator, able to detach himself from rebellious desires and thus pass judgment on characters who have such desires. By distancing them, he can see them as comic. Thus the object-world seems much less enclosing and threatening than in Richardson. As long as uncontrolled desire is isolated in the object, we need not share it and feel a need to deal with it so seriously. And because Fielding also locates strong control in his protagonists, they do not seem so threatened by rebellious desires, in themselves and therefore in other characters. Consequently they have more ability to act, dealing with object-characters and bringing about plot resolutions fairly easily. Like Fielding's narrator, the protagonist can distance the object-world and so need not be so enclosed in it. Thus that world seems wider than in Richardson, allowing more freedom of action, and so making possible a more complex plot.

But Fielding's approach has its disadvantages too. For one thing, it tends to create a division within the novel. Fielding deals with the conflict between character and plot by largely separating the two,[6] so that in one area of the novel plot is dominant and in another area subsidiary characters are left relatively free of plot's control. As a result, there are two kinds of character: those who are largely plot-determined, and minor comic characters whose main function is to display their tension. The protagonist serves plot because he is acting for a strong control; the object-characters are mostly distanced and so not allowed to act for that control. Novelists like Scott and Dickens who resemble Fielding in characterization also split their characters into these two categories. The world of Little Nell or Agnes Wickfield, for example, seems quite different from the world of Dick Swiveller or Wilkins Micawber. The two sets of characters hardly talk to each other, existing in worlds of different kinds.

I think minor characters are limited by being cut off from the serious characters in this way. They can't engage in serious plot interaction with those characters. In Fielding they collide with the protagonist but are quickly put in their place, seen through and rejected, so that plot action remains fairly episodic. Our response to minor characters is diminished when we see them as members of an inferior order who can't be allowed the importance or privileges of central characters. The narrator distances them because he opposes the uncontrolled desire they serve. When character tension is located in them, we do not respond as strongly to that tension as we do when it is in a subject-character. If we do not take them at least partly as subject-characters, we do not share their desires and thus their tensions. Dickens largely overcomes this disadvantage, as I shall show later, but in Fielding the comic characters' tensions are not seen as those of a subject-character would be. The characters seem to lack serious inner conflict because they do not have the serious desires a subject has. Instead of being caused by desires within the character, their tensions seem imposed from outside. The conflict in a character like Lady Booby is between her desire and the social mask with which she tries to hide that desire, but the mask does not seem to be an inner reaction caused by desire (as Clarissa's guilt is caused by her desire). We do not feel Lady Booby guiltily fears her own passion, but rather that she thinks she ought to conceal it. Desire is in conflict with an external, social control. As a result, the desire does not seem serious enough to cause an inner reaction. And desire and control remain separate; the mask can be removed. In contrast, desire and control interact in a character like Clarissa, combining to create compromise formations; no unmasking is possible, only a gradual readjustment of the opposing forces. Fielding's characters usually do not exhibit this kind of interaction, but rather talk in alternating voices as Lady Booby does, one side of the character separate from the other. In Parson Adams, Fielding does use compromise formations (for example, Adams's snapping his fingers implies both a desire for expression and self-restraint); but normally Fielding sees character as composed of separate parts such as reason and passion. Thus we do not feel the characters have as much inner tension.

This division between kinds of characters also limits the protagonist. Since tension (though comically diminished) is largely shifted to minor characters, we respond less intensely to the protagonist and the other serious characters. Because Fielding distances desire, his protagonist does not serve or arouse it as much as in Richardson. And because the protagonist is somewhat separate from the object-world, he can't act upon it very fully and seems to lack power. The ideal he represents remains on a separate plane from the social reality around him. In his attempt to integrate the two, Fielding grafts a romancelike framework onto his episodic form; but the sublimation provided by the happy ending still seems contradicted by the rest of the work. Since in much of *Tom Jones* and especially *Joseph Andrews* the ideal acceptance of control which the protagonist usually embodies remains separate from the rebellious desire located in the object-world, the sublimating ending which attempts to reconcile desire and control seems unconvincing. The protagonist also seems weakened because the narrator partly replaces him. For example, it is usually the narrator, not the protagonist, who unmasks hypocrites and thus deals with them. Because Fielding doesn't fully believe that the ideal control he seeks to impose can exist in and deal with social reality, he locates the main embodiment of that control outside the fictional reality in a narrator. But although that narrator is attractive, he cannot enter the fictional world as a protagonist can; he cannot directly serve desire and act on the narrative object. Thus he does not offer the kind of fulfillment we seek through characters.

The tension between control and intensity affects the treatment of point of view not only in Richardson and Fielding but in later writers too. If we see the narrator as a manifestation of the basic narrative subject, we can relate what the novel does with narrators to what it does with protagonists. The example of *Clarissa* has shown us that the novel introduces conflict into the subject, and we can expect to find this conflict not only in protagonists but in point of view as well. As more uncontrolled desire finds expression in the subject, a second aspect of the subject becomes separated out—an aspect which opposes that lack of control. In the case of *Clarissa,* that aspect is located within the character; but even so, it functions like a narrator, standing apart and criticizing desire. Most novelists don't locate this critical attitude merely in characters as Richardson does; they also locate it in a narrator. As a result, there is a conflict between narrator and protagonist: the protagonist tends to be rebellious and the narrator tends to be critical of him. Desire and control can no longer be completely reconciled; the protagonist expresses a desire that can no longer completely submit to control, and the narrator expresses a control that cannot completely accept desire. This conflict resembles that between Sancho and Quixote; already there we can see a conflict between desire, unable to accept rational control, and a rationality that stands apart from desire and criticizes it and is therefore separated out in another character, Sancho.

We can see protagonist and narrator as expressing two aspects of the self, an active and a contemplative side.[7] The active self seeks to serve desire, translating it into action in the object-world; the contemplative seeks to resist desire by becoming aware of what opposes it. We can relate these to the pleasure and reality principles. In traditional romance there does not seem to be much conflict between these aspects of the self. The narrator can accept the protagonist's desires and need not become critical of him. But in the novel, point of view begins to express an opposition to desire. It may be this tendency Northrop Frye has in mind when he speaks of the development of ironic narrative.[8] I would describe an ironic narrative as one in which we see the protagonist as negative. When a writer becomes critical of his protagonist in this way, he tends to transfer more of the subject function to the narrator. Thus the narrator tends to oppose character.[9] The character attracts us into sharing his desire, but the narrator asks us to oppose that desire. The more a novelist seeks to use character to arouse an intense response, the more he wants us to respond to the desires the character serves. And the more we value intensity of response, the more we are likely to resent the intervention of a narrator asking us to criticize the character's desire. Thus, as I have mentioned, the novel often prefers dialogue, in which we respond directly to characters, rather than summary, in which the narrator distances and rationalizes events. But at the same time that its attraction to character tension pulls the novel away from narrative intervention, it is also pulled in the opposite direction, seeking to criticize its characters' uncontrolled desires. One clear example of this tension between character and point of view is the conflict between Thackeray's attraction to Becky Sharp and his critical attitude toward her.

But although there are these tensions in the novel between character and the means by which novelists seek to control or criticize the desires that characters arouse, the novel did succeed in working out at least a temporary synthesis, evolving a form able to accommodate the increased demands of characterization. We can better understand this synthesis by looking at the writer who, I think, most successfully achieved it: Jane Austen. She manages to combine some of Fielding's ability to distance, judge, and laugh at characters with some of Richardson's sympathetic presentation of character tension.[10] She does this by shifting some of the narrator's function to the protagonist as Richardson does, yet retaining a separate narrator able to function somewhat as Fielding's does. Thus she combines a narrator's detachment with a protagonist's desire; her protagonist arouses desire as in Richardson yet is also partly detached, resisting desire, like Fielding's narrator. Where Fielding largely relegates uncontrolled desire to the negative object, Austen (like Richardson) allows more uncontrolled desire in the subject, even though this means the subject acquires greater conflict. Because she makes her protagonist important, the main manifestation of the subject need not be a narrator critical of desire as in Fielding. We primarily share the protagonist's view of the fictional world rather than a detached narrator's. She usually avoids making her narrator an "I," minimizing the degree to which we take the narrator as subject so that we are not attracted away from accepting the protagonist as the main representative of our "I." And it is the protagonist, not the narrator as in Fielding, who mainly deals with object-characters, seeing through them and laughing at them. At the same time, Austen doesn't go to the opposite extreme as Richardson does, allowing the protagonist's negative desire to become so powerful it threatens his detachment and restraint. Rather, she allows control to remain dominant. But instead of embodying that control mainly in a narrator, she locates it mainly in her protagonist where it can interact with desire, restraining it. Thus the protagonist can be a compromise formation, joining control like a narrator's with desire like a simple protagonist's. A protagonist like Elizabeth Bennet is able to become aware of her uncontrolled desires, to criticize and oppose them, more easily and with less emotional suffering than Clarissa is. Where Clarissa is threatened by and afraid of her desires, Elizabeth can laugh at hers. In other words, Elizabeth has some of the detachment and independence of a Fielding narrator. It is as if Fielding's narrator has given up some of his detachment and entered into the fictional world and become a protagonist, a protagonist who (as in Richardson) has to stay within one social world and who has to work out a way of living within that world, dealing with the uncontrolled desires and inner conflicts it causes, rather than escaping to new places as in Fielding. Or—more accurately—it is as if the protagonist of *Clarissa* were Anna Howe, able to laugh at and so deal with her family and Lovelace.

By shifting much of the narrator's rational awareness to the protagonist, Austen can make her narrator less obtrusive than Fielding's and concentrate more on her protagonist. A rational protagonist enables awareness to enter into the fictional world and deal with it in a way that a separate narrator cannot do. And the protagonist can thus work out a fulfillment within the fictional world by overcoming the negative object, not merely standing apart and criticizing it. Because Austen's protagonists can serve rationality like this, they are able to resolve their inner conflicts more than Clarissa can. At the same time, because they have more uncontrolled desire, they have more conflict to resolve than a Fielding protagonist has. There can be more interaction between desire and control because these are combined within the same character. And the presence of more desire in a protagonist like Elizabeth makes us respond to her with more sympathetic intensity than to a Joseph Andrews. Thus Austen can arouse a fairly strong response to character tension and yet retain control over the forces causing that tension. She can do so because she follows Richardson's lead in working through character, dealing with conflict through characterization.

Perhaps Austen was able to work out a more complete reconciliation of desire with control than her predecessors because of changes in the relation of the individual to social authority. In the mid-eighteenth century there still seems to have been a strong conflict between middle-class individualism of the sort implied by Clarissa's inability to accept her parents' control and aristocratic social control of the sort represented by Squire Allworthy. In Austen's society, authority seems less absolute. Darcy resembles Allworthy, but he is less all-powerful and threatening and is easier to reform. As a result, the individual need not rebel against the social control Darcy represents as Clarissa rebels against the Harlowes; Elizabeth Bennet resents social control, but she doesn't run away from home. This reconciliation of the individual with authority may reflect the gradual reconciliation of the middle class with traditional social control, the compromise that began in the late seventeenth century but does not seem to have reached its culmination until the nineteenth century.

Perhaps also social authority seemed less repressive to Austen because she was a woman. For a man growing up, the main embodiment of authority (his father) is also the object of Oedipal resentments and fears, feelings that he is likely to associate with authority in general. But for a woman, especially in the eighteenth century, parents could seem less threatening because the mother, though a sexual rival, had less social power and the father, though perhaps powerful, was not sexually threatening. Thus in Austen's novels mothers and motherlike characters like Mrs. Norris tend to be the villains but lack power (Mrs. Bennet can't make Elizabeth marry Collins), and fathers tend to be sympathetic or at least unthreatening.[11] Furthermore, a woman of that period had little opportunity to rebel and therefore a greater incentive to come to terms with social control. Whatever the influences on her, they helped Austen to create fiction in which opposing forces reach almost perfect equilibrium.

In the remaining two chapters, then, I will analyze the characterization in two writers who I think represent the high point of the two traditions I have been discussing. Just as Austen brings the Richardsonian tradition of psychological intensity to its culmination by combining with it an objectivity like Fielding's, Dickens raises the Fielding tradition of comic characterization to its highest development by giving comic characters a subjectivity like that in Richardson.

Austen & the Conscious Character

chapter 6

ALTHOUGH most characters in the classic English novel exhibit inner tension like that in Richardson's characters, there is of course a great deal of variation among characters. What gives a particular character his individuality is the nature and relationship of the desire and control implied in him. We can define the character with implied tension as a particular way of expressing tension, a particular balance between desire and control which expresses those forces in some typical, distinctive kind of compromise formation. The character functions as a way of allowing desire expression and to some extent balancing that desire with forces opposing it (both inside and outside the character), at least partly responding to and dealing with those forces, restraining and deflecting desire to accommodate them. Characters deflect desire in distinctive ways, arousing more or less desire in us and opposing it in different ways. And the relationship between these inner forces is implied through the ways a character typically expresses and restrains desire and the ways he responds to objects of desire and to opposition to desire. To get at the individuality of a given character, we can ask what his desire is—what it seeks, how strong it is, how much it can accept control. And we can ask what kind of control he manages—how repressively or tolerantly he controls desire, how successfully he balances desire with control; desire and control may be in strong conflict or may be combined, interacting with each other in various ways. We can consider how successfully the character deals with that conflict, how he deals with what opposes desire or with desires that cannot be fulfilled, whether he is able to work out some compromise between the two forces. I think characters seem "realistic" when the form in which they express desire seems related to the way they try to control it, and when the balance between desire and control remains consistent or changes in a way which is consistent with their tension. Probably we also feel a character is plausible when the balance between desire and control implied in him is one we can temporarily accept, accepting the control he offers us as a way of dealing with the desire he arouses in us. In evaluating characters, however, we should bear in mind not only their consistency and plausibility but also the intensity of the response they cause; a character may seem "realistic" yet lack vividness.

Although many varieties of character are possible, two main kinds are typical of the English novel. The divergence I have described in the novel's form was accompanied by a divergence in characterization. Novelists who concentrated on the subject located tension primarily in the protagonist, developing one kind of character; and novelists who concentrated on the object located tension primarily in object-characters, developing a different kind of character. It is these two kinds that I wish to examine in these final chapters, looking at examples of each to show how the details of characterization work.

Many critics have pointed out the presence of two different kinds of character in the novel. E. M. Forster's distinction between "round" characters, who can change, and "flat" characters, who can't, is best known. David Daiches contrasts characters who are presented all at once, as known constants, so that the work merely displays their constancy, with characters who emerge gradually, defined by events. John Bayley distinguishes between characters who are presented from the outside, as we see others, and characters who are presented from within, as we see ourselves. W. J. Harvey contrasts complex protagonists with simpler background figures. And Scholes and Kellogg make a distinction between two kinds of representational character, the psychological and the sociological.[1]

Although these categories don't coincide exactly, they all seem to be getting at the same basic distinction among characters. The various qualities typical of each kind of character are related. It is because a character has an implied inner consciousness that we can have an inside view of him. If that inner consciousness is complex, the novelist may take longer to make the character emerge. And a character with such consciousness is likely to be a protagonist. Protagonists serve desire, and it is desire that arouses conflicts; thus it is likely to be the protagonist who encounters conflict and has to develop the awareness to deal with it. Since the protagonist is the character we associate most closely with ourselves, we want him to have an awareness like ours. And if he has conflict and an implied awareness of that conflict, he is also likely to be able to change. His tension makes us want him to change, resolving conflicts, and his awareness enables him to change. Thus we can group these traits together as the interrelated qualities of one kind of character—a character with an implied inner self which enables him to become aware of and deal with (or at least try to deal with) both inner and outer conflicts.

This kind of character is usually called "round," but the term is not very helpful in understanding how such characters function. And if we rely on Forster's criterion that round characters change, surprising us convincingly, some difficulties arise. Characters who don't grow as "round" characters do can still surprise us in other ways. Nor is any change at all sufficient to make a character "round"; different kinds of character change in different ways. I would prefer to call characters of this kind *conscious* characters.[2] Conscious characters are not the only kind with implied tension, but they deal with their tension in a different way from "flat" characters. They respond to the forces opposing their desires by altering the form in which they express desire, and this response makes us feel they have at least some awareness of the forces (inner and outer) causing tension. In this way the conscious character resembles a detached narrator, able to stand apart from desire and criticize it. Since this function is within the same character as the uncontrolled desire it opposes, it can not only be aware but can interact with desire in ways a narrator cannot. The conscious character can deal with his desires by restraining them, working out a compromise between desire and control. And he can use his awareness to come to a similar compromise with external forces opposing him. Instead of releasing energy in uncontrolled, irrational ways, he behaves in a moderate, restrained way which implies his ability to control the irrational forces he is aware of in himself. His individuality lies in the particular way he controls those forces, the kind of compromise he works out. When the conscious character changes, then, he typically moves toward this compromise with what opposes desire, a compromise made possible by increased awareness and resulting in diminished tension.

One advantage of the term *conscious* is that it enables us to allow for differing degrees of consciousness; it need not be an either-or term like *round* and *flat*. Some characters exhibit a greater ability to deal with their tension than others. Some characters seem conscious yet retain strong inner tension. The characters of Emily Brontë and of Dostoevsky, for example, seem self-aware yet driven by impulses their consciousness can't fully control. Lovelace is another character in whom self-awareness and uncontrolled desire remain in strong conflict. The more tension a protagonist exhibits, the more likely he is to be self-aware, since we want a protagonist to have the ability to deal with his tension. Even if he cannot resolve his inner conflict, his awareness provides us with a way of partly dealing with it, distancing it and judging it. Whether he deals with it fully or not, the conscious character must have inner tension so that we feel his consciousness is an expression of an ability to deal with inner forces. Otherwise the character will seem merely the writer's mouthpiece; his consciousness will not seem to come from within, to be a response to inner tension.

As novelists themselves became increasingly self-conscious, they located more and more consciousness in their characters; the protagonists in most novels are quite conscious. Among all these conscious characters, one of the most effective is Elizabeth Bennet in *Pride and Prejudice,* since she has both clear inner tension and considerable ability to deal with that tension. To analyze the way conscious characters work, then, I would like to look at the way Austen presents Elizabeth. In doing so I hope to show how writers make us feel characters are conscious.

The main trait Forster ascribes to his round character is the ability to learn; however, though learning is an important sign of awareness, it is not a quality but a way—one of many ways—of manifesting a quality. A conscious character need not learn something to convince us he is conscious. Characters can impress us as having awareness on our first acquaintance with them, before we have had a chance to see them change. Jane Bennet, for example, never changes, and yet one feels she has the consciousness that would enable her to change if the plot required it. Another way a novelist can make a character seem conscious is by giving us an inside view of the character's mind or by having the character tell us his thoughts. But here again, this is not necessary to make us feel a character is conscious; we never get an inside view of Jane Bennet, nor does she tell us much about the depths of her mind.

There is another, less obvious way of implying consciousness which I think is more important. The main way novelists make characters seem conscious is by using the details of speech and action in the way Richardson does, making the character's behavior a continual series of small compromise formations that imply both some uncontrolled desire and at the same time a consciousness of that desire that attempts to control it. In addition, the details of behavior can imply a character's awareness of the uncontrolled desires of other characters and show his attempts to deal with those desires as well. And he can adjust his desires to external forms of control in ways that imply consciousness of both desire and what opposes it. He can react sensitively to his world, understanding others' unexpressed feelings, adapting his behavior tactfully to complex relationships with them. To do this he must control his own desires to some extent, moderating them in response to outer demands. It is through this kind of behavior that we feel a character is conscious, and if he does not show awareness in this way, neither making him change nor giving inner views of him will convince us he is a conscious character.

To show how this technique works, I will examine the scene in which we first see Elizabeth close up. It is not a scene in which she does anything surprising, but it is sufficient to establish her as a conscious character. Austen has just shown us (in the opening chapters) that Elizabeth is enclosed in a society that opposes the desires we attribute to her and instead gives power to her mother—and to Darcy, who has just snubbed her. We want Elizabeth to deal with this opposition to desire, if only by providing some expression within the fictional world for our criticism of negative characters, validating our response and acting as an extension of the critical awareness the narrator has induced in us.

In the fourth chapter Elizabeth and Jane withdraw from the restrictive social world we have seen up to now. By the very act of withdrawing they are dealing with social control, showing they can detach themselves from it and view it as a narrator might. It is particularly Elizabeth who is able to be detached and critical; Jane remains fairly submissive to social control. We can also contrast Elizabeth with Clarissa, who remains obsessed with moral control (especially as represented by her father) even in solitude, and who when she does withdraw from her family condemns herself to total isolation, unable to re-enter the social world. Elizabeth, on the other hand, can find a balance between public and private selves.

In their privacy the sisters are free to talk about the people who make up the social world, and the way Elizabeth talks about them enables her to deal with the frustration they have caused. She shows her awareness of them—and thus her superiority, since they are less aware. And she shows she is more aware than Jane as well, since Jane tends to accept people simply as their social selves. Notice how this little scene shows Elizabeth expressing her awareness of what people are like and how they are different from each other:

> When Jane and Elizabeth were alone, the former, who had been cautious in her praise of Mr. Bingley before, expressed to her sister how very much she admired him.
> "He is just what a young man ought to be," said she, "sensible, good-humoured, lively; and I never saw such happy manners!—so much ease, with such perfect good breeding!"
> "He is also handsome," replied Elizabeth, "which a young man ought likewise to be, if he possibly can. His character is thereby complete."
> "I was very much flattered by his asking me to dance a second time. I did not expect such a compliment."
> "Did not you? *I* did for you. But that is one great difference between us. Compliments always take *you* by surprise, and *me* never. What could be more natural than his asking you again? He could not help seeing that you were about five times as pretty as every other woman in the room. No thanks to his gallantry for that. Well, he certainly is very agreeable, and I give you leave to like him. You have liked many a stupider person."
> "Dear Lizzy!"

"Oh! you are a great deal too apt you know, to like people in general. You never see a fault in any body. All the world are good and agreeable in your eyes. I never heard you speak ill of a human being in my life."

"I would wish not to be hasty in censuring any one; but I always speak what I think."

"I know you do; and it is *that* which makes the wonder. With your good sense, to be so honestly blind to the follies and nonsense of others! Affectation of candour is common enough; —one meets it every where. But to be candid without ostentation or design—to take the good of every body's character and make it still better, and say nothing of the bad—belongs to you alone. And so, you like this man's sisters too, do you? Their manners are not equal to his." . . .

Elizabeth listened in silence, but was not convinced; . . . with more quickness of observation and less pliancy of temper than her sister, and with a judgment too unassailed by any attention to herself, she was very little disposed to approve them. They were in fact very fine ladies; . . . but proud and conceited. (1.4.14–15)

This passage, like the one from *Clarissa,* contains many compromise formations in which two opposing character functions are joined. Elizabeth functions partly as what I have called a negative subject, expressing a desire that opposes control. As there is a side to Clarissa that is attracted to Lovelace and opposes her parents, there is a side to Elizabeth that is attracted to Wickham and rebels against the social control represented by her mother and (she thinks) Darcy. It is this side I am calling negative. The clearest desire Elizabeth expresses here is a desire for Bingley. It is of course a desire that Jane win Bingley, but perhaps we can see this as a displaced version of Elizabeth's own desire for an attractive man. With his ease and good looks, Bingley resembles Wickham, so that he can elicit the same kind of desire from Elizabeth. Elizabeth is willing to allow desire more than Jane is; she is more willing to acknowledge that Bingley is a desirable object. And by praising Bingley not for his breeding as Jane does but for his handsomeness, Elizabeth shows she is more willing to allow desire to be personal, not merely controlled by social forms. She also speaks for this desire in asserting that she expected a compliment to Jane; she is saying that desire deserves to be fulfilled. This statement implies a rebellious element in her desire.

Her comparative rebelliousness is suggested by the way she opposes Jane, who embodies a greater submission to social control. For example, Jane's modesty here shows that she opposes her own desires more than Elizabeth does, not asserting a strong claim to fulfillment. We can see Jane as a secondary subject-character reflecting the positive function in Elizabeth. Elizabeth's criticism of Jane, then, externalizes her conflict against her own self-restraint. She points out here that submission like Jane's dulls one's awareness, one's ability to see faults in others. Her own critical awareness is the main way Elizabeth expresses her negative function: her criticism of negative object-characters is a way of rebelling against them, refusing to believe in their right to exercise authority over her.

Other aspects of Elizabeth's behavior also imply her opposition to control.[3] She is more active, energetic, and independent than a passive, submissive romance protagonist or a fairly romancelike protagonist like Clarissa. We can see her energy in the fact that she talks so much, saying more than the situation requires, not merely accepting what Jane says but asserting her own independent opinion, showing her lack of "pliancy of temper." She also refuses to accept mere social forms of speech. The manner of her speech is assertive and emphatic.[4] She emphasizes "I" and "me." She energetically opposes restraint by exaggerating, saying "five times as pretty," "a great deal too apt," "never," "all the world," "every where," "every body." She indulges in italics, exclamation marks, and dashes, seeming in a hurry to speak, to say as much as possible as strongly as possible. And this way of talking is clearly in contrast with Jane's quiet restraint.

Furthermore, Elizabeth's speeches express opposition to submissiveness like Jane's. She mocks polite forms and those who uncritically accept them. She implies her critical attitude toward social forms by detecting the selfish motives they hide, the "design" beneath the "affectation." She values the ability to "see a fault" in people and asserts that she knows what is "natural" in people, unlike Jane, who is sometimes taken in. It seems to be in behalf of natural feelings such as attraction to a handsome man that she resents social control, seeing social forms as affected because they deny natural impulses.

But although Elizabeth talks in a more rebellious way than Clarissa does, she can do so because she keeps her rebelliousness less serious than Clarissa's. Unlike Clarissa, Elizabeth does not run away from home and is not strongly attracted to an embodiment of highly rebellious passion like Lovelace. Austen makes Elizabeth's home less repressive and the character embodying passion, Wickham, weaker, less fiery and attractive. And just as she diminishes these external forces, she also moderates the opposing forces within Elizabeth that correspond to these external forces—control and desire. By diminishing Elizabeth's desires she makes Elizabeth seem less rebellious and irrational. In this passage, for example, she does several things to keep Elizabeth from seeming too passionate. For one thing, it is Jane's desires, not her own, that Elizabeth is defending. Thus she need not take desire too seriously here; she can be detached about it, like a narrator speaking of a protagonist's desires. In addition, even when Elizabeth does express desire, she does so in a relatively restrained manner, not becoming violently resentful of restraint as her mother or Lydia would. Even though she is partly in the wrong, is too attracted to desire and not yet fully aware of the need for restraint, she nevertheless behaves in a way that shows she can restrain herself and can thus learn greater self-control. Thus the fact that her desires are moderated makes us feel there is a force in her able to become aware of and so restrain desire.

One way Elizabeth controls desire through awareness is by putting it into words. Speech is a fairly rational, controlled form of behavior. Speaking to another character does not serve desire as fully as attempting to coerce that character physically (or fleeing him like Clarissa). By speaking to him, one tacitly acknowledges his independence; one accepts that he is not simply the object of one's desire, to be controlled by that desire. One acknowledges that he is the subject of his own actions—that he will answer back, and not necessarily say what one wishes. Thus speech (especially speech like Elizabeth's, responsive to other characters) can imply an awareness of the limitations on one's ability to make reality conform to one's desires. Even if the speaker is still trying to control another character, he accepts that he must only do so indirectly. And language like Elizabeth's implies self-control because her language is relatively social, restricted by decorum.[5] Furthermore, Elizabeth's way of talking here, even while implying her capacity for desire, also implies her awareness of others. She talks mainly about character, comparing and judging people, and although her way of talking implies desire by criticizing people who oppose her desire, it also implies restraint. She shows she can accept the otherness of people, not merely seeing them as objects of her desire (as her mother would).

In resisting her own desire like this, Elizabeth is partly functioning (like Clarissa) as a positive subject, one who serves control and seeks to sublimate desire. The main way she expresses this positive function is by detaching herself from desire, somewhat as a narrator would. Like Clarissa, she makes herself the topic of her own sentences, standing back from herself as a narrator would and describing herself, separating herself from her negative function. Because of this detachment she can be ironic in her way of expressing desire, as narrators often are. The opening sentence of *Pride and Prejudice* presents a narrator who treats desire ironically in much the way Elizabeth does here. That sentence says that a goal-character (a single man) "must" be fulfilling (must want a wife); and Elizabeth here says that a goal-character "ought" to be fulfilling (desirably handsome). Both of these statements mock the way desire distorts perception (as it does in Mrs. Bennet's case) by making the desirer think that the object-world is a function of his desires, that others ought to be as he wishes. By adding "if he possibly can," Elizabeth mocks this attitude, implying an awareness that what one desires cannot always be possible. Thus instead of allowing desire to control perception, she is using her awareness of her world (an awareness like the narrator's) to restrain her desire.

Irony is a compromise formation. It enables Elizabeth both to express and to mock her desire. She treats herself as desirer ironically. For example, she says compliments never take her by surprise, implying that she expects the world to fulfill her desires. Yet as she says this she stands apart from herself and observes this desire, implying that she doesn't fully believe in it. Thus (as with Clarissa) her statement is a compromise formation expressing two opposing functions—a positive, critical "I" mocking the negative "I" that speaks for desire. At the same time that she doesn't take desire too seriously, she also doesn't take restraint too seriously; neither dominates her. Just as her negative function is less seriously rebellious than Clarissa's, her positive function is less repressive, not so adamantly opposed to rebelliousness. She neither desires too much nor tries to restrain herself too much. Instead of condemning her desires as Clarissa does, she can mock them and can allow them freer expression. And she can treat self-control ironically too. For instance, she says she gives Jane leave to like Bingley. This exaggerated way of stating her meaning implies an awareness that one cannot really control affection in this way and therefore mocks the attempt to control it. We see, then, that Elizabeth is controlled neither by desire nor by society. Instead she replaces a repressive self-control like Clarissa's, seeking to submit to society, with a more moderate kind of self-control, an awareness that is able to distance both desire and repressive control, seeing them ironically, and is thus able to work out a compromise between them. Rational awareness depolarizes the conflict between desire and control by not allowing either to become too serious. Irony is a way of remaining aware of both opposing forces at once, so that neither dominates one's attitude and seems all-powerful; each can be limited if one remains aware that something opposes it. Reason can thus avoid being completely taken in by either force.

Elizabeth differs from Clarissa, then, in that her negative and positive functions are less polarized, more restrained and mixed together. The way she expresses rebelliousness is quite restrained, and the way she seeks to control her desires still allows those desires expression. Thus Austen continues the process of depolarization which I have described as typical of the novel. She not only depolarizes the conflict among characters but also that within characters. This makes the character of Elizabeth seem more conscious—that is, seem to have a stronger force within herself capable of dealing with her tension.

Elizabeth's energy and ability to restrain it are implied throughout the novel. Her opposition to restraint is implied by the way she resents Darcy, seeing him as an embodiment of a social control she feels is repressive, and prefers Wickham, whom she sees as representing the ability to overcome restraint and allow feeling. We also see her opposition to control in the way she answers back to people like Darcy and Lady Catherine, asserting her independence of them. She often speaks with "great energy" (1.6.24; 2.11.192), not restraining herself as much as Jane does. Where Jane "only smiles," Elizabeth can "laugh" (3.18.282). Her laughter is often directed against people who are too submissive to social control and are thus unable to allow their desires adequate expression. The clearest example of such excessive submission is Mr. Collins, but Elizabeth also mocks Darcy (not entirely fairly) for a similar inability to take social forms lightly enough to reconcile them with private desires and so express those desires. By trying to make Darcy talk she seems to be trying to overcome his inner repression, so that here again she is opposing repression.

We see more of Elizabeth's energy in the first half of the novel; later on her self-restraint increases. But even at her liveliest she always combines some restraint with her energy. She restrains herself even when she attacks Darcy. She neither advances into open conflict nor retreats; she keeps within the bounds of decorum yet implies more than can be said, adjusting private meaning to public forms of expression by using ironic implication and by mockingly exaggerating the desires she expresses so they won't seem too serious. Her behavior may be "bordering on the uncivil" (3.18.380), but it doesn't cross the border. Her ironic awareness enables her to find compromise formations that "unite truth and civility" (2.15.216), combining some self-expression with some submission, not rejecting control too much but accepting a "mixture"—both "sweetness and archness" (1.10.52). She doesn't take her resentment too seriously and so can make it arch and playful. Though she evades social restraint, she does not directly challenge it.

Her self-restraint is shown more directly by her attitude toward those positive object-characters who represent a good kind of control. She values Jane, which suggests she sees value in an acceptance of social control like Jane's. Her going to help Jane when Jane is ill shows her willingness to subordinate her desires to the needs of others. And, most important, her eventual acceptance of Darcy is an acceptance of the kind of social control Darcy represents—a control now seen as fulfilling, not repressive.

A conscious character like Elizabeth seems to induce a dual response in us. We have both an emotional response as we do to a character like Clarissa (and even more to Lovelace) and a rational response as we do to a narrator like Fielding's. At the unconscious, irrational level of what I have called primary response, we want a character to gratify our desires as fully as possible. Thus we are attracted to that side of Elizabeth I have called negative, the side expressing uncontrolled desire. When Elizabeth restrains herself she fails to gratify our desires and we feel frustrated. We project our tension onto her, feeling that tension as a conflict between her desires and restraint. But if one side of us is frustrated and reacts emotionally, rationally we respond to the side of Elizabeth I have called positive, the side that restrains desire. We are grateful that she avoids a guilty, violent expression of desire. And we rationally appreciate the skill and wit with which she does so, managing to express desire yet control it. This rational response we also seem to project onto a character, inferring that to deal with his tension he must have a rational awareness like that we feel in responding to him. We feel that if he can deal with his tension, he must have some entity within him that can be aware of the forces causing that tension. We also feel a rational appreciation for the aptness with which a character like Elizabeth adjusts the way she expresses desire to the constraints of the world around her so that desire can find some fulfillment in that world. And the conscious character appeals to our reason by judging other characters for us, at the same time embodying a standard of comparison to help us judge how rational those characters are. In these ways the conscious character not only induces us to respond rationally but also provides a way of channeling our response, giving it expression in the fictional world. His rational self-control replaces our own, enabling us to be rational without having to make the effort our own rationality requires of us.

The nature of the conscious character affects the work in which he occurs in various ways. For one thing, the more consciousness a character has, the more important he is likely to become. Since he has the ability to perceive, understand, and deal with his world, we will want to see through his eyes, to share his subject relation with the world; and the more he attracts us, the less sympathy we are likely to feel with other characters. For example, Austen stays close to Elizabeth, whereas Dickens's protagonists exhibit less awareness and so are less important, while his object-characters become more important.

The conscious protagonist is likely to be at the center of a plot based upon a learning process. Such a plot is likely because it dramatizes the process implied within the character. Within the character we feel the presence of a rational self-control which is able to resolve the conflict between rebellious desire and repression, and this process of resolving conflicts is usually acted out in the plot. In the first half of *Pride and Prejudice*, for example, Elizabeth functions partly as a negative subject serving uncontrolled desire. In the second half her positive function becomes dominant, controlling her desire and thus transforming it. Like Clarissa, she learns to reject her negative desire and the lack of proper control embodied in the negative goal-character (Wickham). This process involves working out a compromise between desire and control, and thus it resembles the way Elizabeth is constantly compromising (if imperfectly) between these two in the details of her behavior. It is in the climactic central scene where she refuses Darcy and then receives his letter that she discovers how inadequate has been her rational control over her feelings. This scene makes explicit the tension between desire and restraint implicit in Elizabeth's character and shows Elizabeth using her conscious self-control to oppose desire. At first her "power of comprehension" is weakened by "strong prejudice"—that is, by a tendency to let desire distort perception, to see the world as she wishes it were. But then that power of comprehension—her consciousness—is able to overcome the "wishes" that have "flattered" her—that is, to control desire. She sees that desire has "driven reason away." But now reason can reverse that process. She does this by turning her consciousness on herself, seeing the way desire has misled her. When she sees this she exclaims "Till this moment I never knew myself!" (2.13.204–8). Thus her capacity for consciousness is dramatized, and the process that dramatizes it is her learning—first about others, and through that about herself.

When the conscious character affects the plot in this way, that effect extends to the other characters involved in the plot. Because the conscious protagonist has an inner conflict, other characters can correspond to the inner forces causing that conflict, so that their interaction reflects the inner process by which the protagonist deals with his conflict. As in *Clarissa,* characters reflecting forces in the protagonist can interact with him and cause him to change. Because Elizabeth has this kind of relationship with object-characters, she can engage in a more complex interaction with them than we find in Fielding. Since the characters correspond to aspects of her inner conflict, she is more affected by them. She cannot deal with them as easily as Fielding's protagonist can deal with object-characters. However, because Elizabeth has the ability to deal with her inner conflict, she can also deal with these characters. In this respect Austen seems close to Fielding. As I have said, her protagonist has the kind of consciousness and detachment Fielding locates in his narrator. Elizabeth does not seem trapped in conflict like Clarissa, controlled by the forces within her causing conflict and by the characters (Lovelace and Mr. Harlowe) corresponding to those inner forces. She is able to control her own desires fairly well, and thus repressive characters need not react against her desires so strongly and she need not feel very threatened by them. And just as she can detach herself from her own desires, so she can detach herself from the characters embodying uncontrolled desire and not take them too seriously. Thus negative characters are distanced and seem as comic, as in Fielding, although since they correspond to aspects of Elizabeth's inner conflict they remain more important than in Fielding.

In other words, Austen's object-characters exist primarily to arouse a rational response in us (as they do in the conscious protagonist) rather than an emotional response (attraction, fear, hate) as in Richardson. Because the conscious protagonist encourages us to value rational awareness, we are not attracted to irrational characters. Instead, along with the protagonist, we distance them and judge them. Austen influences us to judge them by making them similar in various ways which induce us to compare them with Elizabeth and each other. We compare characters who play similar roles—parent, child, suitor. When we make such comparisons we are remaining aware of something outside the character himself, so we do not feel so close to the character; and most of these comparisons make us see a character's shortcomings, which also makes us see him as an object. Thus our response can be less emotional. For instance, the improper desire that Wickham represents is not very attractive or powerful; Elizabeth's desire for him does not stir the emotional depths that Clarissa's attraction to Lovelace does. Instead we are concerned with comparing Wickham to Darcy, deciding which is the better man; and Elizabeth can finally put Wickham in his place, passing judgment on him, unlike Clarissa, who cannot fully escape Lovelace and the conflict he causes except by dying. The world Austen creates, then, is one that allows (and even forces) the protagonist (and us) to become conscious. It both induces her to judge it and leaves her free (unlike Clarissa) to behave rationally and to learn to become more rational. In contrast to Clarissa's world, her world does not repress her so seriously that she is driven into rebellion; and it does not make uncontrolled desire attractive enough to induce her to abandon her rational self-restraint.

Because Elizabeth can detach herself from both uncontrolled desire and the repressive reaction against it, the characters representing those impulses are diminished, as I have mentioned. Less uncontrolled desire is located in the negative object, and thus less repression need be located there. Instead, more positive desire reconciled with positive control is located in the positive object and in the subject. In other words, since desire can be largely reconciled with control, it need not be seen as negative and rejected, located in negative characters. The main representative of desire in *Clarissa* is Lovelace, a character in whom desire is rebellious and unacceptable. The main representative of desire in *Pride and Prejudice* is not a villain but Elizabeth herself; she and Darcy can replace Wickham as the most powerful characters. And the main representative of control in *Clarissa* is Mr. Harlowe, embodying an unacceptable, repressive authority, whereas the main representatives of control in *Pride and Prejudice* are Elizabeth and Darcy, embodying a self-control that can be reconciled with desire.

As a result, the negative object in *Pride and Prejudice* is relatively depolarized. Since Wickham is rather weak, uncontrolled desire is less rebellious and threatening. And there are no repressive figures of authority like Mr. Harlowe; the nearest equivalents, Mrs. Bennet and Lady Catherine, are distanced and seen as comic, and they do not have much power over Elizabeth. Just as she is not overpowered by the negative object-characters, so she is not overpowered by the corresponding inner forces, rebellion or repression. Since she is not so repressed, not internalizing repressive parental control as Clarissa does, she can replace that control with her own conscious, rational self-control.

It is because opposing forces are not strongly polarized that Elizabeth can work out a compromise between them. That is, she can replace negative desire and control—rebellion and repression—with their positive counterparts. Her inner compromise is accompanied by a compromise worked out in the plot. Whereas Clarissa has no alternative except repression or rebellion, embodied in her two suitors, Solmes and Lovelace, Elizabeth can find a suitor who is neither too repressive nor too rebellious. Her choices are represented by three sets of characters: three subordinate protagonists embodying alternative selves for her, and three goal-characters, suitors representing the goals she can choose. Rebelliousness is represented by Lydia and Wickham, Lovelace's equivalent. Its opposite is represented by Charlotte and Collins, whose role is like Solmes's; this set of characters embodies a submission to social control which denies desire almost entirely. But Elizabeth need not choose either of these two extremes: unlike Richardson, Austen provides a set of positive object-characters embodying the fulfilling control Elizabeth learns to accept. Elizabeth can combine desire and restraint like

Jane, the good alternative offered her. And Austen offers her a good suitor, Darcy, who also represents a middle ground, love tempered by control. In the world of *Pride and Prejudice,* where rational restraint is made fulfilling, the alternative Darcy represents is more attractive than either extreme. He enables Elizabeth to fulfill desire yet accept some control, just as she compromises between these forces within herself. Thus Elizabeth's world not only fosters rational restraint but justifies it by rewarding it. It is because she learns restraint that she comes to value the control Darcy embodies and can also teach him to moderate it, and so can win him. Her union with Darcy acts out on the level of plot her inner balancing of desire with control, since Darcy embodies a self-control like that she accepts within her mind.

Austen dramatizes Elizabeth's inner change by presenting a corresponding change among the object-characters. Since those characters are related to forces within Elizabeth, the transformation of her inner forces is accompanied by a transformation of the narrative object. When Elizabeth functions primarily as a negative subject, serving rebellious desire, her desire creates a false set of object relationships. She sees uncontrolled desire (embodied in Wickham) as positive, fulfilling; and she sees control (embodied in Darcy) as negative, repressive. It is because these object relations are unfulfilling that Elizabeth herself seems negative here, unable to attain sublimation. But when she is forced to confront the fact that the object-world does not fit her view of it, and thus to become aware that desire has distorted her perception, her reason alters its relation to desire, learning to control it more. This inner change is accompanied by a redefinition of the object-characters: Darcy replaces Wickham as the positive goal-character. And as her perception of Darcy is transformed, Darcy himself undergoes a corresponding change, learning to allow for feeling (by learning to accept Elizabeth) just as Elizabeth learns to accept control in accepting him. Wickham also changes, acting in a more negative, uncontrolled way (running off with Lydia) once he is cut off from Elizabeth. Just as Elizabeth learns to become critical of Wickham, she learns to detach herself from uncontrolled desire within herself, standing back and judging it as a narrator would, seeing the self-as-desirer as an object.

Because desire is inherent in the subject-character's function, that desire is dealt with through a negative process, subjecting the subject-object structure that desire creates to a negative transformation. In other words, Elizabeth discovers the way desire has created a false object, and in order to find the true object she must reverse that process of distortion, transforming it so that the good character is seen as bad and vice versa. This transformation resembles the rejection of romance we find in early Austen works like *Northanger Abbey*. Elizabeth is somewhat like Catherine Morland in first seeing the object-world as if it were in romance, seeing Wickham as hero and Darcy as villain. Naïve romance defines characters by their relation to desire: those opposing it are bad and those fulfilling it are good. The transformation of this pattern acts out a rejection of the kind of uncontrolled desires to which romancelike fiction often panders. By replacing Wickham with Darcy, Austen implies that fiction should not simply appeal to our desires but should teach us (like Elizabeth) to accept some rational and moral restraint.

This transformation in the goal-character is accompanied by other transformations in the object-world. Other characters are changed mainly with respect to their power over Elizabeth. In the first half of the novel, since she resents control, those characters who embody control are more important and often seem threatening. It is in the first half of the novel that bad parentlike characters such as Mrs. Bennet and Lady Catherine are important, as well as other characters who represent the way society seems to oppose Elizabeth's fulfillment—for instance, Miss Bingley and Mr. Collins. When these characters return later in the novel they no longer seem threatening; they are much less important and powerful and we can laugh at them more completely. It is also in the first half of the novel that Jane is important, evidently to embody the kind of restraint Elizabeth needs to acquire. In the second half of the novel Elizabeth becomes primarily a positive subject and can restrain herself; thus we no longer need to have Jane held up as an example to make us criticize Elizabeth. In the second half of the novel, the characters who become more important are those like the Gardiners, who represent a good control that exists to help Elizabeth rather than make us criticize her, so that Elizabeth can now accept and profit from that control. In other words, control is now seen as positive. There is a similar change among the alternative protagonists, the examples Elizabeth reacts against. In the first half it is social control that seems negative, and so the negative protagonist Elizabeth criticizes is Charlotte (and to some extent Jane, who seems a bit too restrained). In the second half, it is rebelliousness that Elizabeth has learned to see as negative, and so the negative protagonist she reacts against is Lydia, who becomes much more important, while Charlotte loses importance and Jane is wholly accepted.

In order for these transformations both in Elizabeth and in other characters to take place, Austen gives characters dual functions. If a character is to change convincingly, we need to believe that the capacity for change has been in him all along. In Elizabeth's case, not only do we see from the start that she tends to be somewhat rebellious but also, mixed with that negative function, we see her ability to control herself. Thus when she changes, her inner tension does not vanish; both functions remain present, but the balance of power shifts. Elizabeth still resists control somewhat, as we see in her playfulness with Darcy at the novel's end, but now her positive function, accepting control, is dominant. And Austen uses the mixed nature of her object-characters in working out Elizabeth's learning process: Elizabeth perceives one function of the object-character but must learn to see the opposing function as well. If Darcy were all good, it wouldn't be convincing that she first sees him as negative. And she is misled by Wickham because he combines the traits of an attractive goal-character with traits of the negative transformation of that kind of character, the lustful villain—each set of traits moderated by existing in compromise formation with its opposites. It is because the object-world is complex in this way that the protagonist must develop the consciousness to understand it in order to enter into a fulfilling relation with the object.

This process of judging resembles that done by Fielding's narrator (and partly by his protagonist). But in Fielding the protagonist and the characters he judges are fairly simple, and so the act of judging is relatively easy. One can soon discover the true self beneath a character's mask. In Austen's characters, however, as in Richardson's, social and private selves are more interrelated and so less separable. And the protagonist is also divided, the side of him serving desire resisting the control of the side that tries to perceive the world objectively. This conflict makes it harder for him to judge; he needs to become self-aware and deal with his desires before he can judge accurately. Furthermore, since desire and control are not separable, when he judges he cannot simply reject social falsity as Fielding's characters can, both at the end of a scene and at the novel's end when they leave behind the corrupt social world. Instead Austen's protagonists must reach a compromise with social control, and that is a more complex and difficult process. As a result, judging and dealing with characters is not a simple action that can take place in a short episode as in Fielding; rather it is a gradual process which can become the basis for the plot of the whole novel. Thus the more complex the protagonist's consciousness becomes, the more complex becomes the plot based on him.

Pride and Prejudice can be described, then, as an education (for us as well as Elizabeth) in what character is and should be, teaching us to see it as complex, not simple as in traditional romance. We compare characters associated with the acceptance of social control (such as Darcy, Collins, Jane, and Lady Catherine) with characters who partly elude that control (such as Elizabeth, Bingley, Wickham, and Lydia), and we need to develop the ability to see that these categories are inadequate for some of them. That is, we need to see that submission and rebellion are not as simple as they at first appear, nor desire and control as polarized. We find that the characters who accept social control are not all good, since they tend to oppose genuine feeling in themselves and others, but also that those who resist social control are not all good, since they tend to lack strong moral and rational restraint. Thus we see that people should not be simple, either submissive or rebellious, but rather should seek complexity, working out a balance between desire and control.

Austen evidently sees the capacity for this balance as inherent in character. Character has two aspects; there are the qualities of "nature" one is born with (for example, disposition) and the traits one acquires through "education" in "society" (1.15.70). These are in tension, and they seem to correspond to the two functions I have been describing in her characters. Natural qualities are those associated with desire, to some extent opposed to control. Social qualities come as a result of the control one is taught to accept. As Darcy says, "understanding" should try to "overcome" the "feelings" through "education" (1.11.57–58), though (as he needs to learn) feelings must be allowed their place. Thus natural qualities should be balanced with social; that is, desire should be joined with control. The novel teaches us to see these two aspects of character in order that we may understand how they should be balanced.

In addition to plot, the presence of a conscious protagonist also influences the way a novelist treats point of view. A novelist like Austen who values rational awareness tends to use point of view to encourage such an awareness in us. We are asked to judge characters along with Elizabeth. By transferring much of the narrator's function to Elizabeth, Austen can avoid a narrator who imposes judgments on us. Thus she leaves us fairly free to judge for ourselves, like Elizabeth, so that we too can make mistakes. This eventually teaches us to develop the ironic awareness Austen wants us to have. At the same time that we, along with Elizabeth, judge other characters, we are also asked to compare her with other characters and judge her.[6] Thus even though Elizabeth is conscious enough so that we can often see through her eyes, allowing her partly to replace the narrator, we must keep some ironic detachment from her. By doing so we learn to restrain our own desires, balancing them with critical awareness much as Elizabeth learns to. This dual attitude is reflected in Austen's dual point of view, partly showing us what Elizabeth sees and partly using a detached narrator who can give us information that enables us to be somewhat critical of Elizabeth, seeing that she can be mistaken.

Most novelists probably follow Austen to some extent in taking a critical attitude toward the conscious protagonist. The fact that the character is conscious does not mean that he is always right. The kind of awareness that conscious characters embody involves an awareness that reality is imperfect, not wish-fulfilling; and this awareness is likely to be located not only in the protagonist but in the narrator, so that he will see the protagonist too as imperfect. As I have said, we feel the character is conscious because his consciousness exists as a way of dealing with an implied inner tension, and if the character has tension he is imperfect. In other words, the best way for a character to show he is conscious is by dealing with his tension through a learning process, and if he is to learn something he must be imperfect.

In the case of Elizabeth Bennet (as with most conscious protagonists), the imperfection we are asked to judge is her tendency to allow desire to control consciousness, letting vanity mislead judgment. Austen evidently feels there is a danger that reason can be led astray by selfish desires, can become too critical of social control and attracted to independence. She feels it should serve some higher authority instead of merely mocking those it sees as inferior and displaying its own cleverness. Wit alone is not enough; it needs to serve some moral control, just as Austen's own wit serves her moral purpose.[7]

One reason the narrator remains detached from the protagonist is so that the narrator can embody this state in which reason serves moral control. The narrator has the rational awareness that the protagonist must learn to attain. The narrator provides us with a standard against which to judge the character and gives us a sense of the qualities the character should seek. In *Pride and Prejudice* the narrator is close enough to Elizabeth so that we feel Elizabeth can become as conscious as the narrator is; but the narrator is detached enough so that we can see that Elizabeth has not yet attained that state. The narrator is thus a second embodiment of the positive side of Elizabeth, the detached consciousness able to be critical of uncontrolled desire. As Elizabeth learns, she comes closer to the narrator, seeing and judging as the narrator does. Thus later in the novel the narrator need not be so detached but can give us inside views, largely sharing Elizabeth's point of view. Yet even then the narrator retains some detachment, distancing the desires aroused through Elizabeth by using a fairly abstract, general vocabulary, rationalizing what she presents. Thus the narrator reinforces our sense of the value of rational awareness, its ability to deal with feelings.

The narrator's relationship to Elizabeth, then, has the same tension in it that Elizabeth's character induces in us. Like the narrator, we partly feel close to Elizabeth, taking her as a subject serving the desires the work arouses in us, but at the same time we partly feel critical of her, standing back from the desires she arouses and seeing the need to control them. Thus Austen's treatment of point of view seems to result from the kind of tension she locates in her protagonist. She is able to balance sympathy and ironic awareness because her narrator is neither too distant from Elizabeth as in Fielding nor too close as in Richardson; she retains some detachment but keeps the narrator unobtrusive enough so that we do not feel we are being pulled away from Elizabeth. In other words, Austen's use of point of view involves another compromise formation, one that allows a romancelike attitude toward the protagonist, seeing her as wish-fulfilling, yet at the same time includes a sense of the need to be critical of the kind of desires romancelike fiction arouses. Like Elizabeth herself, Austen doesn't deny the desire for fulfillment, but she balances that desire with restraint.

Of course many later novelists also make their characters seem quite conscious, and much of what I have said here can apply to conscious characters in other works. George Eliot and Henry James seem especially close to Austen in the way they organize their works around a conscious protagonist. In my final section I will consider ways in which they and other later writers modify the conscious character.

Dickens & the Unresolved Character

chapter 7

THE other kind of character typical of the English novel is one to which I think critics have not done justice. Forster's term "flat" sounds pejorative, as if something is missing from these characters. But they can be just as effective, though in a different way, as "round" characters are. Indeed, the master of this kind of characterization, Dickens, created characters who can arouse as much tension in the reader as any characters. Their conflicts may be less obvious than those of conscious characters, but that does not mean we do not feel there is conflict in them. Probably critics have been less successful with characters like Dickens's because of a bias in favor of more "realistic" and self-conscious fiction. In any case, I go into greater detail in this chapter to try to compensate for this shortcoming, and because Dickens's characterization is so rich and effective that I think it merits especially detailed examination.

The so-called "flat" character is best exemplified by the comic subsidiary characters not only in Dickens but in Fielding, Scott, and for that matter Shakespeare. Forster's term "flat" might also apply to simple plot-function characters, but those characters are quite unlike the ones we shall examine here. Indeed, these comic characters are often very little controlled by their plot function; they tend to exist as ends in themselves, to entertain us by being "characters." They are what W. J. Harvey calls "Cards,"[1] though I think he sees them as simpler than they really are. I would prefer to call them *unresolved* characters. Though they have implied tension as conscious characters do, they do not exhibit an ability to resolve that tension. They seem to lack the consciousness and rationality to do so, or even to express their conflicts directly, so that critics have often overlooked their inner life. The terms *flat* and *round* imply that the two kinds of characters are opposite and that there is no middle ground between them. I prefer terms that allow for a continuum of different characters; characters can seem more or less conscious and their tension can seem more or less resolved. And I prefer terms that allow for some combining of the two character types. A character can be somewhat conscious of his conflicts yet unable to resolve them, as for instance Clarissa and Heathcliff are, at least until the ending of their novels. And a character can have an unchanging persona, implying an inner tension he cannot resolve, yet still exhibit some awareness, as Sam Weller does, for example. However, unresolved characters tend to lack much consciousness, since the more consciousness a character exhibits the more he is likely to seem able to resolve his tension.

Where conscious characters are transformations of the subject, unresolved characters seem to be transformations of the object. Since they lack the consciousness to attract us into taking them fully as subjects, we tend to see them mainly as object-characters. But they are object-characters that have been transformed, like other novel characters, so that tension is implied within them. The simpler unresolved characters like Fielding's exhibit an unresolved tension between two object roles: a character like Parson Trulliber pretends to be a positive object-character, a fatherlike embodiment of good authority, but turns out to be a negative transformation of this, a repressive character. However, the characters I shall concentrate on here are more complex, like Parson Adams; they are still mainly object-characters, but they also function partly as subjects. Parson Adams, for example, functions mainly as what Trulliber pretends to be, a good father-figure embodying Christian self-control, but when he thinks his son has drowned he acts like a subject-character, expressing desire, not control. Here, and much more in Dickens, the object-character has been transformed by being made to express some of the desire earlier fiction located in subject-characters. This transformation seems to be a result of the change we saw in Richardson; desire is no longer so fully sublimated and so it finds secondary, less controlled outlets in the object, for example through Lovelace. In Dickens, comic characters also tend to function partly as subject-characters. Where Austen sees subject-characters partly as objects, Dickens treats object-characters partly as subjects. We feel they desire something they are unable to do, and we partly share their desire. We can see their tension as a conflict between their subject- and object-functions; the object-function remains dominant, preventing them from functioning fully as subjects.

Unresolved characters like those in Dickens differ from conscious characters, then, in that they cannot function as subjects as adequately as conscious characters can. That is, the desire they serve cannot be sublimated or controlled enough to be accepted and used fulfillingly by the self. Thus their desire remains fairly negative, not reconciled to control, often irrational, even violent. As a result, the side of them that opposes their desire remains strongly opposed to it. The more their desires rebel against control, the more repressively that control reacts against those desires. The conscious character can restrain his desire and thus reach a compromise with inner opposition to desire, but the unresolved character cannot make such a compromise. The force opposing his desire thus finds expression in his other function: he partly functions as a negative, repressive object-character opposing his own desire. It is as if he is trying to function as a subject, serving desire, but there is a negative force in him preventing him from doing so, preventing his desire from becoming controlled enough so that he can allow it direct expression. The character seems to fear his own desires; because he evidently cannot control them, they remain too rebellious to express directly and must be repressed. The force that opposes desire and makes it rebellious we can locate in his object-function. Like a repressive object-character, that force opposes desire. In the conscious character, control is positive, since it is a control that is able to accept desire. But in the unresolved character, control is repressive, opposing desire, and thus is seen as object not subject. And in the conscious character uncontrolled desire, though partly accepted, is largely rejected as negative. In contrast, uncontrolled desire is all the unresolved character has, and (especially in Dickens) it need not seem so negative. However, the relation between desire and control within the unresolved character resembles that in the negative object: the two are polarized, strongly opposing each other, so that they usually seem unfulfilling and somewhat negative.

Because these two functions are in conflict, we respond to unresolved characters by feeling tension. Insofar as we respond to them as subject-characters, they arouse desire in us: we want them to be like protagonists, able to express and fulfill desire, able to resolve their tensions and deal with the forces opposing desire. But unresolved characters frustrate this desire in us. This is what makes us feel there is some other force in them opposing desire.

One of the main ways the two character-functions are combined is through distortion. The character looks, talks, or acts in a distorted way—that is, his subject-function seems distorted. Here, as in other kinds of character, two character-functions are being expressed simultaneously: to some extent he is behaving like a subject-character, but the opposing function is combined with his behavior, transforming it into a distorted, unfulfilling form. This makes us feel there is some force within the character preventing him from acting as we wish, making him behave in an indirect, irrational, incongruous way. This combination of functions is a kind of compromise formation, but unlike those used in presenting conscious characters, the compromise is less complete and the opposing forces remain in stronger conflict.

Although unresolved characters frustrate us in such ways, they also offer us a compensatory pleasure. Whereas the conscious character offers us the satisfaction of dealing rationally with tension, the unresolved character enables us to respond more intensely. Because in the conscious character desire is restrained and moderated, the character is likely to seem less energetic. The unresolved character can create more local intensity, a stronger immediate response. In the case of Dickens this intensity was especially desirable because he normally serialized his novels, so that the parts had greater importance in relation to the whole than in most novels.

The unresolved character, then, is used primarily to arouse tension, whereas the conscious character is used primarily to deal with it. With the unresolved character, it is we ourselves who must deal with the tension; the character does not do so for us—at least not very fully or directly. Thus, as in Richardson, the character is a means of making us suspend our self-restraint and feel tension for its own sake. Like Richardson, Dickens seems to value intensity as an end in itself. He uses characters somewhat the way Keats uses imagery, to load every rift with ore, to make each detail as intense as possible. And with Dickens's characters the tension we feel can be comic and pleasing because, since the character is not a subject-character, we need not take his tension seriously and desire its resolution. Because he is not very conscious, he does not seem bothered by his tension. An unresolved character who is self-conscious, like Clarissa, becomes pathetic; but Dickens's subordinate characters can remain comic because they lack such awareness. We see that the character's tension can't be resolved, but we do not feel threatened by this because we have not invested serious desire in the character and because he himself doesn't seem to take desire seriously enough to need to deal with frustration. As a result, we can accept the lack of resolution; we need not try to deal rationally with the tension we feel, or worry about resolving it. The unresolved character thus enables us to become rather childlike, allowing desire a less controlled (because less serious) expression than normal. We can laugh when the character fails to deal with his tension because his failure makes us feel that rational self-control isn't as important as we thought it was; he can get along without it. We can enjoy this evasion of control because it is childlike, playful, not demanding serious gratification but rather converted into a form of expression for its own sake. In other words, the unresolved character can enable us partly to deal with the tension he causes by making that tension comic, presenting it in a form we need not take seriously and try to control.

We can differentiate unresolved characters according to how much they function as partial subjects, serving desire, and how much they function as negative objects, opposing desire, and according to how negative these two functions are. In some characters desire is dominant, a relatively uncontrolled, even rebellious desire. These include villainlike characters such as Lady Booby, Lydia Bennet in *Pride and Prejudice,* and Dickens villains such as Quilp. In other characters, the opposition to desire is dominant so that the character seems too repressed to allow his own desires much expression. These include Solmes in *Clarissa,* Uncle Toby, Mr. Collins in *Pride and Prejudice,* Jos Sedley in *Vanity Fair,* and many bashful characters in Dickens such as Mr. Toots in *Dombey and Son.* We can also compare the way unresolved characters deal with their tension. Even though they cannot fully reconcile desire and control, some unresolved characters like Parson Adams and Sam Weller are able to avoid the extremes of rebellion and repression and at least partly deal with their tension, in ways I shall discuss later in this chapter.

Unresolved characters occur mainly in novels like Fielding's, which place more emphasis on the narrative object than on the protagonist. Novelists who are primarily concerned with a central consciousness usually relegate unresolved characters to minor roles, mocking their lack of consciousness as Jane Austen does with Mr. Collins. Similarly, Henrietta Stackpole in *The Portrait of a Lady* and Captain Mitchell in *Nostromo* lack the consciousness that these novels value and so are not treated as major characters. On the other hand, the novelist can convert object-characters of this type into secondary subjects, as George Eliot often does with Casaubon and Bulstrode in *Middlemarch;* but when the writer does this, the characters cease to be simple unresolved characters to be laughed at. Instead they are a combination of unresolved and conscious character like Clarissa, claiming our sympathy because we feel they have a serious desire for fulfillment like a protagonist, yet cannot attain that fulfillment.

One reason Dickens's characters have such intensity is that he combines these two tendencies, often making us see his characters as comic but at the same time asking us to sympathize with them. Thus he increases the tension between their subject- and object-functions. Like Richardson, he locates characters in an enclosing, repressive world and gives them a correspondingly strong inner repression, thus making them pathetic victims of the forces opposing desire. Whereas Fielding's comic characters seem to wear their masks by choice, to be in control of themselves, Dickens's seem caught in their selves, so that we take their tension more seriously—but not too seriously, since they usually remain object-characters enough so that we can laugh at their failure to resolve that tension. At the same time, since we take them partly as subject-characters, we laugh with them as well as at them, enjoying the way they evade the forces opposing their desires.

Dickens uses many devices to imply unresolved tension in his characters; I cannot cover them all here, but I would like to describe some that seem most typical. I think the techniques of characterization that reveal most about his concept of character are based on a metaphor of pressure, the metaphor that underlies the words *express, suppress,* and *repress*—words he often uses. He visualizes characters as having an inner pressure, a force within them that seeks some outlet—that is, some form of expression. This force is opposed by another which seeks to hold it in—to suppress it. By translating the character into an image of a physical force pushing against a physical resistance, Dickens makes us respond kinesthetically, feeling the character as if he were a force expressed in some distinctive physical movement, a way of moving that suggests an inner process, a particular way of channeling his desires. This metaphor was evidently suggested to Dickens by the steam engine. By using such a comparison he implies that industrialized society has turned people into machines, denying expression to the natural impulses he feels are in their hearts.

We can use terms Dickens himself uses for the two conflicting forces in his characters—energy and repression. Each of these forces is implicit in the other: the character's energy pushes outward so strongly because it is being held in so tightly, and his repression holds it in because it demands an outlet so aggressively. In other words, repression makes energy rebellious, and the rebellious desire for self-expression arouses a repressive counter-reaction. As Dickens puts it, "energy" becomes "all the more forced" because of "long suppression" (*MC,* 52.796).[2] When a character "represses" his feelings, an inner "struggle" results (*DS,* xv). That is, the characters seem to have an inner conflict that implies the presence of both repression and a force it represses. As a result, the stasis that E. M. Forster says is typical of "flat" characters can make us feel, not that a character lacks inner life, but that he has a strong inner tension. His inability to change can imply that the conflicting impulses in him are so strong and uncompromising that they are stalemated. For example, Dickens tells us that Miss Wade's "composure"—her apparent lack of feeling—is what implies the presence of an "unquenchable passion" which has been "repressed" (*LD,* 1.27.327–28). The character's very inability to express himself adequately can thus make us feel that there is an unresolved conflict in him.

The force that Dickens calls energy seems to correspond to what I have called desire in characters. We can see a character's energy as the form in which he expresses desire: energy is a force causing action, and the action serves the desire we impute to the character. The energy in Dickens's characters is usually violent, expressing an uncontrolled desire which cannot be sublimated and which we therefore cannot fully accept as the desire of a subject-character. And the repression in characters seems to correspond to the part of them that functions as a negative object, opposing desire as a repressive villain would.

There is of course great variety among Dickens's characters; some are highly energetic, some highly repressed. In his early novels characters are relatively free to display their tension and we need not take seriously their failure to resolve it. In the later novels characters seem to have less energy, partly because he encloses them within tighter fictional structures which control them more fully, and perhaps partly because Dickens has become less optimistic about how much freedom of expression the individual can manage. The uncontrolled desire within characters becomes a problem he takes more seriously, seeking to resolve the conflicts it causes. He becomes increasingly conscious of the need for control, as shown in his greater concern with form and in his use of more self-conscious narrators.[3] Thus he locates more consciousness within characters, so that even those who remain quite unresolved (like Flora Finching in *Dorrit*) often show some awareness of their tension. As his characters become more aware of their own conflicts, they become less comic and more pathetic. Nevertheless, despite the variation among his characters, I think the same two conflicting forces are implied in almost all of them, especially in his most effective characters, the comic and grotesque ones. Thus it seems possible to make some generalizations that will apply to most of his successful characterization.

Although repression and energy are implicit in each other, we can distinguish techniques of characterization that primarily imply the presence of one or the other. Among the many ways Dickens implies repression, there are several based on the metaphor of pressure. He often describes a character as a container, suggesting that what is within him is being held in. He gives characters a hard, stiff surface that encases them. For example, Dombey has a "cold, hard armour" which opposes his "soft emotion" (*DS,* 40.560–61). His hardness is thus a negation of an inner impulse, preventing the heart from finding expression. This outer hardness is related to the self-enclosure Dickens often attributes to characters—for example, the jailer Chivery, who has "locked himself up" so that he expresses very little (*LD,* 1.25.298). Here Dickens associates inner repression with the way society imprisons the individual, evidently picturing that repression as an internalization of outer enclosure, a restrictive social self which opposes the heart. He sometimes uses images of external enclosure (for example, the way Mrs. Clennam sequesters herself in her room) to represent inner repression so that we can visualize the way a character is "shut up within himself" (*DS,* 20.285).

The image of the character as enclosed in some sort of shell is implicit in many of the descriptions that treat characters as if they were physical objects or associate them with objects.[4] The character's hardness makes him like an object; he is too repressed to become fully human, to express what is within him. A good example of this imagery can be found in the characterization of Miss Murdstone, who is "metallic" (*DC,* 4.48) and is associated with hard objects which suggest "what was to be expected within" (*DC,* 26.393)—for example, a bag like a "jail" that shuts up "with a bite" (*DC,* 4.47–48), as she shuts up her feelings within herself. Similarly, Barkis's more involuntary, passive repression is imaged by his box: he is "as mute and senseless as the box, from which his form derived the only expression it had" (*DC,* 30.445); he is not only closed up like the box, but he seems so repressed that the box has replaced him and his own identity is lost. And if a character thus seems to be a physical thing, we clearly see him as an object, not a subject.

Dickens also uses the names of characters to make them seem thinglike. A character's name enables him to function as a subject and object, but some names encourage us to see the character as subject and some as object. At one extreme, if the character is represented as an "I," we obviously take him as subject. In addition, there are various names that seem conventionally appropriate for protagonists—for example, Tom Jones, an ordinary enough name so that we can imagine ourselves bearing it. In contrast, Dickens often uses names that are highly eccentric, even names that do not sound human, so that we are less likely to accept them as signifiers for the self, representatives of our "I." A name like Wegg or Quilp seems to turn the character into a thing, as if his humanity has been denied expression.

Another way Dickens makes characters seem repressed is by making them oppose the desires we attribute to them. They often seem unable to obtain the fulfillment we want them to obtain and unable to express feelings Dickens makes us infer they have. For example, Mr. Toots's behavior implies that he is attracted to Florence Dombey, but he evidently opposes his own desire, either preventing himself from expressing it at all or reacting guiltily against it when he does express it, saying it is "of no consequence" (*DS,* 56.782). Characters often have trouble releasing the energy within them, as if something obstructs it, like the "stoppages" in Uriah Heep's nose (*DC,* 25.384). And when characters are unable to change, we can infer that they are too repressed to do so even though they desire to. In addition, self-opposition can be implied by a character's clumsiness when he does manage to express himself. When, for example, Mr. Toots speaks, his speech is "awkward" because it combines "chuckles and emotion" (*DS,* 32.464)—that is, the emotion he desires to express is opposed by an inhibition that makes his self-expression comic. Repression distorts self-expression into indirect, even pointless forms, preventing it from becoming purposeful and fulfilling. Thus when Peggotty tries to write a letter, she exhausts her "utmost powers of expression" yet can only produce an utterance that is "incoherent and interjectional" (*DC,* 17.247).

One way characters are deflected away from asserting their desires is by being made submissive—excessively propitiatory like Micawber or defensive like Wemmick in his fortress. Such behavior makes us feel the character is afraid of something, and since we see no adequate outer cause for his fear we can infer an inner cause, a fear of being too direct, of expressing too much desire. Often Dickens's submissive characters are like children, submitting to parent-like characters even if those characters repress them. The submissive character thus seems afraid to rebel against authority, as if such rebellion would arouse Oedipal guilt. Submissive characters also act overawed, like Captain Cuttle with his "reverence" for things he doesn't understand (*DS,* 4.42); it is as if he fears to question what controls him. Characters who submit to control in such ways usually seem childlike, unable to assert desire in a direct, fulfilling, adult way. One clear example of a childlike, submissive character is Mr. Dick, who accepts Aunt Betsey's control as if she were his mother.

When characters seem too repressed to assert their desires directly, they often become trapped in static behavior patterns they seem unable to alter. Dickens frequently describes characters as being in a particular "state," a stasis evidently caused by opposing impulses "wrestling with each other" (*DS,* 56.791). For example, he says of Betsey Trotwood that "a curious process of hesitation appeared to be going on within her, while she preserved her outward stiffness" (*DC,* 34.498); thus we feel that her stiffness is the result of an unresolved inner conflict caused by some force preventing her from expressing herself. One way Dickens makes characters seem static is by substituting nouns or verbals for verbs so that a character's action seems a permanent state, something he is always doing. When characters keep repeating pointless behavior, we feel they are too repressed to find a fulfilling outlet; they keep on acting because their desire remains unsatisfied, still seeking an outlet, but as long as they can only repeat themselves it can never be satisfied. Mr. Dick keeps writing of King Charles's head because he wants to express himself and yet cannot put into words what he really wishes to express, so that he can only keep trying and failing over and over.

However, it is the energy that Dickens implies in his characters that makes them so vivid. This energy is implicit even in the way they repress themselves. Their inner pressure is so strong that it is difficult to repress; repression thus requires energy. For instance, Aunt Betsey twitches "as if her old wrongs were working within her and she repressed any plainer reference to them by strong constraint" (*DC,* 1.7). There seems to be a force within her seeking an outlet so strongly that it can only be held in with considerable effort. Similarly, Rosa Dartle looks "compressed, as if she . . . must keep a strong constraint upon herself" (*DC,* 50.720), and Mrs. Snagsby is "violently compressed" (*BH,* 10.128). Here again Dickens is using the metaphor of pressure. Repressed characters are not merely like containers, but like pressurized containers. By opposing self-expression so energetically, the character seems to have converted (or perverted) his energy into self-denial. At the same time, it seems as if self-repression has created this inner pressure; by denying an outlet to his energy, except through self-denial, the character has made that energy more demanding. The more the container compresses its contents, the more explosive those contents become. In other words, the more a character must repress himself, the more we feel there must be some force in him to be repressed. Thus we feel the character's inner pressure as a force pushing against repression. For example, Carker has "long-tightened springs" which seek "release with a quick recoil" (*DS,* 58.816). Even as repressed a character as Mrs. Clennam contains "hydraulic pressure" (*LD,* 1.5.52). And Mr. Toots is so repressed he is like "a bottle of some effervescent beverage" (*DS,* 22.315), a pressurized container that seems about to pop.

Dickens often uses the container image to imply inner pressure by describing a character's outer surface as tight, even swelling, so that we feel he can barely hold in the energy he contains. We are told, for example, that Flintwinch's "energy, always contending with a second nature of habitual repression, gave his features a swollen . . . look" (*LD*, 1.3.37). Creakle must make an "exertion" to release any energy, and even then he cannot release much (he can only whisper); because he is full of pressure he cannot let out, he can only swell "thicker" (*DC*, 6.82). When characters do release their energy, Dickens often uses metaphors that compare their action to the release of something under pressure (such as steam). He uses the image of venting, as in describing a character's feelings "constantly struggling for a vent" (*DS*, 56.790). The image of a vent implies that the character is a container through whose surface inner pressure has managed to make a hole. In other words, the character's energy is so strong it can at least partly overcome his repression. But a vent is only a small outlet, implying that much of the energy remains repressed. The need for such an outlet is also implied when Dickens says that a character finds "relief" in some action; this locution suggests that inner pressure has built up painfully.

Probably the most distinctive way in which Dickens's characters vent their energy is in bursts of action.[5] This behavior makes us feel their inner pressure has escalated until it can overcome repression and force its way out. Since an outburst alternates action with the absence (or negation) of action, it implies the presence of two opposing forces, a desire to act and a force seeking to repress that desire. We can see this alternation between extremes in the case of Mr. Toots, who alternates silence with a "burst" which shows the "vehemence of his feelings" (*DS*, 32.464). One example that clearly shows the tension between energy and repression is the "bursting . . . of the smouldering fire so long pent up" in Mrs. Clennam, who tried "to repress herself, but broke out vehemently" in an "explosion" of "passion" (*LD*, 2.30.773–74). This description implies that repressing her energy has made it explosive, turning it into a passion she can no longer hold in. Pancks is one of the characters most notable for acting in bursts; Dickens describes him as "loaded with" a "heavy charge" which he "fired off" (*LD*, 2.13.582). Pancks's very name sounds like an outburst, like one of his snorts. Similarly, we are told that Mr. Dick "shot" a communication "out of himself as if he were loaded with it" (*DC*, 44.651). Peggotty's buttons burst off when inner pressure makes her swell up; and when she speaks through a keyhole (as if she can only find one limited outlet for her inner force) she is described as "shooting in each broken little sentence in a convulsive little burst of its own" (*DC,* 4.61). Micawber alternates circumlocution with sudden bursts of confidence, expressing the feeling his circumlocutions have attempted to conceal. His most notable "burst" is his exclamation of "HEEP!" described as "An explosion of a smouldering volcano long suppressed," its suppression causing "an internal contest" (*DC,* 49.711–12; 52.747, 751).

The image of a character swelling up until something bursts out of him may suggest some unconscious associations. We might see the characters as phallic, and their desire to release energy as a distorted expression of erotic desire. In other words, characters may have provided Dickens with a kind of displaced outlet for his own sexual energies. This might explain why the desire implied in them seems so strong and irrational and why it is repressed so strongly. The characters' intense bursts of energy seem almost orgasmic. On the other hand, the venting images also sound excretory; Michael Steig, for example, believes that Dickens's characters seem as if they are trying to expel excrement.[6] Again, this association makes the characters' desire to release energy seem all the stronger, indeed elemental. It also makes them seem rather infantile and antisocial. Perhaps it would be most accurate to guess that these unconscious desires underlie and are associated with Dickens's desire to release imaginative energy through his characters, giving that desire much of its intensity.

In addition to alternating between bursts of energy and stasis, characters alternate between release and repression in other ways. For example, Micawber is alternately hopeful and despairing. In Micawber's "vacillations between an evident disposition to reveal something, and a counter-disposition to reveal nothing" (*DC,* 49.709), we can see the tension between repression and the desire for expression. And Wemmick is alternately social and adult in the outer world, and rather childlike at home. When characters oscillate in this way, it seems as if they lack the rational ability to reconcile their opposing impulses as conscious characters do.

A burst of action is one of the ways in which Dickens's characters concentrate their energy in order to express it. They often concentrate on one outlet to which they give great intensity, evidently because it is the only outlet they can find for their energy. Thus we feel repression has prevented them from finding any other outlet. And when a character gives his action an intensity disproportionate to its ostensible purpose, we feel that the action exists not primarily for that purpose but rather for self-expression. The character seems to be using that action to replace all the other things he would like to do but can't, making it as intense as possible to make up for the fact that it is his only outlet. Among the examples of this kind of concentration, there is Mrs. Clennam's "concentrated air of collecting her firmness" (*LD*, 1.30.356), so that her appearance seems to replace speech. It is as if the act of repression (her "firmness") has become an outlet in itself. We are told that "the whole power" of Rosa Dartle's "face and character seemed forced into" her "expression," and the "concentration" of her rage is described as compressed into her face (*DC*, 50.720; 32.470). One of the ways Dickens gives us the sense that a character is narrowed down to one distinctive outlet is through synecdoche and metonymy, making one part or possession of the character stand for him.[7] For example, by making Carker's teeth represent him, Dickens makes us feel there is a voracious, catlike energy within Carker which is otherwise suppressed, finding an outlet only through this one vent; and we feel that this energy *is* Carker, has taken him over entirely, gaining control of him.

Dickens's more repressed characters are frequently able to find no more satisfactory outlet than staring, on which they concentrate all their energy. When a character stares, we feel he is too repressed to act in a more direct way, even too repressed to speak; but we also feel there is a force within him seeking some outlet despite that repression. We feel the intensity of that force because Dickens's characters stare more fixedly than they would if they were merely trying to see things. For example, Dickens tells us that Major Bagstock's eyes "strained and started convulsively" (*DS*, 7.85); this intensity can make us infer that staring has become a means of self-expression. The way Kit Nubbles stares at Little Nell shows how staring replaces a more direct outlet for his desire: "Kit looked at her with his eyes stretched wide; and opened and shut his mouth a great many times; but couldn't get out one word" (*OCS*, 10.81). We are told that a character's "fixed" look expresses "the most vehement passion" precisely because that passion is repressed; her staring shows "the effort that constrained" her desires, thus "bespeaking" her "violent and dangerous character" (*DS*, 34.490–91), implying the presence of the rebellious energy she tries to suppress. Similarly, the "wasting fire within" Rosa Dartle, unable to find a direct outlet, finds "a vent in her gaunt eyes" (*DC*, 20.292).

Dickens's characters engage in other actions that are similarly indirect, actions that do not deal fulfillingly with the character's world. When action thus exists mainly for self-expression, it turns into a kind of display. The release of energy becomes an end in itself, making us feel the character is too repressed to find a more fulfilling outlet, but also that the character needs self-expression so much that he will accept any available outlet, no matter how pointless. Micawber's flowery language and the volubility of Mrs. Gamp and Flora Finching are good examples of this kind of display. Characters like this often delay the object of their sentences, implying some inhibition against directly expressing the desire to act on an object, an inability to function fully as a subject serving desire. But this very delay allows a pleasing release of energy for its own sake, an indirect expression of that desire.

Dickens also uses the physical appearance of characters for a kind of display. He frequently describes the appearance or behavior of characters as expressive. For example, Mrs. Chick's "choking" manner is "expressive" of her "suppressed emotion" (*DS*, 1.5); the distortion of her behavior and appearance imply a tension between emotion seeking release and the force suppressing it. Here, as in the case of staring, appearance and behavior become a substitute for the direct expression of emotion, so that the very failure to express what we infer the character desires becomes an indirect means of expressing character tension. One example of how indirect such expression can be is Dickens's use of hair; he often sometimes makes it an outlet for repressed energy, standing up (like eyes bulging out) as if seeking to relieve inner pressure. For instance, Pancks's hair seems to be seeking "liberation" (*LD*, 2.30.763)—that is, seeking to escape the control of a force trying to hold it in, which we can associate with the force repressing his own energy.

When characters behave in this indirect way, they seem distorted, their energy deflected away from a fulfilling outlet by their repression. But though distortion implies repression, it also implies energy, since their energy still finds an outlet, even though an imperfect one. Dickens tells us that a character's energy is "unsubduable," that if you "cover" one outlet, energy will find other "channels of expression" (*LD*, 1.2.24). It cannot be wholly repressed; but it can be distorted by the attempt to repress (cover) it. The image of a channel, like that of a vent, makes energy seem to be forcing its way out of containment; and if it is not allowed a direct outlet, it will come out in an indirect, distorted way. For example, we are told that Flintwinch is so "wry"—so distorted, as if by repression—that even the smoke "came crookedly" out of him (*LD,* 2.23.680), as if unable to find a direct outlet. Similarly, Uriah Heep's repression seems to distort him, so that he is "all awry as if his mean soul griped his body" (*DC,* 25.381)—as if he is held in (gripped) by a repression that prevents his body from expressing itself naturally. Yet this crookedness is not merely a sign of repression but also functions as an indirect outlet for his energy; we are told it is "his only compensation for the outward restraints he put upon himself" (*DC,* 54.778). Thus distortion such as his "writhing" is used to "express" feeling (*DC,* 16.235), though in a distorted form, as if simultaneously opposing that feeling. In comic characters, energy is usually distorted into incongruous, awkward forms. Kit Nubbles, unable to acknowledge directly his desire for Little Nell, seeks "relief" in "contortions" (*OCS,* 10.79–80). And a similar character, Mr. Toots, is so inhibited that his energy can "find a vent in nothing but extravagance" (*DS,* 50.706).

When a character's energy is partially denied in this way, it tends to become rebellious; that is, it opposes control, creating inner tension. For instance, Dickens says the "fire" within Louisa Gradgrind is distorted from a "natural" into an "uncertain, eager, doubtful" form (*HT,* 1.3.12); because it is not allowed a natural outlet, it causes inner conflict. The fire in Mrs. Clennam is similarly "suppressed" so that it creates conflict too; in her case the suppression is more severe, so that her energy becomes self-destructive, preying "upon itself" (*LD,* 1.15.178). In a natural state, desire and control would evidently be in harmony; but repression polarizes them. The more rigid the repression, the more violent and destructive the form into which energy is distorted. Dickens tells us that when a character's inner force is "imprisoned" and "suppressed" it can become destructive, "a sullen . . . devil," a force "striving to work out" from within (*MC,* 40.632)—that is, rebelling, like the devil. "All closely imprisoned forces rend and destroy," becoming distorted into "unwholesome" forms (*HT,* 3.1.224). Thus when Rosa Dartle has "chained . . . up" her rage it becomes self-destructive, tearing her "within" (*DC,* 50.721).

One way we can see rebelliousness is in the tendency of many Dickens characters to act defiant without apparent cause. For instance, he describes a character behaving "as if . . . in passionate contention with some unseen opponent" (*DS,* 58.824). When a character acts this way, we can infer he must be defying some opposition within himself. Among characters who act defiant for no apparent reason, one of the best known is Mrs. Micawber, who keeps asserting that she will never desert Mr. Micawber even though no one has suggested that she will, and who typically expresses herself in an argumentative manner.

Even when characters are less hostile, they often exhibit an energy that opposes control. For example, they often act in an excessive manner; Dickens's characterization is full of superlatives and descriptions of extremeness. We thus feel that such a character's energy is too strong to be restrained rationally; evidently it has been driven to this extreme in reaction against the attempt to repress it. For example, we are told Mr. Micawber's "passion for writing letters was too strong to be resisted" (*DC,* 49.712); his energy insists on an outlet so assertively that he cannot prevent its finding expression. Flora Finching is "quite unable to overcome" her habit of addressing Arthur Clennam in a way that betrays the desire she is trying to suppress (*LD,* 3.17.623). We can see a lack of rational restraint in the way characters keep repeating the same behavior even though it is unfulfilling. When Micawber keeps hoping that something will turn up despite continual frustration, we feel that his desire is too strong to learn restraint, that his need to hope is greater than his rational awareness of reality.

One way Dickens often makes us feel that a character's energy is strong enough to overcome restraint is through the use of the "so . . . that" construction. He tells us a character has *so* much inner force *that* it cannot be rationally controlled, that it is able to overcome repression and manifest itself externally. We are told that Miss Nipper's "feelings were so much excited . . . that she found it indispensable to afford them . . . relief" (*DS,* 5.47). Mr. Toots is "so entirely conquered by his feelings" that he must burst into action (*DS,* 56.793). The dog Jip is described as barking "to such a furious extent that he couldn't keep straight" (*DC,* 48.699).

By implying the presence in his characters of these strongly opposing forces, then, Dickens makes us feel they lack the kind of rational awareness through which conscious characters are able to resolve their tensions. This lack is implicit not only in their lack of restraint but in their unawareness of their world—for example, when they use staring for self-expression rather than for perception. An extreme case is Bunsby in *Dombey,* who seems "to have no ocular knowledge of anything within ten miles" (*DS,* 23.335). Indeed, characters can actively resist awareness, as Mrs. Gamp does in angrily rejecting the insinuation that Mrs. Harris is imaginary. A lack of consciousness is also implied by characters' inability to express directly, verbally, what they feel or think. This evident unawareness of what is within them is reproduced by the narrator's refusal to tell us what they really think, as if whatever is in their minds cannot be verbalized because it resists rational control; for example, Dickens says Dombey has "something secret in his breast, of the nature of which he was hardly informed himself" (*DS,* 3.29).

Yet despite the fact that Dickens's characters usually seem unable to resolve their tensions, they of course give us pleasure. I think they do so because, although they cannot express desire fully, they nevertheless find ways of circumventing repression and expressing it indirectly in a kind of displacement activity. Their actions can thus offer a compensation for their inability to fulfill our desires completely. Although they have inner pressure, they are able to relieve that pressure—to let off steam. In other words, they offer us relief from the frustration they cause. One example of the way Dickens's characters find substitute outlets is Barkis, who though apparently too repressed to speak "hit upon a wonderful expedient for expressing himself in a neat, agreeable and pointed manner, without the inconvenience of inventing conversation" (*DC,* 10.137–38). Although his behavior is indirect, it is pleasing because it provides a partial victory over his inhibition. I think such behavior is comic because it combines awkwardness—distortion that deflects energy away from direct expression—with this kind of victory over the distortion. We can thus laugh with the character as well as at him; we need not see his awkwardness as disabling and frustrating and so can enjoy it. In fact it is the character's very failure to be direct that enables him to obtain his victory. It is because he does not seek to release energy in a way that is too demanding, too direct, too adult, that he is able to disarm repression. By including some submission to repression in the form in which he releases energy, keeping that release indirect, even rather childlike, he avoids the guilt he would arouse if he expressed desire more seriously, demanding greater fulfillment. In other words, we receive pleasure from the way the two opposing functions of the character interact. Even though they don't moderate each other as in the conscious character, they do alter each other, each converting the other into a comic form. Both rebellious desire and repressive control are diminished so that we need not take them seriously, since neither is effective. Thus even though the character causes tension, he also helps us deal with it, making it bearable.

One character who is especially adept at finding substitute outlets for his energy is Mr. Micawber. Although some of his outbursts (such as his defiance of Heep) imply rebellious feeling, resentment of his social frustration, he is usually able to find ways of expressing that feeling in diminished, comic form. As a result, he need not become a seriously rebellious character like Heep or Steerforth. By expressing himself through circumlocutions he can avoid too direct an outlet, evidently because his repression makes him afraid of "strong expressions" (*DC,* 54.773). And by writing letters he can express himself even more indirectly, avoiding speech. Even though this deflection of his energy involves a partial denial of it, he is able to compensate for that denial by turning the indirect release of energy into an end in itself, a pretext for display: "Mr. Micawber's enjoyment of his epistolary powers . . . seemed to outweigh any pain or anxiety that the reality could have caused him" (*DC,* 52.751). If reality frustrates him, he can evade it. Another example of the efficacy of such substitute outlets is the way Traddles finds "comfort" in drawing skeletons (*DC,* 7.91). The shift to a deflected outlet deals with tension because deflecting rebelliousness makes it harmless. For instance, Traddles's hair seems to "have taken all the obstinacy out of his character" (*DC,* 41.591), as if the potentially rebellious energy in his character has all been transferred to this indirect, comic outlet. By thus diminishing desire, the character can express it (even if indirectly), offering us a pleasing victory over the repression that tries to prevent his expressing it. It is because the substitute outlet offers this victory that it can be made an end in itself. The actions of comic characters, then, are often like play—action for its own sake, not a serious attempt to act on an object as a serious subject-character would.

One way characters find substitute outlets is by creating fictions.[8] By believing in a "fiction . . . which is better than any reality" (*DS,* 62.874), a character like Captain Cuttle can console himself for the frustrations in his reality. He can replace actual fulfillment with an illusion of fulfillment, a playlike version of it. A fiction makes possible the safe expression of desire—safe because imaginary, not opposed by the forces that would oppose it in reality. Among the characters who create such fictions, the best example is probably Mrs. Gamp, who creates Mrs. Harris to give herself an excuse to release energy while not seeming responsible for it. She uses the name of Mrs. Harris as "a talisman against all earthly sorrows" (*MC,* 49.759), evading awareness of her world, replacing it with the imaginary. Similarly, Dick Swiveller is able to believe in a "pleasant fiction" in which he demands "Implicit faith" against "all reason, observation, and experience" (*OCS,* 7.53–54); the very act of giving up reason, with its need to control desire and adjust it to the requirements of reality, offers the pleasure of escape.

Characters often use fiction-making to transform themselves so that they need not take on a serious subject-function, evidently because they are too repressed to serve desire fully and seriously; Mr. Micawber, for example, creates a fictional role for himself, pretending that he is genteel, adult, in control of circumstances. However, we see that the role is clearly inappropriate, and so we need not take it seriously; nor does Micawber himself seem to take it seriously, since he only uses it for display, not acting on it. His fictional roles seem to be ways of evading being a serious "I," a subject serving desire. For example, he ends his letters by referring to himself in the third person. It is as if he has to become someone else in order to express desires (though only in playful form) to which he cannot allow direct expression through his "I." Similarly, Barkis creates the "fiction" that his box belongs to Mr. Blackboy (*DC,* 31.446), as if he is so afraid to acknowledge his own desire (for money, here) that he tries to replace himself with someone else. Miss Mowcher makes "a jest" of herself, playing a childlike role in order to evade social control (*DC,* 32.462) by preventing her desires from seeming serious. Dick Swiveller acts the role of melodramatic hero, but in a parodic way which need not be taken seriously; thus he seems to express both a desire to be heroic and an inhibition preventing him from being so.

Like the conscious character, the unresolved character bears a distinctive relation to other elements of the novel in which he occurs. The relationship is less obvious, since unresolved characters seem to exist more as ends in themselves, not necessarily serving plot. Whereas the conscious character enables the novelist to present tension in one central character who can use plot to deal with his tension, Dickens diffracts the novel's basic conflict into many characters, each an imperfect reflection of that conflict. Since these characters do not function primarily as subjects, they exist mainly to display tension rather than resolve it. Dickens thus works out another way of dealing with tension than that used by novelists like Jane Austen; but, as in her case, his way of dealing with it is closely related to the kind of characterization he uses.

The conflict between energy and repression, implied within characters, can be seen as a transformation of the underlying conflict upon which each novel is based. That conflict seems to be between a strong desire (primarily for parental love) and a strongly repressive reaction against that desire. We can guess that this conflict is analogous to one in Dickens himself, that the work functions as a way for him to seek imaginative expression of desires that are opposed by a repressive force. This conflict, then, also finds expression in plot. In the plot, the conflict is between agents of repression, corresponding to the repression within characters, and agents of desire, corresponding to the desire within characters. The negative object-characters whose main function is to serve repression—for example, Dombey, Murdstone, Gradgrind, Mrs. Clennam, Miss Havisham—are related to other characters in a way that resembles the relation of repression to desire within themselves. Within these characters repression is dominant, attempting to deny "natural" expression to the heart—that is, to prevent sublimation. Similarly, they seek to dominate characters who primarily serve the heart (especially the protagonist in each novel), denying sublimation to those characters. As repression seeks to imprison and punish energy within characters, so these repressive characters seek to imprison and punish characters seeking self-expression. Dickens typically makes these repressive characters parentlike and makes their relationship with their victims like the relationship of harsh parents to children. He evidently equates repression with the adult, social self, seeing it as imposed on and separate from the part of the self that desires fulfillment. There are also weak parentlike characters in Dickens who, although they are not repressive, fail to provide an adequate parentlike control and so are unable to counteract repression, unable to protect childlike characters from becoming victims of repression. Sometimes these characters are merely comic, like

Micawber and Captain Cuttle; but in later Dickens, parental failure is sometimes taken more seriously, as in the case of Mr. Dorrit. To the extent that such weak characters are seen as inadequate, they seem to function partly as secondary agents of repression, allowing it to happen and potentially causing filial resentment.

The desire for sublimation which repressive characters oppose is embodied in characters who are usually childlike, at least in their relation to the parentlike characters.[9] The nature of these characters resembles that of the analogous entity within characters, the heart. Dickens visualizes the heart as seeking some form of self-expression, as these characters do. And for him the heart, like childlike characters, is (at least originally) pure and innocent, but also weak and largely at the mercy of repression, which like a parent can punish it and force it into various forms. Dickens evidently sees the desire for self-expression within characters as analogous to a child's desire for parental love; the heart seeks to placate inner repression just as childlike characters seek to placate parentlike ones. Each tries to disarm repression so that it can be allowed self-expression and escape guilt.

The childlike characters serving desire include not only the protagonist but also various partial, subordinate protagonists, some more childlike and positive, others less so. Among these childlike characters we can distinguish two extremes, corresponding to the two extremes that repression can cause within characters: submission and rebellion. Submissive characters function primarily as victims of repressive characters, corresponding to the way a character's desires are often largely denied by his inner repression. Since Dickens values submission, he allows these characters to function more fully as subjects than most. The characters who are most completely victims are the submissive protagonists like Oliver Twist and Florence Dombey. In addition, there are other submissive characters who are less pure but remain partly victimized, characters like Mr. Toots and Frederick Dorrit. These characters (especially those who function more as protagonists) are usually accompanied by satellite object-characters reflecting the balance of desire with control in them. Since they submit to a repressive inner control, there is usually a repressive object-character embodying the same kind of control, a parentlike character they must submit to; Oliver Twist is dominated by Fagin, and Chuffey by Anthony Chuzzlewit. Since they must avoid resenting control, often there is also a rebellious character who threatens them, as rebellious desires threaten their submissiveness. This character seeks to arouse the selfish desires they must avoid, as Quilp tries to arouse Nell and the Game Chicken tries to make Toots resent Dombey. The repressive object-characters are those one might expect to find accompanying a rebellious character; they seem to exist to test the submissive character, to let him prove that he can avoid rebellion even though his world pushes him toward it. But the submissive character often differs from the rebellious character in being able to replace these object-characters with positive alternatives. The more he functions as a subject, the more he is likely to find idealized parentlike characters to submit to, characters like Aunt Betsey and John Jarndyce, and a goal-character to fulfill his desires. However, since the submissive character partly suppresses his desire, the positive object-characters accompanying him tend to embody restraint as well as fulfillment. The goal-characters tend to be weak and asexual, like Walter Gay in *Dombey* and Agnes in *Copperfield;* and the parentlike characters also seem rather powerless, perhaps so that the control they represent will not seem authoritarian and threatening as it would to a rebellious character. And when a submissive character is less central, functioning less as a subject, the positive object-characters accompanying him are correspondingly diminished.

Submissive subject-characters are usually repressed by the object-characters accompanying them, just as desire is repressed within them. They often seem imprisoned; their world frequently seems like a container or enclosure preventing their desires from finding an outlet. Just as inner repression reacts punitively against energy for seeking an outlet, so repressive characters often try to make victim characters feel guilty and suffer. For example, the subordinate characters who run Creakle's school, functioning as extensions of the repressiveness whose main embodiment is Murdstone, place a sign on David Copperfield, as if seeking to fasten guilt onto him. Just as inner repression distorts the forms in which characters can find expression, the repressive social world in which they live affects victim characters, causing "deformity of mind and body," producing "stunted" children (*DS,* 20.281; 47.646–47) because it opposes their natural, childlike impulses. As inner repression seeks to destroy the energy within characters, so repressive characters can try to destroy their victims. The deaths of Little Nell, Paul Dombey, and Jo, for instance, seem to reenact the way repressive social control and parental inadequacy can deny the needs of the heart.

In contrast to these submissive victims, there are other childlike characters who function primarily as rebels against authority. These characters seem less childlike than the submissive characters; but they are childlike in their inability to accept control, like children rebelling against parents. Their function corresponds to the way energy within characters often opposes repression, refusing to be suppressed. Just as inner energy tends to oppose control and seek as much expression as possible, so these characters demand excessive fulfillment, for example by seeking power, and oppose anyone who would restrain them. This rebellious aspect of desire finds its purest manifestation in Dickens's greedy, lustful villains like Quilp and Uriah Heep. Uriah seems to desire sublimation (embodied in Agnes); but he seems unable to attain it because he cannot reconcile his desire with his repression and convert it into a controlled, sublimated form. As a result, that desire finds expression instead in an energy that rebels against control. This implied inner conflict is analogous to the way a child can be driven into rebellion by a parent's repressiveness (as when David Copperfield bites Murdstone). Rebellious characters like Uriah usually engage in this kind of conflict with a parentlike character: Uriah usurps Mr. Wickfield's power, Quilp usurps Mr. Trent's, and Carker usurps Dombey's, each rebelling against parentlike control by taking it away from the father-figure. It is as if the parentlike character's failure to provide good control has caused their rebellion. In the absence of good control, rebellious characters take the place of submissive characters, cutting them off from parental love as Uriah cuts Agnes off from her father. By doing this, a villain like Uriah causes a state in which desire and control can be reconciled to be replaced by a state in which those forces are polarized, rebellion opposing repression: instead of the relation between Agnes and her father, a submissive child accepting benign control, we have the Heep-Wickfield relationship. Thus the rebellious character creates a plot conflict that resembles the highly polarized tension within characters. Unresolved characters are likely to generate strong plot conflicts of this sort because they lack the conscious restraint to work out compromises with each other and instead are dominated by impulses that lead them to oppose outer as well as inner control.

Like Dickens's submissive characters, the rebellious characters are usually accompanied by certain kinds of object-characters. There is usually a negative parentlike character who seems to cause or react against their rebellion. The rebellious character acts out the opposite response to this control from that represented by the submissive character (indicating he is a negative transformation of the submissive character); instead of submitting, he resents and rejects control. Thus he is unable to replace the negative object with a positive one, as the submissive character can: because he cannot accept control, there is no good parentlike character to help him, and because rebellious desire cannot be sublimated, there is no positive goal-character to provide him fulfillment. For example, Steerforth lacks a good parent to guide him and can only find a negative goal-character, Emily—negative in that she does not give him fulfillment. Similarly, Richard Carstone cuts himself off from Jarndyce and so loses the fulfillment that Ada embodies; Pip cuts himself off from Joe and loses Biddy; and Carker can only find a negative goal-character, Edith.

In addition to Dickens's villains, there are also less extreme, more comic characters such as Mrs. Gamp or young Bailey, who display some similar rebelliousness, though in a form we need not take so seriously. These characters seem partly negative and partly positive; it is hard to classify Mrs. Gamp morally.

Dickens's novels put much of their energy into intensifying and exploiting conflicts, both within characters and in the plot conflicts those characters cause. But with such highly polarized conflicts, how can he work out a plot resolution? In his last novels he does begin to locate more consciousness in a protagonist, enabling that character to learn and thus resolve conflict; but in most of his novels there is no character embodying a strong central consciousness. The emphasis is rather on the unresolved characters. Thus he cannot base plot resolution on learning to reach a rational compromise of the kind we find in Austen. Indeed, Dickens often expresses a mistrust of the learning process, showing education as one of the ways society represses or deforms what is natural within the child, as in the case of such schools as Squeers's, Blimber's, and Creakle's, and in Gradgrind's education of his children. Dickens does not show rationality as fulfilling. Rather he makes his most rational characters negative—characters like Carker and Steerforth. These characters show that he feels the danger in rationality is that it seeks to control and fulfill desire for itself rather than submitting to some higher control. In other words, he seems to share the Christian belief that one should give up reason and submit to a higher authority. Since he does not believe that reason controls desire adequately, he does not base his plots (except in the last novels to some extent) on the rational process of learning to restrain desire, as in Austen. Instead of restraining desire, his characters seek to allow the heart full expression by freeing it from a false, repressive control. Yet desire, to be sublimated, must be reconciled with some positive embodiment of control, an idealized parental authority. Dickens's plots thus seek sublimation through submission to such control.

In order to bring about a resolution of this kind, the novel must first act out the rejection of negative, repressive control. Just as we can distinguish two extremes in the way his characters respond to parental control, we can distinguish two contrasting ways Dickens uses plot to deal with the absence of adequate parental control. One alternative corresponds to the way characters deal with repression by rebelling against it. Dickens offers us negative plot resolutions which, although they do not provide positive fulfillment, at least offer us the satisfaction of rejecting repression. Just as characters overcome inner repression by building up pressure until they release energy in a burst, so Dickens's plots typically build up to a similar kind of burst, an explosive climax.[10] Instead of gradually resolving conflicts, he increases tension to the breaking point and then suddenly releases the energy that has hitherto been frustrated. For example, he suggests that Mr. Merdle dies of "Pressure" which has evidently built up until he is "self-exploded" (*LD*, 2.25.709; 26.711). Repressive social control (which Merdle represents, although he is also its victim) becomes self-destructive because it denies inner energy, forcing that energy to oppose it by finding a violent, destructive outlet. Similarly, the repressive authority represented by Dombey is "undermined" until Dickens finally makes it "fall down in a moment," like Mrs. Clennam's house. With this collapse of repression, the inner force Dombey has denied can finally be released in a "burst of tears" (*DS*, 59.842–44). Similar sudden collapses befall other parentlike characters who have denied the heart both in themselves and in their childlike victims—for example, the collapse of Mr. Dorrit and the death of Miss Havisham. In these cases too the removal of an embodiment (though also a victim) of repression allows the heart to find expression. Another example of the way repression can become self-destructive is the death of Krook, who is associated with repressive control by being related to Chancery. *A Tale of Two Cities* builds up to a similar climactic outburst, the Revolution. *David Copperfield* climaxes with two explosions whose juxtaposition implies an interrelationship: Micawber's "burst" of defiance against Heep (*DC,* 52.751) is followed by the tempest, in which the sea looks *"swelled"* (*DC,* 55.791), as if building up pressure before the storm's destructive outburst. In this case the burst of violence destroys an embodiment of rebellion (Steerforth), not repression, but since repression and rebellion cause each other both must be rejected before sublimation can replace them.

In addition to this kind of negative resolution, Dickens also deals with plot conflicts in a positive way that corresponds to the way his submissive characters deal with repression. Instead of rebelling, those characters disarm repression by submitting, remaining inhibited. The plot equivalent of this is the virtuous protagonist's submission to a parentlike character. This submission makes possible a reconciliation of positive desire (the childlike heart) with control, a sublimation that is acted out on the level of plot by a transformation of control, repression replaced by a positive control that accepts the heart's desire. This transformation involves replacing the negative, repressive parentlike characters with positive ones. We can see this replacement, for example, in *Copperfield:* as David learns to reject uncontrolled desire and submit to control, he is able to replace the negative, repressive fatherlike character Murdstone with a series of increasingly fulfilling substitutes, from the weak Micawber through the loving but still strict Aunt Betsey to Agnes, who functions at the end not only as a goal-character but also as a reincarnation of the ideal parent, loving rather than repressing—an ideal glimpsed (though in imperfect form) at the start in the person of David's mother. David earns this ideal because he gradually separates himself from characters embodying uncontrolled desire—for example, Steerforth and Dora—and thus disavows the rebelliousness or inability to submit to control that they represent. Thus his sublimation involves rejecting the polarized forces in the negative object embodying repression and rebellion—forces corresponding to those that cause tension within characters. This rejection can take the form of an explosive outburst of the kind I have described. Once polarized forms of desire and control have been rejected, they can be replaced by embodiments of positive desire and control that accept each other.

Sometimes, instead of replacing the bad parent, Dickens converts him, so that the same transformation is acted out, but within one character. The character can change in this way because the conflicting forces within him are analogous to those in plot conflicts, repression opposing the heart. Dickens often uses the words "hard" and "soft" to make these two entities concrete. Hard characters are enclosed in their shell of repression; soft characters are those who lack this hardness and can thus express the heart's feelings.[11] The same two entities can be found within one character; Dickens contrasts the "hardness" of a character's outer surface with the "softness of his heart" (*LD,* 1.18.218), enclosed by that surface. A good example of the way a protagonist's submission can overcome the hardness of repression is Florence Dombey's conversion of her father from repressiveness to a "docile submission" (*DS,* 59.845) like her own. Dickens often describes such a conversion as a softening. In *Dombey,* as in *Copperfield,* submission only disarms repression after rebelliousness and repressiveness (the negative object) have been rejected: Carker's death acts out the rejection of rebelliousness, and Dombey's fall purges him of repressiveness. This process resembles what takes place within Dickens's submissive characters; they disavow their desire to release energy as the plot rejects uncontrolled desire in Carker, and by being submissive they make their inner repression bearable as Florence softens her father.

However, these two extremes, rejection and submission, are not the only kind of resolution Dickens offers. In addition to his rebellious and submissive characters, he also creates an intermediate kind of character, one capable of balancing repression and energy;[12] and in his plot structures he offers us ways of attaining a similar balance. Among the intermediate characters of this sort I would include Sam Weller, Dick Swiveller, Micawber, and to a lesser extent more grotesque characters like Sairy Gamp and Flora Finching. These characters manage to release considerable energy and yet avoid becoming seriously rebellious like villains. In later Dickens such characters become weaker or more serious, apparently reflecting a growing sense of the difficulty of finding any fulfilling expression of desire. Perhaps the closest equivalent in late Dickens to Sam

Weller is a serious character like Eugene Wrayburn, who is more serious because he must try to work out a balance between desire and control; that balance is a problem for him, whereas for Sam the balance has already been attained, apparently without effort. I think that the balance Dickens is striving with difficulty to recapture through Eugene is like that which his earlier novels offer us in less conscious, more comic ways.

I have already described the way these intermediate characters deal with their tension: they deflect desire to indirect outlets which can evade repression because they are not seriously rebellious. Dickens often deals with plot conflicts through a similar process of deflection. Like his characters, he converts his imaginative energy into indirect forms, forms which if they do not resolve conflicts at least make them bearable—even pleasing. Like his characters, he deals with conflict by giving up the attempt to resolve it rationally. He apparently values the expression of intense, rather irrational impulses; but he also values submission to some sort of fatherlike (or godlike) authority. These two cannot be fully reconciled. Thus he seeks some way of allowing both, accepting their conflict. Since reason cannot reconcile them, he partly suspends rational control, somewhat as Richardson does. Instead of trying to diminish tension, he heightens it and emphasizes its unresolved nature, perhaps to make us feel the impossibility of working out any rational compromise so that we too will partly suspend rationality. I think this suspension is what makes possible Dickens's deflection of desire.

One of the main ways sublimating narrative controls desire is by expressing it through the subject, binding it to an "I" who seeks to reconcile it with control, a protagonist attempting to submit to authority and thus overcome the uncontrolled desire embodied in the negative object. But Dickens diffracts desire by shifting much of it away from the subject. It is as if he wants to release more energy than the ego can accommodate, perhaps because much of his imaginative energy is so strong it seeks as intense an expression as possible and thus is unwilling to accept rational control. Like his characters, he has so much energy that it keeps bursting out, finding new outlets. And like his characters, he enables that energy to find expression by deflecting it. His characters, as I have mentioned, also tend to shift desire away from the subject: they often lack a strong "I," a rational ego able to control their energy, and sometimes they replace their own inadequate "I" with a fictional persona. Similarly, Dickens largely replaces his main protagonist (the central "I") with characters who express desire in indirect, deflected ways.

It is in this way that Dickens typically transforms basic narrative structure. Although of course he retains protagonists, he shifts much of his interest (especially in the novels before *Dombey*) to the narrative object. His protagonists are so submissive that desire cannot be expressed through them very satisfyingly. Dickens evidently does not want to allow the rebellious, uncontrolled aspect of desire to find expression through the subject, perhaps because he feels this desire threatens to gain control of the self. He segregates uncontrolled desire from the protagonist, and as a result his protagonists lack the energy that desire could give them. Instead they typically represent the heart, which Dickens shows as pure but rather weak and passive. Even when a plot seems to require that the protagonist have guilty desires, Dickens usually keeps the protagonist quite submissive and shifts those desires onto other characters. For example, although we are told David Copperfield has an undisciplined heart, we do not see him behaving in a very undisciplined, rebellious way. Instead, lack of discipline is transferred mainly to Steerforth, as well as to other characters like Uriah Heep, Jack Maldon, and more comic versions like Dora and Micawber. Because Dickens's protagonists have been thus purified of assertive energy, they remain submissive to parentlike control rather than seeking to convert desire into action. For instance, David Copperfield accepts the control of parentlike characters like Aunt Betsey and Agnes. This submission seems analogous to submission to a strong superego, preventing the self from developing a strong ego serving the reality principle. Thus Dickens's protagonists (again, especially in the earlier novels) do not seem to have much ability to deal with reality. Characters like Little Nell and Florence Dombey are virtually imprisoned, cut off from the outer world as if unable to face it. And Esther Summerson, although less passive, is cut off from the Chancery world by Dickens's use of a dual narrative; it is as if she does not wholly belong in reality, separated from it by being largely idealized. Dickens's protagonists also seem separate from reality because they lack the inner tension we would expect their world to cause in them, a tension it does cause in the secondary characters who belong to it. Unable to deal actively with their world, the protagonists often become its victims, suffering because they cannot overcome the repression their world embodies.

Although Dickens does not follow Richardson in deleting a central narrator, his treatment of the narrator also shows his tendency to shift away from the subject. He does not usually employ a narrator, as Fielding does, to distance and judge his unresolved characters. Occasionally the narrator intervenes to moralize, but these interventions are usually kept separate from character presentation. Dickens, like Richardson, generally transfers most of the subject function to his characters and primarily uses the narrator to increase the intensity of our response to the characters by making us see them at least partly as subjects. He keeps a separate narrator, unlike Richardson, probably because his characters are not conscious enough to serve as narrators. Nevertheless, his narrator mainly serves character tension, not trying to deal with or explain tension but rather displaying it. The narrator often reproduces the characters' distorted view of their world or gives us a view like that an unresolved character might have, causing tension in us. For example, he often presents imagery without much rationalization, and often distorts that imagery in ways that arouse desire or fear. The narrator's view of the world often seems rather like a child's. In a young child's view the object-world is probably dominant and the subject, the self, does not have a clear, separate existence but rather is wholly taken up with seeing and desiring the object. Dickens often gives us a similar view of his fictional world, most clearly when he explicitly presents a child's view of the world, as at the start of *Copperfield* and of *Great Expectations*. It is as if he is trying to deprive us of the sense of an ego observing, understanding, and judging what it sees. Thus he makes us partly suspend rationality (like his characters) and allow tension to be comparatively unresolved. Perhaps the clearest example of the way he shifts emphasis to the object, treating it partly as subject, is the opening sentence of *Bleak House*, which consists of one word: "London." Here (as in a child's first utterances) there is no "I," no subject at all. We are left with nothing but the object—a negative object. We can see the negative object-world of the whole novel (primarily the world of the impersonal narrator) as an expansion of this one word, making clear its implications. Beginning with *Copperfield*, Dickens does move toward a new use of the narrator, a more clearly separate, conscious "I," but in his later fiction he still often seeks to avoid distancing the object. The dual narration in *Bleak House* betrays the tension between his wish to distance and judge the fictional world and his desire to become absorbed into it.

The way Dickens transforms the subject affects his treatment of the narrative object in various ways. In the positive object, as in the subject, emphasis is shifted from desire to control. Since the protagonist is highly submissive, the most important positive object-characters are those embodying the control to which the protagonist seeks to submit. Since the protagonists are usually fairly childlike, these authority figures are correspondingly parentlike. These parentlike characters take over much of the function of goal-characters. Sometimes the goal-character is also parentlike, as in the case of Agnes Wickfield, who is quite maternal. Sometimes there is a nominal goal-character apart from the parentlike character, but he becomes relatively weak and unimportant. For example, the goal-character Walter Gay in *Dombey* is offstage during most of the novel and is not very interesting when we do see him. And for Little Nell the goal-character has been deleted entirely. Goal-characters are largely replaced by parentlike characters; the love Florence Dombey mainly seeks is her father's, and Little Nell seeks her grandfather's love. Such a transformation of the goal-character implies an avoidance of the sexual aspect of desire. Submission partly replaces fulfillment. And because the subject's desire is partly repressed, it seems rather weak. As a result, the characters embodying its fulfillment are also weakened. Thus, even though Dickens emphasizes parentlike characters, he does not make the good ones very powerful or fulfilling.

As he weakens the positive object, Dickens shifts power to the negative. Whereas desire expressed through the subject is likely to be controlled, desire expressed through the object is separated from the ego's control. Thus that desire tends to become rebellious and as a result finds expression primarily through the negative object. This emphasis on the negative object seems to be a reaction against the submissiveness of the protagonist; if desire is denied full expression through the protagonist, it seeks compensatory expression elsewhere, an expression through which it can react against that denial. Rebelliousness can be allowed in the negative object, since there it is seen as bad and is distanced. Thus it is as if the protagonist's submissiveness causes the characters around him to oppose him and become rebellious, as in the case of the grotesques surrounding

Little Nell, existing to contrast with her and to oppose her submissiveness, threatening to replace it with rebelliousness. As I have said, Dickens's rebellious characters seem to embody a temptation to resent parentlike authority. The protagonist must avoid this temptation even though the negative characters try to make him rebellious (as Murdstone makes David Copperfield bite him and Steerforth tempts David toward lack of discipline). Quilp tries to turn Little Nell into a sexual being instead of the pure, idealized child she is; and Heep tries to make David resentful (for example, against the parentlike Dr. Strong).

In later Dickens, as he decreases the degree to which energy is deflected away from the subject, more rebelliousness remains within the protagonist and so the rebellious villains are weaker. In other words, Dickens makes an effort to redeem rebellious desire, returning it to the subject in an attempt to come to terms with it and thus control it more consciously. Beginning with *Copperfield* (although we can see the character of Martin Chuzzlewit as a preliminary attempt) Dickens implies a rebelliousness within his protagonists like that in his villains (as in David's attraction to Steerforth and Pip's to Estella). Yet Dickens still deflects much of his imaginative energy away from the protagonist.

When Dickens shifts desire to object-characters in this way, they tend to function partly as subjects. The desire in the highly villainous characters is too negative for us to accept them very fully as subjects. Nevertheless, they exercise a certain attraction, increasing the tension with which we respond to them, a tension caused by the conflict between their subject- and object-functions. Villains like Quilp and Carker behave as if they are trying to become subject-characters, take over the novel and replace the protagonist, filling the vacuum left by the protagonist's weakness. Although these characters are extreme, I think other object-characters similarly function partly as subjects because Dickens shifts desire to the object.

Increasing the rebellious energy in the narrative object causes a repressive reaction, so that some object-characters become highly repressive. The rebellious characters tend to take power away from good authority figures, so that power shifts instead to repressive figures (or sometimes the good parentlike character is transformed into a negative one). For example, Quilp takes power from Nell's grandfather, Uriah from Mr. Wickfield. Carker not only takes power from Dombey but helps make Dombey repressive. Weak parentlike characters are often replaced by repressive ones, as Murdstone replaces David Copperfield's mother and Miss Havisham replaces Joe as the main influence on Pip. Negative parentlike characters like Fagin, Pecksniff, Grandfather Smallweed, Mrs. Clennam, and Podsnap usually have more power than good ones—at least until the end of the novel.

We can see Dickens's deflection of desire to the object, then, as generating the highly polarized conflicts between repression and rebellion that are typical of his novels. By deflecting desire, he can express it in a less controlled form which causes conflict. Furthermore, we can see the same process of deflection as the cause for the similar tension within characters. As Dickens expresses more uncontrolled desire through his secondary characters, the repressive reaction against that desire also finds expression through those characters. Because this repression opposes desire, it prevents the characters from functioning entirely as subjects; they function partly as negative object-characters, opposing the desire they arouse. Repression keeps desire from being expressed except in partial, indirect forms. Thus it is as if the subject-function is divided up among many characters, each only an imperfect, mixed expression of that function. The negative object-function remains dominant in almost all the secondary characters, although some, like Sam Weller, are able to function primarily as subjects.

Desire is diffracted, then, not only into Dickens's rebellious villains, but to some extent into all of Dickens's comic characters. It finds its most direct, violent expression in rebellious characters; but a subjectlike desire is also implied, in a less demanding form, in other characters. The different characters are like partial, distorted reflections of the protagonist, expressing the same basic desire but in different ways, some submissively, some in more uncontrolled forms. The more rebellious characters are like negative versions of the protagonist, examples of what he should avoid, and the more submissive characters are like secondary protagonists, his allies or alter egos, submitting to the same kind of control. Yet even in these submissive characters there is usually more uncontrolled desire than in the protagonist. Because desire occurs in these secondary characters in deflected form, it need not be so seriously restrained. Thus these secondary characters can be more active, serving desire. Even a character as inhibited as Mr. Toots can do more than Florence Dombey can; he can move about in the fictional world and at least try actively to express and fulfill his desires. However, since comic characters like this have more uncontrolled desire, they also arouse a repressive reaction opposing that desire, causing tension (though in less rebellious characters that tension can remain mainly comic). Because of their tension they do not function as subject-characters as fully as the protagonist does. Thus the desire given them, though more active, is less serious and so is allowed less fulfillment. As a result, the object-characters accompanying them are less fulfilling. For example, Caddy Jellyby is like a diminished version of Esther Summerson, diminished because she has a negative side which resents her mother's inadequacy and therefore resists submission like Esther's. Because of this tension, positive desire is not allowed as fully in her as in Esther. Thus Caddy is less fully a subject-character than Esther, not so central in the novel, and the object-characters accompanying her are similarly diminished in comparison with Esther's: her father, though good, is much weaker than Jarndyce, and her goal-character, Prince Turveydrop, is even weaker than Allan Woodcourt. Because her object-characters are less fulfilling, offering desire less sublimation, she does not arouse as much serious desire as Esther.

In later Dickens we find less deflection of desire to the object. As more desire remains in Dickens's later protagonists, he emphasizes them rather than their comic counterparts. As conflict becomes more serious and central, the tension in the protagonist becomes more important and that in the comic characters less important.

Because each secondary character provides only a partial outlet for desire, Dickens tends to keep on deflecting his imaginative energy, seeking yet more outlets. It is as if he starts with a protagonist who is too virtuous to allow desire much expression, so he shifts from that protagonist to other characters, trying to find some way of expressing desire that will be more intense and satisfying yet not guilty. However, since that desire finds expression in quite repressed, submissive form or else in rebellious, guilty form, no one expression of it is satisfactory. Dickens seems to keep seeking to escape repression, but in each new form of expression the repressive reaction recurs. As a result, he keeps deflecting more and more, creating a larger and larger world around the subject, moving out from the work's center, seeking outlets for a desire he can't fully express through any one character. As each new character proves to be an imperfect outlet, Dickens deflects some desire away from him.

Thus, as they become partial subjects, characters tend to acquire a little secondary object-world of their own, onto which their energy is deflected. As I have mentioned, they often acquire satellite characters who represent some aspect of them. Dickens even deflects energy onto physical objects so that they too function as partial subjects. He often transfers the subject-function from a character to a thing which then metonymically represents that character. It is this tendency that I think George Orwell has in mind when he describes Dickens's elaboration of the marginal.[13]

As a result of this deflection, the various plot conflicts in a Dickens novel can be seen as alternative versions of each other. Thus the process of deflection provides a way of generating a complex fictional work based on the same fundamental conflict we have seen within Dickens's characters. However, I do not think these alternative conflicts are related as they are in a writer who uses conscious characters and asks us for a rational response, as we compare characters. In later Dickens, where he is more self-conscious, he rationalizes form more and does seem to expect us to compare and judge characters to some extent. But basically the different conflicts in a Dickens novel seem interrelated as parts of one large process seeking to reconcile desire with control. The secondary plots present deflected versions of the central conflict between the heart's desire for sublimation and a control that opposes desire and must be placated by submission. In its deflected versions, this desire can take on rebellious forms and the control opposing it can thus become repressive. Where the protagonist wants parentlike love, the rebellious villain has guilty desires which create a different relationship with parentlike authority; the villain wants to escape that authority and replace the parentlike character, a desire resembling the Oedipal desire to replace one's father. Nevertheless, we can usually detect a kinship between the protagonist's desire and the desires of other characters. Uriah Heep resembles David Copperfield in desiring Agnes, even though his desire takes a guilty, rebellious form. Steerforth resembles David in desiring Emily, a character whom (like Dora) we may see as a deflected, flawed version of Agnes. In Steerforth's case, as in Uriah's, the desire is guilty because accompanied by an opposition to parentlike characters (Mr. Peggotty, whom Steerforth defies, is like Mr. Wickfield, whom Uriah opposes—a good parentlike character to whom one should submit). Among positive characters, Traddles's love for Sophy resembles David's for

Agnes. Annie Strong's submission to her husband resembles the submission to parentlike control embodied in Agnes, a submission David learns from her. Emily's submission to Mr. Peggotty and even Mr. Dick's to Aunt Betsey reflect the same pattern. Thus in *Copperfield*, as in other Dickens novels, we can relate the various plots by seeing them as related versions of one subject-object relationship, the subject either desiring or (in the negative versions) rebelling against a positive object which embodies parentlike control over desire. We can compare the relationships among these characters to a series of parent-child relationships. There are positive parents who allow sublimation and negative ones who oppose it, as well as intermediate ones like Micawber who show some capacity for parentlike affection but also seem partly inhibited from becoming adequate parents. There is a related spectrum of childlike characters, some rebellious, some submissive, many intermediate. In the case of *Copperfield* they correspond to aspects of the central child, David; he moves from rebelliousness like Steerforth's toward submission like Agnes's. We keep encountering relationships in which parental failure to help the child fulfill his desire for an authority he can believe in creates a temptation to rebel against parentlike control, a temptation that Dickens seeks to counteract through submission.

In addition to providing a structural principle, the process of deflection provides Dickens with a way of dealing with the basic conflict out of which each novel is generated. One way it does so is by making the protagonist's submission more bearable. If the protagonist cannot release much energy, Dickens can use secondary characters to make up for him. He can keep the protagonist pure by separating out the rebellious aspect of desire and deflecting it to other characters. In addition, those characters act as a kind of safety valve, enabling the novel to get uncontrolled desire out of its system.[14] Once the secondary characters have let off steam, we can more easily accept the submission required of the protagonist. For instance, we can accept the submission David Copperfield learns because we have been allowed a compensatory (though only partial) release of energy in such events as Micawber's defiance of Heep. Just as Micawber makes his own partial submission bearable by expressing rebelliousness in deflected, indirect, comic ways, so the novel as a whole makes the final virtuous submission bearable by using characters like Micawber to provide a deflected expression of desire. Thus a Dickens novel works out a balance between release and repression in a way resembling the balance achieved within his intermediate characters.

Like his comic characters, Dickens deflects desire in order to make it less serious. Even though the deflected forms in which his characters express desire are often violent, we need not take them entirely seriously because the desire expressed has been shifted away from the subject; taking desire seriously means accepting it as the desire of our "I," of the subject. Where Richardson keeps unresolved tension in his protagonist to make us feel a strong need to deal with it and feel pity if it cannot be resolved, Dickens locates tension in characters we can see as object-characters so that we need not care so much if they fail to resolve their tension. We can distance desire, seeing it as outside the self, and so we are not so bothered if it is uncontrolled. And by expressing desire in a way that does not demand fulfillment as seriously as a subject's desire does, the comic characters can partly evade the repressive reaction that opposes desire. In other words, Dickens uses those characters to deflect desire into a form that can coexist with repression, making their tension bearable.

Unresolved characters, then, have a structural function in Dickens: they are the means whereby he deflects energy in order to deal with tension. By expressing desire through comic characters, he converts it into an indirect, playful form. He can do this because of the mixed, unresolved nature of his characters: they are both an outlet for desire and a way of partly opposing and therefore diminishing it. Thus we need not feel too frustrated if repression opposes that desire. Instead we can feel that the character's inability to resolve tension is comic.

Because Dickens's subsidiary plots are less serious, they can be treated differently from his central plots. Within his intermediate characters, desire and repression (since they are not taken so seriously) can be allowed to coexist. Similarly, in his comic plots the characters are usually intermediate, not purely villainous or heroic, and so their plot conflicts need not be wholly resolved. Negative characters can be reduced to a playful form—for example, Mrs. Gamp—and so need not be seriously defeated or rejected. Positive characters like Mr. Toots are similarly diminished, so that their victories remain merely comic. In contrast, in his serious central plots (especially in the earlier novels) conflicting forces are highly polarized, the heart victimized by cruel repression aroused by wicked rebelliousness. In comic plots the heart is less pure and so need not be pitied as much, and what opposes it is less strongly polarized against desire and so less threatening.

One example of the way Dickens deals with conflict by deflecting energy is the case of Micawber. David Copperfield is apparently too virtuous and serious a character to oppose Uriah Heep actively himself; when he does slap Uriah, he feels guilty. So Dickens allows Micawber to act for David, thus absolving David of any rebellious energy. Uriah has usurped Mr. Wickfield's place, becoming like a repressive father-substitute, and opposing him might imply resentment of fatherlike control or of Wickfield's weakness. But we need feel no such reservations about Micawber's opposing Uriah, since we do not take Micawber so seriously. That is, we do not wholly accept him as a subject-character. Thus the potentially rebellious energy Dickens seems unwilling to express through David is deflected to Micawber, through whom it finds a partial, comically distorted, and therefore acceptable form of expression. Micawber does not seek to serve desire too directly—to become a subject completely—and so he can get away with defying Uriah. Similarly, Aunt Betsey replaces David in defying the Murdstones. By letting a parentlike character replace him in this way, Dickens keeps David submissive to parentlike control even while the novel is rejecting bad parent-figures.

Another good example of the way Dickens deflects the subject-function to subsidiary characters in order to deal with conflict is the way he uses the fulfillment attained by Dick Swiveller and the Marchioness to compensate us for the death of Little Nell. They are able to replace her because, even though Dickens may value Nell more, she lacks their ability to circumvent repression. Nell dies the victim of a world in which good parentlike control (her grandfather) has been weakened and thus replaced by a cruel, repressive control, a control mainly exercised by Quilp, who although he rebels against others' control seeks to gain power for himself. Being a purely submissive character, Nell offers no outlet for the desires that seek to oppose that repressive power. Dick, on the other hand, is rebellious enough to circumvent repression to some extent; he is able to resist the control of Quilp and Quilp's agent, Sally Brass. He can do this because, being a comic, mixed character, he does not seek to allow the heart full expression as Nell does; his desires are not as serious as hers. As I have mentioned, he is able to evade repression by diminishing desire, not seeking to function fully as a subject. And, as with Caddy Jellyby, when his subject-function is diminished, the characters functioning as his objects are diminished too. If he does not take his desire too seriously, he need not take opposition to it seriously either. Just as Micawber can reduce Uriah to a "Heep of infamy" (*DC,* 52.751), making him ridiculous rather than villainous, Dick can reduce Sally Brass to a "Dragon" (*OCS,* 34.253), like a child's version of a villain, one we need not fear much. It is as if imagination can transform reality; by making reality seem imaginary the character need not fear it. And, just as Dick does not insist on directly defying Sally's repressiveness and so is able to placate her, he does not insist on winning complete fulfillment as embodied in Nell. Instead he is willing to accept a substitute fulfillment with the Marchioness, a secondary goal-character in whom the goal function is diminished by being combined with some rebelliousness, causing a tension that makes her comic and so less fulfilling. Instead of serious fulfillment, Dick finds with her a childlike, playful version of fulfillment, one that accepts some repression and does not demand too direct an expression of desire. He turns the Marchioness into a parody of a romance goal-character and himself into a mock-hero, thus keeping desire from becoming too serious. It is because he accepts this diminution that he can obtain any fulfillment at all. In other words, Dickens uses these characters, like other comic characters, to deflect desire into a form that can be partly fulfilled because it is indirect and limited.

Once Dickens has dealt with tension in this way, he can reverse the process of deflection. The many partial outlets can be reunited with the subject from which they were deflected: the subordinate characters join forces with the protagonist so that they all seem to function together as one outlet for desire. For example, almost all the good characters in *Copperfield* come together in defeating Uriah, all acting as aspects of one subject. Apparently once deflection makes desire acceptable, purging it of rebelliousness, it can be returned to the subject in a properly submissive form. When this has been done, a set of relationships embodying the polarity between rebellion and repression can be replaced by a set embodying a desire and control that can accept each other so that desire can be sublimated. Dickens makes this reconciliation resemble the reconciliation of a submissive child with a loving parent. This sublimation seems to be made possible not only on the plot level, by the rejection of the rebelliousness embodied in the villain, but also in characterization, by the partial disavowal of rebelliousness implicit in the way characters deflect their desires, avoiding a direct challenge of repression. We could say, then, that the inhibition implied in the unresolved characters is part of the price paid to earn the final sublimation. It is as if they give up part of their fulfillment so that the protagonist may have more.

I think we can better understand the way Dickens attempts to reconcile desire with submission by relating it to his experience with his own parents. Judging by his autobiographical fragment, the central experience of his childhood was his feeling that he had been abandoned by his parents when they sent him to work in the blacking warehouse.[15] In his novels similar experiences keep recurring, in which parents somehow fail their children. In the autobiographical fragment, Dickens betrays resentment of his parents, a resentment also suggested by the way he frequently makes parents weak or even cruel in his novels. I think we can see his fiction as an attempt to overcome that resentment. Perhaps he abandoned the autobiographical fragment because it expressed resentment too directly. By turning what began as an autobiography into *David Copperfield*, he could avoid resentment (and thus rebelliousness) as his characters do, by deflecting the expression of potentially rebellious desires into a fictional form. He replaces an autobiographical "I," a subject directly linked to his own desire, with a fictional subject, just as in his fiction he deflects desire away from central characters to secondary ones. This deflection avoids a direct avowal of filial resentment, just as his inhibited characters avoid directly opposing repression. The fiction replaces a resentful "I" with an idealized self, a protagonist who seems to function as a defense against resenting parental failure; no matter how much characters like Nell or Florence Dombey suffer because of parental (or parentlike) inadequacy, they avoid resentment, especially in earlier Dickens. Dickens seems to be using them to overcome or disavow a tendency to be critical of parents, apparently because resentment arouses Oedipal guilt. Nevertheless, some of that resentment remains; we can see it in the way he makes Murdstone so repressive, making us resent him. So Dickens takes the process of deflection further; he replaces Murdstone with Micawber. The resented aspect of the father is replaced with a diminished, playful version which need not be taken seriously enough to be resented. He does this by also deflecting some desire through

Micawber, making him a partial subject, a childlike as well as a fatherlike character. Thus tension between subject and negative object is partly replaced by tension within the object-character.

Dickens thus uses fiction to purge desire of resentfulness. He tells us in the directly autobiographical part of *Copperfield* that as a child he dealt with his sense of abandonment by telling stories, and I think in his fiction he continues to use story-telling for this purpose. When he was composing a novel, he often went walking back into that same city in which as a child he had felt abandoned, as if to confront again that feeling, perhaps to seek ways of dealing with it. It was as if he were seeking to recapture a childlike state. If he could not regain such a state in reality, he could do so in fiction. In other words, he could use the act of story-telling to transform his resentment into a childlike form in which it was no longer seriously rebellious. He could remove the resentfulness from desire by expressing it through an idealized, submissive, childlike protagonist. Once desire has been made submissive in this way, it can be reconciled with control, a process through which Dickens seems to seek something like reconciliation with his own parents. The idealized, childlike subject can be united with a parentlike character who replaces the inadequate parents who might arouse resentment. This transformation accompanies the rejection of rebellious villains who embody (in an exaggerated form, easier to reject) resentment of parental inadequacy. The novels imply that if only one can regain the innocence and submission of an idealized childhood, one can escape Oedipal guilt and regain the parental love one has lost.

Dickens seeks this sublimation not just by becoming like a child, but by becoming like a child telling stories, like the young David Copperfield. We can see the very act of writing the novels, then, as a means of deflecting desire in order to make it acceptable. Dickens converts it into a playlike, fictional form, avoiding too much seriousness.[16] Here again, what he does resembles what he makes his characters do, creating fictions. Just as Mrs. Gamp creates Mrs. Harris, Dickens creates his characters as outlets for his imaginative energy, an energy so intense that it is probably only within a fiction that he can express it adequately. Within fiction he can partly evade the force that tries to prevent the direct expression of desire. Even if desire is expressed in a form that is somewhat uncontrolled and thus difficult to reconcile with what opposes it, it can be expressed all the more intensely because it is less controlled. And because the form in which he expresses it is playful, that intensity is comic and pleasing.

Dickens's unresolved characters, then, help him to express desire and at the same time to submit to control. By deflecting desire into indirect forms, not trying to express it too directly, he is partly accepting some control over desire while simultaneously allowing it some expression. Thus, although characters function to some extent as parts of a structure that sublimates desire, that sublimation remains imperfect and the characters also function as outlets for some unsublimated desire, a desire existing in unresolved tension with control. It is as if the secondary characters would like to attain a perfect sublimation like the protagonist's but are unable to. Yet I can't help feeling (and suspecting that Dickens too felt) that the comic by-product is more valuable than the sublimation to which it contributes. It is the very impurity of the characters, their ability to evade control, that makes them attractive. They make us feel that we need not take the novel's conflicts too seriously, that those conflicts can be transformed into a source of pleasure; thus we can accept their unresolved tension. Dickens can value his unresolved characters instead of mocking or condemning them as most novelists do. It is their very inability to resolve their tension, to exercise rational control, that he values in them. Their irrationality enables them to remain childlike and playful and thus make pleasing a tension that cannot be resolved.

The Decline of Character Intensity

epilogue

In the later nineteenth century, characterization in the novel began to lose intensity.[1] Many modern novelists of course still create characters with tension like those in earlier novels, but they rarely seem to value character as an end in itself as their predecessors did. Instead, writers became more concerned with what I have called secondary response, with thematic and formal concerns. Modern critics have valued this kind of fiction—preferring novelists like Henry James and Joyce, for example—probably because criticism tends to concern itself with the rationalization of response and to value writers who have awareness like a critic's. However, I think we should recognize that although fiction gained in some respects, there was a resultant diminution in other qualities, especially in the kind of local intensity we value in first readings—in our primary response. This change seems to have been influenced by many of the same tendencies that affected the development of characterization in earlier novels. It is as if there was a point when the conditions affecting the development of the novel produced maximum character intensity, and beyond that point those same trends began to work against that intensity.

This point, I think, was the point at which romance and "realism," desire and resistance, were in maximum tension—when the novel retained much of its affinity to romance and yet had developed much of its resistance to romancelike wish-fulfillment. The synthesis of romance and antiromance was based on an ability to balance belief in sublimation (like that romance offers) with an awareness of the forces that make sublimation difficult. Until the middle of the nineteenth century, English novelists usually seem to have been able to visualize some embodiment of authority that their characters could accept—an authority which, if not identical with social authority, nevertheless seems to be a transformation of it, idealized and often located on a transcendent level. As long as a novelist could create such an idea of authority, he could still believe in a sublimating control, a control that desire could submit to and yet be fulfilled by. Yet that belief could be balanced with an awareness of the ways in which actual social control (in the "realistic," unidealized form in which the protagonist encounters it before the happy ending) opposes desire, threatening to cause rebellion against control and a loss of faith in the possibility of finding a sublimating control. As long as these could be balanced, the novel could keep romance and realism in equilibrium.

I have already mentioned that this compromise was evidently an unstable one.[2] We can see the synthesis beginning to disintegrate in George Eliot's novels. In *Middlemarch* romance and realism are still kept in balance, but just barely. Dorothea's story offers (although in restrained, "realistic" form) some of the idealization and wish-fulfillment of romance; but that half of the novel is balanced by Lydgate's story, which shows social forces opposing such fulfillment and preventing characters from becoming so ideal. The two stories are contained within the same world, obeying many of the same constraints. And their union is made more convincing because Fred Vincy's story provides an intermediate example, working out a compromise between fulfillment like Dorothea's and limitations like Lydgate's. When we turn to *Deronda,* however, these two tendencies are no longer successfully reconciled: Deronda's world seems too idealized to be consistent with Gwendolen's, which is pushed to the opposite extreme, allowing almost no fulfillment.

The novel's disintegration seems to have taken place when novelists lost faith in the existence of any sublimating form of control with which desire could be fulfillingly reconciled. Belief and awareness no longer seemed compatible. I think this change was caused by a shift in the way writers perceived authority, a shift apparently influenced by the changing nature of social authority and its relation to the individual. I have already discussed the way in which social authority came to be seen as more and more alien and consequently was internalized less fully. Perhaps society became too commercialized, too technological, too institutionalized and impersonal to provide forms of authority the individual could internalize. Or it may be that the modern acceptance of individualist desire was like the opening of Pandora's box, an irreversible process: perhaps once the individual's right to fulfillment has been asserted, control can never completely be reestablished and desire will continue to seek more and more expression. Whatever the causes, I think belief in abstract forms of authority like God depends on the ability to internalize some form of social control, creating a capacity to believe in the concept of authority; and so alienation from society is accompanied by a loss of faith in any form of authority as absolute.

In the novel the changed attitude toward authority finds expression in a change in that aspect of the narrative object which embodies the idea of authority. By the end of the nineteenth century, novels rarely offer good fatherlike characters embodying a fulfilling control or goal-characters embodying an attainable sublimation. Instead, many protagonists lack good parentlike guidance and find themselves stuck with negative goal-characters embodying the denial of sublimation, characters like George Eliot's Rosamond Vincy and Grandcourt. But George Eliot still balances this denial of sublimation with some hope of partial fulfillment: Dorothea is able to escape her negative goal-character, Casaubon. Later novelists seem more pessimistic. In Henry James, for example, Isabel Archer finds herself married to a negative goal-character like Casaubon; but instead of killing off Osmond as George Eliot removes Casaubon, James instead kills off a goal-character (although a diminished one) who resembles Will Ladislaw—Ralph Touchett. Tess of the D'Urbervilles similarly finds herself with a negative mate, Alec, who cuts her off from the positive goal-character and whom she can only escape at the price of death. In *Nostromo* Mrs. Gould cannot escape her unloving husband, and Antonia and Linda are denied the men they desire. The negative mates I have listed here (Osmond, Alec, Gould) represent not just the denial of a fulfilling goal but also a social control which effectively thwarts the individual's desires, trapping the protagonist. Thus social control no longer seems fulfilling; the novelist no longer believes in it.

Novelists also continue the tendency to diffuse opposition to desire throughout the protagonist's world, making that world more and more negative. Already in Dickens and George Eliot we can see the world becoming more enclosing; *Bleak House* and *Middlemarch*, for example, show complex social worlds which limit and entangle characters. Hardy shows the entire world dominated by a destiny whose main function seems to be to oppose his protagonist's wishes. Other novelists are less explicit about assigning responsibility, but they still show a world indifferent or hostile to human wishes. Conrad, for example, uses symbols like the Golfo Placido in *Nostromo* and Africa in *Heart of Darkness* to create embodiments of negative control. Setting becomes more important than character, is able to control and defeat characters. Conrad's sense that there are impersonal, pervasive forces beyond our control leads him to create these symbols, locating power not in characters but in objects that oppose characters. As the negative object becomes diffused throughout the work in this way, conflicts become harder to resolve. One can defeat a villain, but not the whole world. Thus the work offers less and less romancelike fulfillment. In Northrop Frye's words, fiction becomes "ironic," opposed to our (and the protagonist's) desire for fulfillment.[3] And as the world opposes and encloses the protagonist more, he becomes weaker and less ideal. One thing that makes a character seem strong is his ability to initiate action, making us feel there is a strong desire in him to act. When the protagonist is acted on by his world rather than overcoming it, he seems passive, as in Hardy. Thus he does not seem to have as strong an inner force; he arouses less desire in us.

As the novel loses its ability to provide sublimation, it seeks something with which to replace sublimating control. I have already discussed the way the rejection of authority led to its replacement with increasingly conscious self-control. This tendency too seems to continue with modernism.[4] As desire became harder to sublimate, people were forced to become more aware both of their desires and of the forces, both social and inner, resisting sublimation. Awareness is a way of trying to accept frustration and the forces causing it, of trying to restrain desires one cannot fulfill. Modernism typically seeks such an awareness. The increased concern with self-consciousness at the end of the nineteenth century is probably best exemplified by Freud, but we can see it also in novelists like Joyce and Woolf.

This concern with awareness finds expression in the modern novel's treatment of protagonists. Where earlier protagonists learn submission to some embodiment of sublimating control, the modern protagonist often learns to deal with desires he can't sublimate by becoming more self-aware. In *Middlemarch,* for example, Dorothea seeks to submit to some sort of godlike control which will enable her to find a fulfilling and purified outlet for her desires; but the dead forms of Christianity, as represented by Casaubon, fail to provide such a sublimating control and instead replace it with a negative object embodying repressive control. Thus Dorothea cannot find the outlet she desires (until late in the novel, and then only partly) and instead must turn inward, as we see her doing on her honeymoon, learning self-awareness and self-criticism, overcoming her "confused thought and passion" through a gradual "struggling forth into clearness" of a "self-accusing" consciousness which seeks to control her egoistic desires (20.224). Many later characters are similarly forced to substitute awareness for action, since society no longer seems to offer any fulfilling outlets in action. After marrying Osmond, for example, Isabel Archer sits alone meditating on the failure of her marriage much like Dorothea. Deprived of a goal-character, her only substitute for fulfillment is an inner one. All she can do is become more aware; consciousness has become an end in itself. In *The Ambassadors* James starts out with a protagonist who has already failed and is consequently mainly an awareness, not an actor. James describes the literary character as a "consciousness," not an actor but a "register" of action, "finely aware" of it.[5] Other characters who must mainly content themselves with awareness include Mrs. Gould, Stephen Dedalus, and Mrs. Moore in *A Passage to India.* D. H. Lawrence seems somewhat different from the writers who emphasize consciousness, but he is concerned with it too; he concentrates on the forces in the self that consciousness tries to become aware of.

This increase in self-consciousness seems to me to cause a decrease in tension. As I mentioned in an earlier chapter, conscious self-control is a function of what Freud calls the ego. Without the support of a strong superego (internalized authority), the ego seems unable to repress rebellious desires fully. Thus it seeks to diminish tension by reaching some accommodation with desire rather than directly opposing it. If we are no longer able to sublimate or repress desire fully, we are constrained to allow it some expression and try to come to terms with it, using self-awareness as a way of partly controlling it, an imperfect substitute for repression. This is a continuation of the tendency toward compromise and depolarization I have already discussed. Although we find compromise formations in Richardson, the opposing forces in his novels remain quite polarized, a highly authoritarian control opposing a highly rebellious passion. Even in Austen, who depolarizes conflicts more, negative and positive forces remain clearly opposed. But in later novelists, these opposing forces become less separate and less strongly opposed. Even if there is less resolution of tension, the tension seems increasingly diffused throughout the work and so less intense. There is less hope of fulfillment and therefore desire is more restrained, decreasing conflict. Richardson seems willing to allow rebellious desire direct, separate expression (for example, through Lovelace) because he still believes he can repress or sublimate it. The modern writer who no longer believes this is less willing to allow that desire such full expression and instead combines it with restraint, diminishing it. We can see this depolarization in plot conflicts; protagonists are no longer so idealized and in sharp conflict with strongly evil villains. Instead, both uncontrolled desire and opposition to it tend to combine within both protagonist and antagonist, so that neither is all good or bad. Desire (and the protagonist who mainly serves it) is weaker, more compromised, and thus creates a less intense conflict.

As outer conflict loses intensity, so does tension within the protagonist. When a writer makes a protagonist more conscious, he uses the character to deal with desire, resisting and criticizing it, rather than using the character to arouse desire in us, as he does in romance. In other words, the protagonist functions more like a narrator, a detached awareness rather than an actor in the plot. This makes us respond to him with less intensity. We do not respond to narrators as strongly as we respond to characters because a character can act, and his action arouses our desire by seeking to fulfill it. The more desire we feel, the more tension we can feel. But if a character restrains his desire, we need not react against it and so we feel less tension. In addition, when a protagonist interacts with the object-world we partly see him in that world, as a being separate from us, unlike a narrator, whom we need not feel is separate at all. This interaction gives us a sense that the character is an entity able to act on the object-world and thus serve desire. We feel force exists in the character because of its external effect, its expression in action and the resistance it encounters. And we take pleasure in feeling that that force can act in the object-world; we feel we are exercising power through something outside ourselves—a feeling we can only have if the character seems separate from us. In addition, when we see the subject-character partly as an object, this creates a tension in our response. Perhaps we need this sense of character as something not identical to ourselves so that we can allow desire to find displaced expression through him. If we felt the desire were literally our own, we might feel guilty about allowing it expression. The character must seem partly an object in order to function as a transitional object, allowing desire a playlike, distanced outlet the way a mask does.

When novelists see character as inner self, they place less emphasis on character as social identity, probably because they no longer believe in social roles. In earlier novels, much of the intensity of our response comes from the conflict between social and inner selves, desire opposing the social self's control. Austen and Richardson are concerned with the inner self, but as it is expressed in conflict with the social side of the self which seeks to understand and control it and make it moral. For writers like them, the inner self can be reconciled with control enough so that it can be expressed in rational, social terms, if only by implication. But when the modern novelist rejects the outer self, he can no longer use it to create that tension between private and social selves. As the positive object-character embodying good social control tends to disappear, so too does such control within characters. When we come to George Eliot, the social self no longer seems adequate to express character fully. She asserts that she is not as interested in "outside estimates of a man" as in "the report of his own consciousness" (*Middlemarch*, 10.110). She evidently feels there are unconscious forces in a character like Casaubon which she cannot merely imply through his own words and actions; she wants to tell us things about characters that are "hardly ever told even in their consciousness" (15.174), things Casaubon for example "did not confess to himself" (10.111) —inner forces which are "indefinable" (66.724) and "invisible"

(16.194). Nevertheless, George Eliot still alternates the inner self with the social, showing us characters from outside as well as within. In late James, however, the novel seems almost entirely given over to inner views of character. And by the time we reach Lawrence, we find an impatience with the social self, a sense that what is external is somehow inauthentic, not really part of the self. In *Women in Love,* for example, Lawrence wants to get at "the source of the deepest life-force, the darkest, deepest, strangest life-source of the human body," escaping the "mind"; it is only at this deeper level that one can become a "complete self" (23.306).[6] He evidently can no longer believe in any form of control and seeks to free desire from it, from social inhibitions and rational restraints. It is the depths of the self that are "reality" (23.311). But as characters cease to have a social self, they become harder to know; like the unconscious they are meant to embody, they become complex and ambiguous. As a result, it is hard to respond to them intensely; more of our effort goes into trying to understand them, dealing rationally with their tension rather than feeling it. And their tension is less sharp, since it is not the strongly polarized conflict between desire and social control but rather the half-conflict between consciousness and desire, partly opposing but partly accepting each other.

Another danger of emphasizing the unconscious is that it can replace characters. Lawrence, for example, no longer wants to see character as the agent of desire but rather as a medium through which desire acts; the actual source of desire—the force motivating action—is located somewhere beyond character, in some "greater, inhuman will" that controls character.[7] Thus in *Women in Love* Ursula feels that "what we must fulfill comes out of the unknown to us"; it isn't something "merely *human*" (29.429). But if the source of energy is not character but "some mysterious life-flow" (23.305), then we will not feel that the character has power, or is an entity within which is located the desire that causes him to act—in short, we will not feel he is a character. Insofar as we do still see him as a character, he is not an actor but a consciousness of this mysterious force. It is the force that acts. As a result, the character seems controlled by some abstraction outside him, almost in the way a romance character can be controlled by love or fortune. In addition, such characters lose the particularity we find in traditional novel characterization. For instance, in *Women in Love* Birkin feels that people "acted and reacted involuntarily according to a few great laws," and so are "all essentially alike" (23.296). They lack the individuality social identity would give them.

An approach like Lawrence's can work against character tension. In practice, Lawrence usually retains a sense of character as tension; but like other modern writers he does tend to create characters who are meant to embody a particular psychic force such as libido or repression. Insofar as a character is controlled by one force, he is no longer a compromise formation, a being within which conflicting forces are implied. Rather, conflicting forces are separated, embodied in different characters. I think we feel more tension when conflicting forces are implied through compromise formations, concentrating conflict at one point. Many other modernist writers resemble Lawrence in making characters represent an inner force; that is, they make character become a symbol. When this happens, the character has ceased to be an end in himself and has become externally determined, serving an idea. For example, in *Heart of Darkness* forces that might have been in tension within a character are largely separated out and represented by symbols instead, embodied in characters and images. The central character, Marlow, is largely a consciousness rather than an actor. His journey is like the journey of consciousness into the depths of the self. He leaves behind the social world, the world of external selves, and journeys into a dark, dreamlike realm within which he discovers a character—Kurtz—who seems to symbolize the uncontrolled, negative desire that lies within the self. But although these two characters seem to represent two aspects of the self, consciousness becoming aware of desire, Conrad has separated them into two characters instead of combining them in one complex self as would a novelist dealing with the world of external selves. It seems that Conrad feels the need to separate consciousness from desire in order to become critically aware of desire. But this separation removes conflict from within character, locating it not within individual units but among separate units.

The tendency to replace traditional internalized authority with self-awareness also affected the novel by making desire less controllable, since desire could no longer be fully sublimated or repressed.[8] Thus tensions tended to become more unresolved. The acceptance that one cannot resolve conflicts seems to be one of the basic characteristics of modernism in general. In the modern novel, then, characters tend to become more unresolved, even though they are also more conscious; they are aware of inner conflict but unable to resolve it. Perhaps self-awareness causes this inability; the more self-aware one becomes the more one realizes that there are depths in the self which cannot be controlled or sublimated. We can contrast this condition with that of Elizabeth Bennet in *Pride and Prejudice;* for her, self-discovery and thus the resolution of conflict are relatively easy and not very painful. Awareness enables her to resolve conflicts and find fulfillment. That resolution seems possible because her self-control still includes an acceptance of internalized authority; the ego gains strength by acting for the superego. In other words, Austen believes in judgment, but she also believes that judgment should serve an absolute moral authority, a set of unquestioned values. In later fiction, as the protagonist must rely more exclusively on self-control without belief in such a higher authority, self-control becomes weaker and less fulfilling. We can contrast Elizabeth with Isabel Archer, for example; Isabel's self-discovery does not enable her to find fulfillment. She can only become aware of her desire, not sublimate it and translate it into action.

This inability to reconcile desire fully with control leads to a disintegration of character. Modern novelists begin to stop seeing the self as a whole, as Leo Bersani has remarked.[9] They seem less certain about what character is, whether it is knowable. As E. M. Forster puts it, "Psychology has split and shattered the idea of a 'Person.'"[10] Traditional characterization deals with tension by containing it within a character who imposes a unity on it and acts to resolve tension by fulfilling desire and dealing with what opposes it. We may see the history of the novel as a gradual increase in conflict within the subject, a conflict leading eventually to the disintegration of the subject. We have already seen this tendency in the way Dickens divides the subject into many partial protagonists; and in *Middlemarch* the subject is split into two main protagonists who cannot be reconciled with each other, as well as numerous secondary characters who also function partly as protagonists. By the time we reach Virginia Woolf the subject seems to have become atomized so that all characters are like partial protagonists. We find a similar disintegration within individual characters. The modern character's function is often not to resolve tension but rather to face it and allow it to exist unresolved. Character becomes not an identity but a search for identity, for some unity and resolution. We can see this change beginning in George Eliot. She speaks of character as a "play of minute causes" (*Middlemarch,* p. 83), a "conflux of emotions and thoughts" (p. 710)—that is, not as one entity but many. The fragmentation of character is especially clear in Lawrence's rejection of "the old stable *ego*" of traditional characterization.[11] In *Women in Love* Lawrence talks of character as something incoherent and incomprehensible: "How curious it was that this was a human being! What Brangwen thought himself to be, how meaningless it was, confronted with the reality of him. Birkin could see only a strange, inexplicable, almost patternless collection of passions and desires and suppressions and traditions and mechanical ideas, all cast unfused and disunited into this . . . man . . . , who was as unresolved now as he was at twenty, and as uncreated" (19.248). I don't think Lawrence completely follows this view of character; he still presents characters as separate beings, relatively knowable, striving to escape personality rather than actually free of it. But insofar as one accepts the view of character this passage implies, character ceases to be an entity at all, a thing able to act in the fictional world, and is replaced by various "passions and desires" which become the actors instead.

As desire becomes less controlled, it grows increasingly rebellious; and since it is mainly the protagonist who serves desire, protagonists become increasingly negative, their desires uncontrolled. Often the writer opposes his protagonist, creating a world to frustrate the protagonist and show that his desires are wrong. Sometimes it is almost as if the protagonist is the villain. Among protagonists who are fairly negative, one can include Henchard in *The Mayor of Casterbridge* and Nostromo. But though Hardy and Conrad oppose these protagonists, they also retain considerable sympathy for them. In the case of Stephen Dedalus in *Portrait of the Artist* and even more in the case of Lawrence's protagonists, the novelist is quite sympathetic to his rebellious character. Nevertheless, these protagonists too serve a desire that opposes control.

When a novelist sees his protagonist as negative, he is likely to decrease the intensity of our response to the protagonist. Hardy, for example, distances his protagonists and does not enter into their inner conflicts much; instead he mainly shows the conflict between them and the world which their desires oppose. They seem to exist mainly to be acted on from outside—to be the victims of fate. They do retain some inner tension, often opposing their desires with a rather dogged awareness of how unfulfilling reality is. But that inner tension seems less important than their outer conflict with reality. Since their desires are hopeless, Hardy ironically distances those desires, diminishing our response to them.

When a novelist feels unable to reconcile desire with control within his protagonist, he often replaces the positive, controlling aspect of the protagonist with some other embodiment of positive control. If the protagonist is negative, he is an inadequate manifestation of the narrative subject, and so the novelist shifts emphasis to other expressions of the subject. Feeling critical of the protagonist, the writer stands back from him, usually speaking through a narrator instead. Since desire can no longer find a fulfilling outlet through the protagonist's actions, the novelist concentrates on expressing the detached awareness that seeks to restrain desire. Sublimation involves a union of desire with control, but once sublimation has become impossible, control must remain more separate from desire, standing back from it, criticizing or seeking to counteract it. Thus this positive function of the subject, seeking to control desire, becomes separated from that aspect of the subject which serves desire (the protagonist). This is another example of the disintegration of the subject. Sometimes novelists locate this critical awareness in characters, as I have said; but often it finds separate expression in an ironic narrator, as in Meredith, Conrad, and Joyce. I have already mentioned Conrad's use of a narratorlike character in *Heart of Darkness*. In *Youth* the tendency to split the subject is even clearer; Marlow is divided into two manifestations of the subject, an old, disillusioned narrator-Marlow standing apart from a young, idealistic protagonist-Marlow.

This shift in emphasis from protagonist to narrator can be found, of course, as early as Fielding; but his narrator functions mainly to supplement his protagonist, not oppose him, and (as we saw in the case of Austen) the classic novel tended to evolve away from this emphasis on the narrator. However, the ironic narrator remains important for novelists like Thackeray who are critical of their characters' desires. George Eliot often uses a narrator because her characters are negative insofar as they are unable fully to understand, control, or express their desires. Thus she needs a narrator to tell us what the characters feel. In *Middlemarch,* for example, much of the action is internal, "inward drama and argument" (64.710); much of our interest focuses on characters' "fading of hopes" or "self-delusion" (10.110)—the disillusion of more conscious characters like Dorothea and Lydgate or the self-deception of more unresolved characters like Casaubon and Bulstrode. Since these characters are often not fully aware of the forces within them or are unable to express those forces, George Eliot uses a narrator to tell us what the characters themselves cannot. Thus the narrator partly replaces and distances the characters, diminishing our response to them. Even when the narrator is not being critical of a character, he often needs to analyze what the character feels, and analysis does not arouse as intense a response because it deals with the character's conflict, decreasing tension by rationalizing it, rather than making us feel the tension as strongly ourselves. It takes more time to explore and explain the character's mind in this way, whereas direct expression of the character's unresolved conflict through compromise formations enables tension to be concentrated in local details where we can feel it all at once. We can contrast this use of a narrator with the way Austen withholds narrative judgment and makes her protagonists deal with their own conflicts and the way Dickens makes us deal with his characters' conflicts.

As narrators begin to replace protagonists, they become more like protagonists, less able to detach themselves as fully from desire and to express the kind of rational certainty and godlike objectivity we find in Fielding. Here again we see the replacement of the traditional concept of control as an absolute with the more self-conscious, relative, uncertain control of the ego, unable fully to replace the superego. In Henry James, for example, it is sometimes difficult to decide whether a character like Strether is a protagonist who resembles a narrator or a narrator who resembles a protagonist. In Conrad too, as I have said, we see this tendency to make narrators into characters within the story. Observer-characters of this kind give expression to the questing, doubting nature of consciousness. But because they resemble narrators they induce a less intense response than would a character who served desire more directly. And the more the narrator is presented as a distinct "I" within the story, the more he stands between us and other characters, making us detach our consciousness from the desire those characters would arouse. Furthermore, if we see other characters as functions of a narrator's consciousness they seem less independent and thus seem to have less power as actors; we see them more as objects and do not accept them as subjects as much as we otherwise would.

In addition to expressing detached awareness through narrators and characters, modernist writers express consciousness in other ways. The modern novel seems highly self-conscious in the emphasis it places on formal and thematic concerns, trying to elicit a self-conscious, critical response. As James puts it, he wishes fiction could make a "direct appeal to the intelligence."[12] Thus fiction becomes more negative, no longer primarily concerned with arousing our desires but rather seeking to restrain and rationalize imaginative energy, creating forms that enclose characters and teach them (and us) to see that reality opposes desire so we need to accept restraint. The work asks us to react against desire, forcing us to develop an ironic, detached awareness, not only through point of view but by creating complex formal relationships, asking us to remain aware of other parts of the work and of the relationships among parts rather than give ourselves up to a direct response to each detail as an end in itself. The more a novelist is concerned with the form of the whole work, the less he is likely to value local intensity.

We can see this concern with form in the modern treatment of character. Already in *Middlemarch,* character is seen not as something that can be fully revealed in particular details but as a gradual "process and an unfolding" (15.178)—that is, as a function of form, of the relationship of the work's parts. In James and Conrad too the form often calls for the gradual revelation of character. As James puts it in *The Portrait of a Lady,* a character's "sentiment" is "not so easily explained," since it is "so composite" that it requires "much time" to develop (2.42.189).[13] Thus characters are presented in a new way. Characters like Madame Merle and Nostromo do not cause an intense response at their first presentation, unlike most characters in earlier novels. Details of characterization are chosen not for their immediate effect but for their relation to other parts of the novel. As a result, the character's conflict is not experienced all at once but is diffused through the work, and so it becomes less intense. Tension exists primarily in ironic relationships among the novel's separate units rather than in compromise formations within its individual details. We must place more emphasis on our secondary response, consciously seeking out those relationships, rather than on our primary response to the desires and tensions characters induce.

Such a concern with form can produce characters of the kind

James calls "ficelles," characters who are "only of the form."[14] These characters exist not to arouse a response for themselves but rather to serve external requirements. Their traits and actions are primarily chosen to fulfill the needs of the work's form; they exist for the sake of their relation to other parts of the work. Thus the novelist leaves less room for the character to display tension free of external determinants, unlike earlier novelists whose form was largely based upon character, allowing such a display. The character is also likely to be simplified, given only those traits the form calls for, and so has less tension. If the character serves external demands, he is likely not to seem to contain the motive power that causes his actions. Much of our sense of character comes from feeling that the character has force and individuality because he originates action; this makes him seem to have desires seeking expression in action. If he seems like a puppet, we feel less force of character in him.

A similar danger arises if the novelist is more concerned with thematic requirements than with character. If the novelist makes the character a symbol (as in *Heart of Darkness*), the character again exists largely to serve external demands and is likely to be simplified (as Kurtz is) and to seem controlled by some force outside himself. E. M. Forster seems to have had some such difficulty with his characters in *Howards End*. The Wilcoxes and Leonard and Jacky were evidently created to embody certain ideas—capitalist materialism and its denial of the heart—and to serve a plot which seems dictated rather by Forster's sense of the way these abstractions interact than by the particular desires and tensions he has implied in his characters. The characters seem inconsistently related: it does not seem likely that Jacky would take both Leonard and Henry Wilcox for positive goal-characters. The desire implied by one object seems inconsistent with that implied by the other. Consequently I feel that Jacky is not so much a character (the locus of one particular desire) as an area in the plot where a character should be. Nor would both Margaret and Jacky be positive goal-characters for Henry and Leonard. These characters, then, arouse different desires in different parts of the novel, which makes us less willing to accept the desires they act for. Once Leonard, for example, has been defined for me as desiring the ideal that Margaret represents, I find it hard to accept him as a desirer of Jacky; I don't believe he is the same character in that relationship. I think we are less likely to accept a character's desire and thus his tension, as in this case, if the forces implied in him don't seem to be functions of each other but rather seem to belong to different characters.

Modern novelists not only shift much of the subject from the protagonist to a detached consciousness finding expression in a narrator and in formal manipulation of the work; they also tend to give increased expression to the subject throughout the work. The process of fragmenting the subject leads (as I have mentioned) to a gradual diffusion of the subject, locating partial manifestations of it in many places—for example, in other characters. The work as a whole rather than individual characters becomes the main focus of interest. The subject is no longer segregated in particular entities. Thus subject and object become less and less distinct from each other, just as conscious self-control becomes less separable from the desire it tries to take as an object and oppose. Insofar as the subject is an expression of consciousness trying to oppose desire, desire tends to be shifted to the object, so that the object tends to initiate more of the action. Object-characters thus become more like protagonists, partial expressions of the subject. As a result, the kind of comic object-character one finds in the novels of Fielding, Scott, and Dickens (though less so in Dickens), a character who lacks awareness and can be seen as an object, tends to be replaced by characters who exhibit much of the same consciousness one finds in the protagonist. Here again we can see this tendency in George Eliot. She starts chapter 29 of *Middlemarch* by suddenly and self-consciously shifting her "point of view" from Dorothea to Casaubon, demanding our "interest" and "effort at understanding" for Casaubon's "consciousness" because he too is "spiritually a-hungered" (p. 312). That is, she makes us see him as a subject, desiring spiritual fulfillment. We can no longer simply dismiss him as an object-character, someone we can dislike or mock because he opposes the protagonist's desires. He cannot reconcile his own desires with control, but this elicits sympathy rather than mockery, since controlling desire has become increasingly difficult—a problem George Eliot takes seriously, a problem her protagonists must face also. Later novelists often seem to convert their object-characters into partial subject-characters too, so that there are no simple villains or fools. Negative characters like Charles Gould in *Nostromo* and Henry Wilcox in *Howards End* are seen with some sympathy—that is, are allowed to have desires of their own, desires that we are induced partly to share. This diffusion of the subject function among the novel's characters tends to detract from our response to the protagonist, since other characters are competing with him for our sympathy. And less desire is located in the protagonist when desire is deflected among many characters. Diffusing desire in this way seems to weaken it. Object-characters like these do not fully replace a protagonist; they do not elicit as intense a response as in Dickens, for example. They have become partly like the modern protagonist, self-conscious and attempting to deal with their desires; so, as with the protagonist, their tension is muted, arousing a less intense response.

In the novels of Virginia Woolf we can find an especially clear example of many of the tendencies I have been describing, since she carried them to an extreme. Even more than the other writers I have discussed, she diffuses the subject's consciousness throughout her work, locating it in almost every character. As a result, the characters are often rather hard to tell apart; they lack much of the particularity they would have if seen as objects. Almost every character is a consciousness; we are constantly shown what that consciousness is aware of—a stream of sense impressions and inner voices. Woolf indicates in *To the Lighthouse* that she is not concerned with action, with "all the being and the doing," but rather with what she considers the real self, the inner depths that consciousness tries to perceive: "one shrunk ... to being oneself, a wedge-shaped core of darkness, something invisible to others." The social self (what is visible to others and interacts with them) is apparently not what matters. Instead of "the surface," mere "personality," Woolf seems concerned (like other modernists) with what is beneath it, "dark" and "unfathomably deep" (pp. 95–96).[15] Since this self is not expressed in action, the character as actor is largely replaced by an awareness like a narrator's trying to get at these inner depths. Even so, the self cannot be really expressed in words. It has apparently become so fragmented that we can no longer see the character as an entity, an object acting in an object-world; he has dissolved into a "mist" (p. 98), something "faint and flickering" (p. 205). Yet a character in a novel can only be presented through language. Thus one disadvantage of this concept of character is that it seeks to verbalize something it asserts cannot be verbalized. In practice, this attempt often seems to me to involve a falsification: trying to put the unconscious into words involves separating impulses that are probably inextricably combined within the self and putting into words feelings that we do not (probably cannot) fully put into words ourselves. When we do glimpse a Woolf character in action, he sometimes seems a different being, not clearly related to the consciousness we usually associate with his name. For example, there is a considerable "discrepancy" in Mrs. Ramsay's case between "what she was thinking" and "what she was doing" (p. 126). The external self is devalued; its actions seem trivial because they are unable to express the inner depths that matter. The inner desire for "some absolute good" is "alien to the processes of domestic life" (p. 199), and inner and outer cannot be reconciled. Instead, a character like Lily feels "violently two opposite things at the same time" (p. 154), and can only deal with this disintegration of self by being conscious of it. It is as if she is half character, desiring, and half narrator, self-aware. It seems that the subject-object conflict has been shifted almost entirely into the character, dividing her. There is little external conflict; there are no villains. Outer relationships are deemphasized, since the social self is not what matters most. Insofar as each character is a consciousness, he is separate from the others, existing in his own world, not interacting much with others, who are largely outside his particular narrative. The object-world thus loses importance. Instead the characters try to deal with an internal object. Each character is subject, desiring some sort of transcendence, and at the same time is the object that his consciousness is mainly concerned with. Or rather, the object is his own perceptions; the object-world has been replaced by its internalization in the character's sensations and thoughts. The object largely loses its objectivity and apartness; our interest is not in what is perceived but in the process of perception itself. It is his awareness—of time, of the world's randomness—that the character as desirer seeks to deal with. This blurring of the distinction between subject and object makes their conflict less intense. Dividing the character into conflicting parts makes him cease to seem an entity within which conflict exists. The conflicting units are separate, and the character seems to be replaced as agent by these fragments of him.

Of course the self-conscious fiction of modernism has its strengths. But we should not let these blind us to the advantages of the traditional novel. The classic English novelists may not be so aware of the depths of the self, but they are able to create intense conflicts through characterization. I think we can respond to those conflicts as deeply as we do to a more conscious presentation of inner depths. Though we may value the complexity of modern fiction, we should not underrate the skill of the great masters of traditional characterization.

notes

See "Works Cited," immediately following these notes, for full publishing information.

Introduction. Developing a Syncretic Criticism

    1. Steiner, *On Difficulty*, pp. 54–55. Steiner is disagreeing with the structuralists and Lacan; even so, he accepts the hypothesis of some minimal sort of structure, which is like what I am arguing for here.

    2. Harvey, *Character and the Novel*, pp. 11ff., 205, and passim; Paris, *A Psychological Approach to Fiction*, p. 4ff. and passim.

    3. Culler, *Structuralist Poetics*, p. 230.

    4. Frye, *Anatomy of Criticism*, pp. 106, 118–19, 136, 164, 199.

    5. Girard, *Deceit, Desire, and the Novel*.

    6. Bersani, *A Future for Astyanax*.

    7. See, for example, Wilden, "Lacan and the Discourse of the Other," p. 262; and Lacan, "The Insistence of the Letter in the Unconscious."

    8. Holland, *The Dynamics of Literary Response*, pp. 12, 27, and passim.

    9. Iser, *The Act of Reading*, pp. 35, 48, 89ff., 96ff., 119, and passim.

    10. Crews, "Anaesthetic Criticism," pp. 18–21, and *Out of My System*, pp. 170–71, 181–82.

11. Holland, *The Dynamics of Literary Response*, p. 27ff.

12. Essentially this same distinction has been made by Guerard, *The Triumph of the Novel*, pp. 20–21; by Iser, *The Act of Reading*, pp. 24–25, 150–51; and by Fish, "Literature in the Reader," p. 89.

13. Paris, *A Psychological Approach to Fiction*, pp. 1, 7ff., 14ff., 24, 28ff., and passim.

14. Other critics who hold that we should analyze the reader's response as it is guided by the text include Iser, *The Act of Reading*, pp. 21ff., 24ff., and passim; and Fish, "Literature in the Reader." This also resembles the approach taken by Paris, *A Psychological Approach to Fiction*, p. 1ff., when he speaks of analyzing the implied author. And in *The Dynamics of Literary Response*, Holland is mainly concerned with form.

15. Crews, "Anaesthetic Criticism," pp. 21–22, and *Out of My System*, p. 182, discusses this weakness in Freudian criticism and argues in favor of historical awareness.

Chapter 1. Character as a Function of a Basic Narrative Structure: The Linguistic Model

1. Todorov, *Grammaire du Décaméron*, pp. 85–87.

2. Propp, *Morphology of the Folktale*, p. 79ff.

3. On the relation of narrative to sentence structure, see Todorov, *Grammaire du Décaméron*, p. 24ff., *Littérature et signification*, p. 59ff., "Structuralism and Literature," pp. 165–66, and *The Fantastic*, p. 145; Barthes, "An Introduction to the Structural Analysis of Narrative," p. 239ff.; and Greimas, *Du Sens*, p. 168ff. Riffaterre, "The Reader's Perception of Narrative," p. 36, also theorizes that a text may be generated from a matrix sentence. Some structuralists hold that a text cannot be generated merely from the sentence; see Van Dijk, "On the Foundations of Poetics," pp. 92, 105. But the sentence seems to me more basic than any larger units; such units only appear much later in a child's learning process and thus probably develop out of the sentence.

4. See Piaget, *Play, Dreams, and Imitation in Childhood*, pp. 99, 131ff.

5. See McNeill, "Developmental Psycholinguistics," pp. 20ff., 63–64. Piaget and Inhelder, *The Psychology of the Child*, p. 85, hold that one-word sentences express perception, desire, or emotion; I would prefer to see emotion as a function of desire, a reaction to its fulfillment or frustration.

6. Frye, *Anatomy of Criticism*, p. 156.

7. Piaget, *The Language and Thought of the Child*, pp. 38, 231ff. This partial regression is discussed by Kris, *Psychoanalytic Explorations in Art*, pp. 26ff., 177ff., 197, 202; and by Holland, *The Dynamics of Literary Response*, p. 74ff.

8. Freud, *The Interpretation of Dreams*, 5.565–66, in *Complete Works*. Schilder, "Studies Concerning the Psychology and Symptomatology of General Paresis," pp. 527–28, theorizes that language originates in this process, expressing the child's desire to possess an object. Holland, *The Dynamics of Literary Response*, p. 73, holds that art uses this same process.

9. Todorov, *Grammaire du Décaméron*, p. 24 ff. Bremond, *Logique du Récit*, p. 112ff., criticizes this assumption that adjectives are basic.

10. Barthes, *S/Z*, pp. 67, 92–95, 191, discusses the way a name enables us to conceive of a character as an entity.

11. Greimas, *Sémantique structurale*, p. 173ff., makes a similar distinction between subject- and object-characters related by desire.

12. Winnicott, *Playing and Reality*, p. 13ff.; on pp. 38 and 100 he relates this play activity to creativity. Piaget, *Play, Dreams, and Imitation*, pp. 93–101, discusses the way play resembles language in substituting a symbol for the object; on pp. 167–68 he says that play avoids accommodation to reality, though symbolizing it. Poulet, "Phenomenology of Reading," p. 56ff., says that when we read we pronounce an "I" which is not the self.

13. The types of character I list here correspond to some extent to character types listed by various structuralists, although they usually fail to define characters in terms of their relation to a subject-character and thus do not distinguish between positive and negative characters. The goal-character corresponds to Propp's sought-for person (*Morphology of the Folktale*) and to the representative of the value sought mentioned by Souriau, *Les Deux Cent Mille Situations Dramatiques*, p. 86ff. The auxiliary character corresponds to Propp's helper, donor, and dispatcher; to Souriau's arbiter and accomplice (p. 101ff.); to the sender and aider mentioned by Greimas, *Sémantique Structurale*, p. 179; to the improver, protector, aider, rewarder, and neutralizer of obstruction mentioned by Bremond, *Logique du Récit*, p. 133; and to the contractor, tester, and judge listed by Scholes, *Structuralism in Literature*, p. 109. The negative object-characters correspond to Propp's villain and false hero, to Souriau's opponent (pp. 83ff., 94ff.), and Greimas's opposer and antisubject (pp. 178–79).

14. Frye, *Anatomy of Criticism*, p. 106.

Chapter 2. Character as a Function of Sublimation: The Psychological Model

1. Perhaps I should distinguish this model from the so-called generative structuralism of such writers as Zolkovskij and Sceglov; see their "Structural Poetics Is a Generative Poetics." They hold that literature is generated from a theme, but they neither define this theme adequately nor demonstrate it to be related to anything basic in the mind. I would say that a "theme" is itself a product of the generative process, a rationalization of

the way the work deals with the desires it arouses; that is, it is a function of secondary response (ours and the writer's).

2. For evidence on children's stories, see Pitcher and Prelinger, *Children Tell Stories,* especially their examples, p. 30ff.; and Leondar, "Hatching Plots: Genesis of Storymaking," p. 176ff.

3. Robert, *Origins of the Novel,* p. 21ff., discusses the Oedipal nature of the novel. For structuralist uses of Freud, see Barthes, *On Racine,* p. 9ff., and *The Pleasure of the Text,* p. 47; Greimas, *Sémantique structurale,* pp. 186ff., 221; and Todorov, *The Poetics of Prose,* p. 109.

4. See Wilden, "Lacan and the Discourse of the Other," p. 160ff.; Brenkman, "The Other and the One," p. 415ff.; and Jameson, "Imaginary and Symbolic in Lacan," p. 359ff. Harding, "Psychological Processes in the Reading of Fiction," p. 309ff., makes a related point, that fiction offers us not wish-fulfillment but a substitute for it.

5. Freud, *The Ego and the Id,* 19.29–34, in *Complete Works.* Bersani, *A Future for Astyanax,* pp. 5–10, discusses sublimation in novel characterization, though without clearly defining what he means.

6. See Segal, "A Psycho-Analytical Approach to Aesthetics," p. 386ff.; and Ehrenzweig, *The Hidden Order of Art,* pp. 102ff., 191ff.

7. Freud, "Creative Writers and Daydreaming," 9.151ff., in *Complete Works,* mentions that the writer splits his ego into components which personify conflicts in the self.

8. Klein, "On Identification," p. 309ff. Jacobson, *The Self and the Object World,* pp. 39–48, 69, discusses fantasies of merging with the love object and rejecting a negative version of it onto which one has projected aggression. Riviere, "The Unconscious Phantasy," p. 348ff., relates this kind of splitting to literature; and Bettelheim, *The Uses of Enchantment,* pp. 9, 67ff., discusses such splitting in fairy tales.

9. Freud, *The Ego and the Id,* pp. 29–30.

10. Frye, *Anatomy of Criticism,* pp. 158, 163–65, 172, 195–99, 216, describes good and bad fatherlike characters of this sort and discusses their Oedipal nature. However, Frye's categories don't coincide with mine, evidently because he is trying to include different kinds of narrative, and because he is not always defining characters in terms of basic plot functions. Girard, *Deceit, Desire, and the Novel,* pp. 8ff., 53ff., and passim, talks of a "mediator" of desire who may sometimes be equated with a repressive character who seeks to control the protagonist's desire, though sometimes his "mediator" seems to be a positive authority-figure whose approval the protagonist seeks.

11. Frye also describes villains of this sort; see, e.g., pp. 149, 196. Some other theorists distinguish between two kinds of villain, like those I discuss here; Propp, *Morphology of the Folktale,* lists a villain and a false hero, and Greimas, *Sémantique structurale,* pp. 178–79, lists an opposer and an

antisubject. Perhaps the distinction closest to mine is that of Barthes in *On Racine*, p. 10: between lust and authority.

12. Kermode, *The Sense of an Ending*, pp. 17–24, 56–58, 161, 164.

13. Withim, "The Psychodynamics of Literature," p. 560ff., discusses the way narrative can represent the interaction of psychic forces like this.

Chapter 3. The Novel as a Transformation of Basic Narrative Structure: The Historical Context

1. Frye, *The Secular Scripture*, p. 38; and see *Anatomy of Criticism*, pp. 51–52, 136–40.

2. For evidence on the kind of fiction popular before the novel, see Wright, *Middle-Class Culture*, pp. 84, 87–90, 96, 110–17, 375ff.; and Haviland, "The *Roman de Longue Haleine* on English Soil" pp. 9–10, 130ff.

3. On the increased importance of the father and the family, see Wright, *Middle-Class Culture*, pp. 201ff.; Ariès, *Centuries of Childhood*, p. 405ff.; Hill, *Society and Puritanism*, pp. 443ff., 461ff., 488, 501ff.; Pinchbeck and Hewitt, *Children in English Society*, 1.18–20, 42–43, 304–7; Hunt, *Parents and Children*, pp. 38–39; and Stone, *The Family, Sex and Marriage 1500–1800*, pp. 117, 150, 216–18, 653–56. Weinstein and Platt, *The Wish To Be Free*, pp. 3ff., 32ff., 145ff., and 105, theorize that the change in family structure involved a change in the father's role to a more punitive one which caused sons to rebel. Erikson, *Young Man Luther*, p. 49ff., discusses the influence on Luther's religious rebellion of his rebellion against his father, suggesting a possible model for the kind of change that took place in the minds of those who were attracted to Protestantism. Watt, in *The Rise of the Novel*, discusses the change in the family and the effect of parent-child conflicts on the novel (p. 138ff.) and the father's economic power over his children (p. 222ff.). And Robert, *Origins of the Novel*, pp. 17ff., 82ff., says that rebellion against the status quo is fundamental to the novel.

4. Watt, *The Rise of the Novel*, p. 60ff.

5. All citations are from the Penguin edition.

6. Frye, *Anatomy of Criticism*, pp. 33–34. Bersani, *A Future for Astyanax*, pp. 60, 66ff., also discusses the way realism weakens heroes and relates the hero's opposition to society to a conflict between desire and ways of controlling it.

7. For a discussion of Puritan self-discipline, see Weber, *The Protestant Ethic and the Spirit of Capitalism*, pp. 36, 156ff.; and Hill, *Society and Puritanism*, pp. 127ff., 219ff. Erikson, *Young Man Luther*, p. 73ff., suggests that Luther's preoccupation with the conscience internalized his father's severity.

8. Wright, *Middle-Class Culture*, pp. 1, 16ff., 43ff., 240, 549; and see Hill, *Society and Puritanism*, pp. 450, 496, 502; Pinchbeck and Hewitt, *Chil-*

dren in English Society, 1.36–37, 286, 293; and Hunt, *Parents and Children,* p. 34ff. Watt, *The Rise of the Novel,* pp. 197–200, discusses some of the effects of literacy on literature.

9. Hill, *Society and Puritanism,* pp. 454, 483ff., 501ff.

10. Trilling, *Sincerity and Authenticity,* pp. 11, 19ff., provides a good discussion of the internalization of control to develop an ego aware of itself. Alter, *Partial Magic,* pp. xff., 87, 98, 144, and passim, discusses the novel's self-consciousness, though he is mainly concerned with self-conscious narrators; I would say that the more typical and important manifestation of self-consciousness in the traditional novel is through characterization.

11. Ariès, *Centuries of Childhood,* pp. 128–29; and see Hunt, *Parents and Children,* pp. 33–35.

12. Brantlinger, "Romances, Novels, and Psychoanalysis," p. 19ff., discusses the way realism reacts against romance wish-fulfillment yet keeps romance elements. Lesser, *Fiction and the Unconscious,* p. 79ff., discusses the way fiction uses compromise formations. The use of such formations may be similar to the depolarization described by Kristeva in *Le texte du roman,* p. 56ff., and *Desire in Language,* pp. 47ff., 77ff. (I should perhaps admit, however, that I find Kristeva almost totally incomprehensible and cannot help suspecting that this is the effect she aims at.) Robert, *Origins of the Novel,* pp. 21ff., 38, 143, and passim, discusses the way the novel grows out of fantasies that express Oedipal desire, transforming them to make them more realistic.

13. Friedman, *The Turn of the Novel,* p. 11ff., describes the novel as composed of fictional units which are not closed so that they can join to form a process. Iser, *The Act of Reading,* pp. 111ff., 129, talks about how fictional units are indeterminate and therefore transitional.

14. Frye, *Anatomy of Criticism,* pp. 49ff., 105ff., 111ff., 136ff., 305, discusses realism as a way of restraining desire by displacing narrative away from romance. Kermode, *The Sense of an Ending,* p. 17ff. and passim, discusses a similar kind of displacement. Other good discussions of realism as a reaction against romance include Levin, *The Gates of Horn,* pp. 31–66; Scholes and Kellogg, *The Nature of Narrative,* pp. 15, 213; and Levine, *The Realistic Imagination,* p. 5ff., 12ff., 22, 40ff., 53ff., 70ff., 139. I disagree, however, with the assumption (in Levine, among others) that realism is basically a way of trying to perceive reality; in the novel, at least, I think it is rather a way of modifying narrative by reacting against desire, increasing the resistance to wish-fulfillment. Levine often uses terms like mine, but seems to confuse this idea of realism with realism as perception.

15. E. M. Forster, *Aspects of the Novel,* p. 26.

Chapter 4. Clarissa and the Transformation of Character

1. Hazlitt, "On Certain Inconsistencies in Sir Joshua Reynolds's Discourses," quoted by Taylor, "'Particular Character'," p. 169. Taylor provides much other evidence of the development of this new concept of character.

2. *Northanger Abbey,* 25.200. All citations of Jane Austen's works are from the Oxford edition.

3. Overbury, *The Overburian Characters,* p. 92.

4. Watt, *The Rise of the Novel,* p. 195, points out that Richardson was apparently the first person to use the word *personality* in its modern sense; and Brissenden, *Virtue in Distress,* p. 13ff., discusses the rise of a new vocabulary concerned with sensibility.

5. Watt, *The Rise of the Novel,* pp. 2–21, discusses Locke's influence on the novel; and McKillop, *Samuel Richardson,* p. 38, mentions the relationship of psychological fiction to empirical philosophy's concern with consciousness. Spacks, *Imagining a Self,* p. 2ff. and passim, discusses the eighteenth-century concern with identity.

6. Harvey, *Character and the Novel,* p. 24, talks about the way character becomes an end in itself in novels and relates this to middle-class individualism.

7. Swinden, *Unofficial Selves,* p. 209, sees character as a mixture of the subjective and objective; and Price, "The Logic of Intensity," p. 370, argues that novels combine external and internal views of character.

8. On the way characters cause and deal with tension, see Holland, *The Dynamics of Literary Response,* p. 274ff., and Iser, *The Implied Reader,* p. 279ff. Iser, p. 89ff., and Fish, "Literature in the Reader," pp. 71ff., 81, discuss ways that literature can go against our desires or expectations, though I think they place too much emphasis on secondary responses.

9. Richardson to Mrs. Watts, 9 April 1755, and to Lady Bradshaigh, 14 February 1754, quoted by Eaves and Kimpel, *Samuel Richardson,* p. 590.

10. *Clarissa,* 1.432; all quotations are from the Everyman edition.

11. *Selected Letters of Samuel Richardson,* pp. 64, 67, 167.

12. Harvey, *Character and the Novel,* p. 26, also holds that novelists have negative capability.

13. Sidney, *The Arcadia,* 1590 edition, 2.4.

14. *Clarissa,* 4.562; and *Selected Letters,* p. 289. One of the prefatory letters to the second edition of *Pamela,* Shakespeare Head edition, 1.xxi–xxii, discusses Richardson's use of a single word ("naughty"), which is a compromise formation, combining Pamela's partial rebellion against control (her "Disdain") with partial submission to it; Richardson's use of this letter indicates that he is quite conscious he is creating a new technique.

15. Richardson, *The History of Sir Charles Grandison,* 1.34; and *Selected Letters,* p. 64.

16. Fish, "Literature in the Reader," pp. 81–82, talks of a similar relation of the sentence to the work.

17. Holland, *The Dynamics of Literary Response,* p. 174ff.

Chapter 5. The Conflict between Character Intensity and Form: Richardson, Fielding, and Austen

1. *Selected Letters,* pp. 50, 167, 234–35.

2. Harvey, *Character and the Novel,* p. 23ff., says the novel existed to reveal and explore character.

3. This conflict between character and form is discussed by E. M. Forster, *Aspects of the Novel,* pp. 66–67; Scholes and Kellogg, *The Nature of Narrative,* pp. 80, 237; Harvey, *Character and the Novel,* p. 188; and Paris, *A Psychological Approach to Fiction,* pp. 4ff., 9. However, we shouldn't oversimplify this conflict. I don't think "realistic" characters are necessarily opposed to formal and thematic controls. Realism usually creates thematic meaning by showing how "reality" opposes desires; and realism usually exists as a function of form, modifying form by including more resistance to desire.

4. Lukács, *The Theory of the Novel,* pp. 60, 72–73, 80; and Ortega y Gasset, *The Dehumanization of Art,* p. 67. Levine, *The Realistic Imagination,* p. 22, describes realism as a process too.

5. Scholes and Kellogg, *The Nature of Narrative,* pp. 212, 232, 237. Harvey, *Character and the Novel,* pp. 133–34, distinguishes between novels that emphasize the self and those that emphasize the world.

6. Muir, *The Structure of the Novel,* pp. 23–27, points out this tendency.

7. Freud, "On Narcissism," 14.95–96, in *Complete Works,* discusses a similar division in the psyche.

8. Frye, *Anatomy of Criticism,* p. 34.

9. Booth, *The Rhetoric of Fiction,* pp. 276–78, 383, and Harvey, *Character and the Novel,* pp. 78–80, 133–34, discuss the relationship between character and point of view and the conflict between judgment and sympathy.

10. Watt, *The Rise of the Novel,* p. 296ff., discusses the way Austen reconciles these two traditions. Hardy, *A Reading of Jane Austen,* pp. 14–20, 35ff., also discusses this synthesis and talks of Austen's use of the unobtrusive narrator. Page, *The Language of Jane Austen,* p. 121ff., discusses her use of indirect speech, combining narrator's and character's viewpoints.

11. Several critics have pointed out aspects of this pattern. Gorer, "The Myth in Jane Austen," pp. 199, 202, talks about maternal persecution in Austen, though I think he overstates her approval of fathers; Harding,

"Regulated Hatred," pp. 360–61, discusses maternal failures in her work. Trilling, *The Opposing Self,* p. 226, points out that her fathers are usually weak. Duckworth, *The Improvement of the Estate,* p. 5, discusses the way parental failure makes her heroines self-reliant and disagrees (rightly, I think) with critics like Harding who feel parental failure leads rather to social alienation.

Chapter 6. Austen and the Conscious Character

1. E. M. Forster, *Aspects of the Novel,* pp. 67–78; Daiches, "Character," pp. 12–13; Bayley, *The Characters of Love,* pp. 34, 45, 384; Harvey, *Character and the Novel,* pp. 55–58; Scholes and Kellogg, *The Nature of Narrative,* pp. 98–102.

2. Wimsatt and Beardsley, *The Verbal Icon,* pp. 78–79, point out that consciousness is the basic principle in the round character.

3. Paris, *Character and Conflict,* pp. 96ff., 180, 199, discusses this aggressive side to Elizabeth and other Austen characters, though I think he overemphasizes it and makes it sound more positive than Austen feels it is; what Austen seems primarily concerned with is how one can deal with one's aggressiveness.

4. Page, *The Language of Jane Austen,* pp. 20, 103ff., 140ff., 146, talks about the way deviation from speech norms implies force of character in Austen's work.

5. Babb, *Jane Austen's Novels,* pp. 53–54, 132–39, 243–44, and passim, provides a good discussion of the way characters use forms of conversation to express feeling.

6. Booth, *The Rhetoric of Fiction,* pp. 245, 253–61, discusses the way Austen uses point of view to balance sympathy and judgment.

7. Some critics would disagree with this. Harding, "Regulated Hatred," p. 170ff., says that Austen opposes social control and desires superiority; and Mudrick, *Jane Austen,* pp. 1ff., 17, 36, 125, also says Austen opposes social control and values ironic wit which mocks it. Duckworth, *The Improvement of the Estate,* pp. 5ff., 23, 28, 118, 126, 132, provides what I think is a good argument against this position, discussing the way Austen accepts social control and opposes excessive individualism.

Chapter 7. Dickens and the Unresolved Character

1. Harvey, *Character and the Novel,* p. 58ff. McCarthy, "Characters in Fiction," pp. 287ff., 292, also offers some interesting comments on characters of this sort, finding complexity implied in their very inability to change; and see Muir, *The Structure of the Novel,* pp. 135–37, 142–44, on inner life in "flat" characters.

2. All references are to the *New Oxford Illustrated Dickens.* I have used the following abbreviations: *BH—Bleak House; DC—David Copperfield;*

DS—Dombey and Son; HT—Hard Times; LD—Little Dorrit; MC—Martin Chuzzlewit; OCS—The Old Curiosity Shop. Among the critics who have suggested that the "flat" mask of Dickens's characters implies that personality is suppressed beneath it are Miller, *Charles Dickens,* p. 90; Stoehr, *Dickens,* pp. 21–23; Frye, "Dickens and the Comedy of Humors," p. 77; Harvey, *Character and the Novel,* p. 71; Sucksmith, *The Narrative Art of Charles Dickens,* pp. 257–58; and Hardy, "The Complexity of Dickens," pp. 38–39, 43, 50–51. Critics often make the suppression of personality sound more serious and damaging than it actually seems in Dickens; Hardy comes closest to my own sense that his characters do not necessarily need pity.

3. Among the critics who have discussed the increased restraint in later Dickens are Trilling, *The Opposing Self,* pp. 63–64; and Hardy, "The Complexity of Dickens," pp. 36–37, 51.

4. For a discussion of the way Dickens characters become like objects, see Van Ghent, "The Dickens World," p. 419ff.

5. Marten, "Gestural Evil," p. 23, makes a similar point about outbursts relieving characters' frustrations; and Steig, "Dickens' Excremental Vision," pp. 345–46, talks about how the repressed energy of Dickens's characters can become explosive. Alter, *Fielding and the Nature of the Novel,* pp. 90–91, makes a similar observation about Squire Western.

6. Steig, "Dickens' Excremental Vision," pp. 339–54.

7. Stoehr, *Dickens,* pp. 77–78, discusses the way objects represent characters in Dickens.

8. Hardy, *Tellers and Listeners,* p. 166ff., discusses ways Dickens's characters use fictions. Miller, *Charles Dickens,* pp. 150–51, describes Micawber using role-playing to escape reality. Stewart, *Dickens and the Trials of the Imagination,* pp. xvii–xx, 85, 89, 105, 111–13, and passim, describes the way Sam Weller, Dick Swiveller, and others use imagination.

9. Among those who discuss parent-child relationships in Dickens are Lindsay, *Charles Dickens,* pp. 59–64, and Wilson, "Dickens on Children and Childhood," p. 208ff. Lucas, *The Melancholy Man,* p. 173ff., relates this concern to *Copperfield.*

10. Stoehr, *Dickens,* p. 168, describes such a pattern of repression and explosion in *Bleak House.*

11. Similar terms are discussed by Miller, pp. 149–50 (*fluidity* and *solidity*), and Moynahan, "Dealings with the Firm of Dombey and Son," pp. 124–26; but Dickens uses the image of softness much more often than that of wetness in discussing the heart.

12. Hardy, "The Complexity of Dickens," pp. 39–40, discusses the way Dickens creates intermediate characters. Kincaid, *Dickens and the Rhetoric of Laughter,* p. 32, makes a similar point about Sam Weller, as does Stewart, *Dickens and the Trials of the Imagination,* p. 89, about Sam and Dick Swiveller.

13. Orwell, *Dickens, Dali and Others,* p. 59ff.

14. Kincaid, *Dickens and the Rhetoric of Laughter,* pp. 79–82, discusses the way Dickens counterbalances pathos with laughter.

15. J. Forster, *The Life of Charles Dickens,* 1.19ff. This episode is similarly analyzed by Hutter, "Psycho-Analysis and Biography," p. 32ff., and Pratt, "Dickens and Father," p. 4ff.

16. Miller, *The Form of Victorian Fiction,* pp. 109–10, describes the way Dickens characters deal with their world through play.

Epilogue. The Decline of Character Intensity

1. This change in characterization is discussed by Bayley, *The Characters of Love,* passim, and "Character and Consciousness," pp. 225–35; Harvey, *Character and the Novel,* p. 135; and McCarthy, "Characters in Fiction," pp. 274ff., 290ff. McCarthy argues as I do that the subject-object distinction has become blurred in modern fiction.

2. Levine, *The Realistic Imagination,* p. 252ff., discusses a similar breakdown in late-Victorian thought.

3. Frye, *Anatomy of Criticism,* p. 34.

4. Levine, *The Realistic Imagination,* pp. 39, 47ff., discusses the increased subjectivity in late-Victorian fiction.

5. James, prefaces to *Roderick Hudson* and *The Princess Casamassima,* in *The Art of the Novel,* pp. 16, 62, 67; and letter to Mrs. Humphrey Ward, 1899, in *Theory of Fiction,* p. 155.

6. All citations are from the Viking edition.

7. *The Collected Letters of D. H. Lawrence,* p. 282.

8. Girard, *Deceit, Desire, and the Novel,* p. 16ff. and passim, talks of the way desire is made false in novels, though I think he overstates this because he excludes from consideration any novels that are not ironic. Friedman, *The Turn of the Novel,* pp. 20, 29ff., and passim, discusses a related failure of control in the modern novel.

9. Bersani, *A Future for Astyanax,* pp. 6–13, 67ff. Bersani relates this disintegration to the breakdown of sublimation. However, he seems to feel that the "destructuring" of character is good; I wish to point out that something is lost when it happens. Bersani seems to be as much the prisoner of a cultural myth as the traditional novelists he criticizes; his myth is that in "reality" character is not ordered—that it is disorder, not order, that is somehow authentic. This seems no more provable than its opposite, and seems unnecessarily prescriptive. Indeed, to attack narrative coherence is to attack the whole cultural enterprise by which the human mind has sought to make order of experience; and I do not see that modernist critics have a good alternative to offer to that enterprise.

10. E. M. Forster, "What I Believe," p. 68.

11. Lawrence, *Collected Letters,* p. 282.

12. James, preface to *The Portrait of a Lady*, in *The Art of the Novel*, p. 54.
13. All citations are from the Scribner's New York edition.
14. Ibid., pp. 53–55.
15. All citations are from the Harcourt, Brace edition.

works cited

Alter, Robert. *Fielding and the Nature of the Novel.* Cambridge, Mass.: Harvard University Press, 1968.
_____. *Partial Magic: The Novel as a Self-Conscious Genre.* Berkeley: University of California Press, 1975.
Ariès, Philippe. *Centuries of Childhood: A Social History of Family Life.* Translated by Robert Baldick. New York: Alfred A. Knopf, 1962.
Austen, Jane. *The Novels of Jane Austen.* Edited by R. W. Chapman. Oxford: Oxford University Press, 1923.
Babb, Howard S. *Jane Austen's Novels: The Fabric of Dialogue.* Columbus: Ohio State University Press, 1962.
Barthes, Roland. "An Introduction to the Structural Analysis of Narrative." *New Literary History* 6 (1974–75).
_____. *On Racine.* Translated by Richard Howard. New York: Octagon, 1977.
_____. *The Pleasure of the Text.* Translated by Richard Miller. New York: Hill and Wang, 1975.
_____. *S/Z.* Translated by Richard Miller. New York: Hill and Wang, 1974.
Bayley, John. "Character and Consciousness." *New Literary History* 5 (1974).
_____. *The Characters of Love: A Study in the Literature of Consciousness.* New York: Basic Books, 1960.

Bersani, Leo. *A Future for Astyanax: Character and Desire in Literature.* Boston: Little, Brown, 1976.

Bettelheim, Bruno. *The Uses of Enchantment: The Meaning and Importance of Fairy Tales.* New York: Alfred A. Knopf, 1976.

Booth, Wayne C. *The Rhetoric of Fiction.* Chicago: University of Chicago Press, 1961.

Brantlinger, Patrick. "Romances, Novels, and Psychoanalysis." In *The Practice of Psychoanalytic Criticism,* edited by Leonard Tennenhouse. Detroit: Wayne State University Press, 1976.

Bremond, Claude. *Logique du Récit.* Paris: Seuil, 1973.

Brenkman, John. "The Other and the One: Psychoanalysis, Reading, *The Symposium.*" *Yale French Studies* 55–56 (1977).

Brissenden, R. F. *Virtue in Distress: Studies in the Novel of Sentiment from Richardson to Sade.* New York: Barnes and Noble, 1974.

Crews, Frederick. "Anaesthetic Criticism." *Psychoanalysis and Literary Process,* edited by Frederick Crews. Cambridge: Winthrop, 1970.

———. *Out of My System: Psychoanalysis, Ideology, and Critical Method.* New York: Oxford University Press, 1975.

Culler, Jonathan. *Structuralist Poetics: Structuralism, Linguistics, and the Study of Literature.* Ithaca: Cornell University Press, 1975.

Daiches, David. *The Novel and the Modern World.* Chicago: University of Chicago Press, 1960.

Dickens, Charles. *The New Oxford Illustrated Dickens.* Oxford: Oxford University Press, 1947–59.

Duckworth, Alistair M. *The Improvement of the Estate: A Study of Jane Austen's Novels.* Baltimore: Johns Hopkins University Press, 1971.

Eaves, T. C. Duncan, and Ben D. Kimpel. *Samuel Richardson: A Biography.* London: Oxford University Press, 1971.

Ehrenzweig, Anton. *The Hidden Order of Art: A Study in the Psychology of the Artistic Imagination.* Berkeley: University of California Press, 1971.

Eliot, George. *Middlemarch.* Baltimore: Penguin, 1965.

Erikson, Erik H. *Young Man Luther: A Study in Psychoanalysis and History.* New York: W. W. Norton, 1962.

Fish, Stanley. "Literature in the Reader: Affective Stylistics." In *Reader Response Criticism: From Formalism to Post-Structuralism,* edited by Jane P. Tompkins. Baltimore: Johns Hopkins University Press, 1980.

Forster, E. M. *Aspects of the Novel.* New York: Harcourt, Brace and World, 1927.

———. "What I Believe." In *Two Cheers for Democracy.* New York: Harcourt, Brace, 1938.

Forster, John. *The Life of Charles Dickens.* 2 vols. London: Everyman, 1966.

Freud, Sigmund. *The Standard Edition of the Complete Works of Sigmund Freud.* Translated by James Strachey et al. London: Hogarth Press, 1953–74.

Friedman, Alan. *The Turn of the Novel.* New York: Oxford University Press, 1966.

Frye, Northrop. *Anatomy of Criticism: Four Essays.* Princeton: Princeton University Press, 1957.

———. "Dickens and the Comedy of Humors." In *Experience in the Novel: Selected Papers from the English Institute,* edited by Roy Harvey Pearce. New York: Columbia University Press, 1968.

———. *The Secular Scripture: A Study in the Structure of Romance.* Cambridge, Mass.: Harvard University Press, 1976.

Girard, René. *Deceit, Desire, and the Novel: Self and Other in Literary Structure.* Translated by Yvonne Freccero. Baltimore: Johns Hopkins University Press, 1965.

Gorer, Geoffrey. "The Myth in Jane Austen." *American Imago* 2 (1941).

Greimas, Algirdas Julien. *Du Sens: Essais Semiotiques.* Paris: Seuil, 1970.

———. *Sémantique Structurale: Recherche de méthode.* Paris: Larousse, 1966.

Guerard, Albert J. *The Triumph of the Novel: Dickens, Dostoevsky, Faulkner.* New York: Oxford University Press, 1976.

Harding, D. W. "Psychological Processes in the Reading of Fiction." In *Aesthetics in the Modern World,* edited by Harold Osborne. London: Thames and Hudson, 1968.

———. "Regulated Hatred: An Aspect of the Works of Jane Austen." *Scrutiny* 8 (1939–40).

Hardy, Barbara. "The Complexity of Dickens." In *Dickens 1970,* edited by Michael Slater. New York: Stein and Day, 1970.

———. *A Reading of Jane Austen.* New York: New York University Press, 1976.

———. *Tellers and Listeners: The Narrative Imagination.* London: Athlone Press, 1975.

Harvey, W. J. *Character and the Novel.* Ithaca: Cornell University Press, 1965.

Haviland, Thomas Philip. "The *Roman de Longue Haleine* on English Soil." Ph.D. diss., University of Pennsylvania, 1931.

Hill, Christopher. *Society and Puritanism in Pre-Revolutionary England.* New York: Schocken Books, 1964.

Holland, Norman N. *The Dynamics of Literary Response.* New York: Oxford University Press, 1968.

Hunt, David. *Parents and Children in History: The Psychology of Family Life in Early Modern France.* New York: Basic Books, 1970.

Hutter, Albert D. "Psycho-Analysis and Biography: Dickens' Experience at Warren's Blacking." *Hartford Studies in Literature* 8 (1976).

Iser, Wolfgang. *The Act of Reading: A Theory of Aesthetic Response.* Baltimore: Johns Hopkins University Press, 1978.

———. *The Implied Reader: Patterns of Communication in Prose Fiction from*

Bunyan to Beckett. Baltimore: Johns Hopkins University Press, 1974.
Jacobson, Edith. *The Self and the Object World.* New York: International Universities Press, 1964.
James, Henry. *The Art of the Novel: Critical Prefaces.* Edited by R. P. Blackmur. New York: Charles Scribner's Sons, 1934.
———. *The Portrait of a Lady.* New York: Charles Scribner's Sons, 1908.
———. *Theory of Fiction: Henry James.* Edited by James E. Miller, Jr. Lincoln: University of Nebraska Press, 1972.
Jameson, Fredric. "Imaginary and Symbolic in Lacan: Marxism, Psychoanalytic Criticism, and the Problem of the Subject." *Yale French Studies* 55–56 (1977).
Kermode, Frank. *The Sense of an Ending: Studies in the Theory of Fiction.* New York: Oxford University Press, 1967.
Kincaid, James R. *Dickens and the Rhetoric of Laughter.* London: Oxford University Press, 1971.
Klein, Melanie. "On Identification." In *New Directions in Psycho-Analysis,* edited by Melanie Klein, et al. New York: Basic Books, 1955.
Kris, Ernst. *Psychoanalytic Explorations in Art.* New York: International Universities Press, 1952.
Kristeva, Julia. *Desire in Language: A Semiotic Approach to Literature and Art.* Edited by Leon S. Roudiez. Translated by Thomas Gora et al. New York: Columbia University Press, 1980.
———. *Le Texte du roman: Approche sémiologique d'une structure discursive transformationelle.* Hague: Mouton, 1970.
Lacan, Jacques. "The Insistence of the Letter in the Unconscious." In *Structuralism,* edited by Jacques Ehrmann. Garden City, N.Y.: Doubleday, 1970.
———. *The Language of the Self: The Function of Language in Psychoanalysis.* Translated by Anthony Wilden. Baltimore: Johns Hopkins University Press, 1968.
Lawrence, D. H. *The Collected Letters of D. H. Lawrence.* Edited by Harry T. Moore. New York: Viking, 1962.
———. *Women in Love.* New York: Viking, 1960.
Leondar, Barbara. "Hatching Plots: Genesis of Storymaking." In *The Arts and Cognition,* edited by David Perkins et al. Baltimore: Johns Hopkins University Press, 1977.
Lesser, Simon O. *Fiction and the Unconscious.* New York: Random House, 1957.
Levin, Harry. *The Gates of Horn: A Study of Five French Realists.* New York: Oxford University Press, 1963.
Levine, George. *The Realistic Imagination: English Fiction from Frankenstein to Lady Chatterley.* Chicago: University of Chicago Press, 1981.
Lindsay, Jack. *Charles Dickens: A Biography and Critical Study.* London:

Andrew Dakers, 1950.
Lucas, John. *The Melancholy Man: A Study of Dickens's Novels*. New York: Barnes and Noble, 1980.
Lukács, Georg. *The Theory of the Novel: A Historico-philosophical Essay on the Forms of Great Epic Literature*. Translated by Anna Bostock. Cambridge: M.I.T. Press, 1971.
McCarthy, Mary. "Characters in Fiction." In *On the Contrary*. New York: Farrar, Straus, and Cudahy, 1951.
McKillop, Alan Dugald. *Samuel Richardson: Printer and Novelist*. Chapel Hill: University of North Carolina Press, 1936.
McNeill, David. "Developmental Psycholinguistics." In *The Genesis of Language: A Psycholinguistic Approach*, edited by Frank Smith et al. Cambridge: M.I.T. Press, 1966.
Marten, Harry. "Gestural Evil: Techniques of Characterization in Dickens' Early Work." *Ball State University Forum* 17, no. 4 (Autumn 1976).
Miller, J. Hillis. *Charles Dickens: The World of His Novels*. Cambridge: Harvard University Press, 1958.
—————. *The Form of Victorian Fiction*. Notre Dame: University of Notre Dame Press, 1968.
Moynahan, Julian. "Dealings with the Firm of Dombey and Son: Firmness *versus* Wetness." In *Dickens and the Twentieth Century*, edited by John Gross et al. London: Routledge and Kegan Paul, 1962.
Mudrick, Marvin. *Jane Austen: Irony as Defense and Discovery*. Berkeley: University of California Press, 1968.
Muir, Edwin. *The Structure of the Novel*. London: Hogarth Press, 1928.
Ortega y Gasset, José. *The Dehumanization of Art and other Essays on Art, Culture, and Literature*. Translated by Helen Weyl. Princeton: Princeton University Press, 1968.
Orwell, George. *Dickens, Dali, and Others*. New York: Harcourt, Brace and World, 1946.
Overbury, Sir Thomas. *The Overburian Characters*. Edited by W. J. Paylor. Oxford: Basil Blackwell, 1936.
Page, Norman. *The Language of Jane Austen*. New York: Barnes and Noble, 1972.
Paris, Bernard J. *Character and Conflict in Jane Austen's Novels: A Psychological Approach*. Detroit: Wayne State University Press, 1978.
—————. *A Psychological Approach to Fiction: Studies in Thackeray, Stendahl, George Eliot, Dostoevsky, and Conrad*. Bloomington: Indiana University Press, 1974.
Piaget, Jean. *The Language and Thought of the Child*. Translated by Marjorie and Ruth Gabain. New York: Humanities Press, 1959.
—————. *Play, Dreams, and Imitation in Childhood*. Translated by C. Gattegno et al. New York: W. W. Norton, 1962.

Piaget, Jean, and Barbel Inhelder. *The Psychology of the Child.* Translated by Helen Weaver. New York: Basic Books, 1969.

Pinchbeck, Ivy, and Margaret Hewitt. *Children in English Society.* Toronto: University of Toronto Press, 1969.

Pitcher, Evelyn Goodenough, and Ernst Prelinger. *Children Tell Stories: An Analysis of Fantasy.* New York: International Universities Press, 1963.

Poulet, Georges. "Phenomenology of Reading." *New Literary History* 1 (1969).

Pratt, Branwen Bailey. "Dickens and Father: Notes on the Family Romance." *Hartford Studies in Literature* 8 (1976).

Price, Martin. "The Logic of Intensity: More on Character." *Critical Inquiry* 2 (1975).

Propp, V. *Morphology of the Folktale.* Translated by Laurence Scott. Austin: University of Texas Press, 1968.

Richardson, Samuel. *Clarissa or, The History of a Young Lady.* London: Everyman, 1932.

———. *The History of Sir Charles Grandison.* Edited by Jocelyn Harris. London: Oxford University Press, 1972.

———. *Pamela.* Shakespeare Head Edition, 4 vols. Oxford: Basil Blackwell, 1929.

———. *Selected Letters of Samuel Richardson.* Edited by John Carroll. London: Oxford University Press, 1964.

Riffaterre, Michael. "The Reader's Perception of Narrative: Balzac's *Paix du ménage.*" In *Interpretation of Narrative*, edited by Mario J. Valdés et al. Toronto: University of Toronto Press, 1978.

Riviere, Joan. "The Unconscious Phantasy of an Inner World Reflected in Examples from Literature." In *New Directions in Psycho-Analysis,* edited by Melanie Klein et al. New York: Basic Books, 1955.

Robert, Marthe. *Origins of the Novel.* Translated by Sacha Rabinovitch. Bloomington: Indiana University Press, 1980.

Schilder, Paul. "Studies Concerning the Psychology and Symptomatology of General Paresis." In *Organization and Pathology of Thought: Selected Sources,* edited by David Rapaport. New York: Columbia University Press, 1951.

Scholes, Robert. *Structuralism in Literature: An Introduction.* New Haven: Yale University Press, 1974.

Scholes, Robert, and Robert Kellogg. *The Nature of Narrative.* New York: Oxford University Press, 1966.

Segal, Hanna. "A Psycho-Analytical Approach to Aesthetics." In *New Directions in Psycho-Analysis,* edited by Melanie Klein et al. New York: Basic Books, 1955.

Souriau, Etienne. *Les Deux Cent Mille Situations Dramatiques.* Paris: Flammarion, 1950.

Spacks, Patricia Meyer. *Imagining a Self: Autobiography and Novel in Eighteenth-century England.* Cambridge: Harvard University Press, 1976.
Steig, Michael. "Dickens' Excremental Vision." *Victorian Studies* 13 (1969-70).
Steiner, George. *On Difficulty and Other Essays.* Oxford: Oxford University Press, 1978.
Stewart, Garrett. *Dickens and the Trials of Imagination.* Cambridge: Harvard University Press, 1974.
Stoehr, Taylor. *Dickens: The Dreamer's Stance.* Ithaca: Cornell University Press, 1965.
Stone, Laurence. *The Family, Sex and Marriage 1500-1800.* New York: Harper and Row, 1977.
Sucksmith, Harvey Peter. *The Narrative Art of Charles Dickens: The Rhetoric of Sympathy and Irony in his Novels.* London: Oxford University Press, 1970.
Swinden, Patrick. *Unofficial Selves: Character in the Novel from Dickens to the Present Day.* New York: Barnes and Noble, 1973.
Taylor, Houghton W. "'Particular Character': An Early Phase of a Literary Evolution." *PMLA* 60 (1945).
Todorov, Tzvetan. *The Fantastic: A Structural Approach to a Literary Genre.* Translated by Richard Howard. Cleveland: Case Western Reserve University, 1973.
――――. *Grammaire du Décaméron.* Hague: Mouton, 1969.
――――. *Littérature et signification.* Paris: Larousse, 1967.
――――. *The Poetics of Prose.* Translated by Richard Howard. Ithaca: Cornell University Press, 1977.
――――. "Structuralism and Literature." In *Approaches to Poetics,* edited by Seymour Chatman. New York: Columbia University Press, 1973.
Trilling, Lionel. *The Opposing Self: Nine Essays in Criticism.* New York: Viking, 1955.
――――. *Sincerity and Authenticity.* Cambridge: Harvard University Press, 1972.
Van Dijk, Teun A. "On the Foundations of Poetics: Methodological Prolegomena to a Generative Grammar of Literary Texts." *Poetics* 5 (1972).
Van Ghent, Dorothy. "The Dickens World: A View from Todgers's." *Sewanee Review* 58 (1950).
Watt, Ian. *The Rise of the Novel.* Berkeley: University of California Press, 1957.
Weber, Max. *The Protestant Ethic and the Spirit of Capitalism.* Translated by Talcott Parsons. London: George Allen and Unwin, 1930.
Weinstein, Fred, and Gerald M. Platt. *The Wish To Be Free: Society, Psyche, and Value Change.* Berkeley: University of California Press, 1969.

Wilden, Anthony. "Lacan and the Discourse of the Other." In Jacques Lacan, *The Language of the Self: The Function of Language in Psychoanalysis*. Translated by Anthony Wilden. Baltimore: Johns Hopkins University Press, 1968.

Wilson, Angus. "Dickens on Children and Childhood." In *Dickens 1970*, edited by Michael Slater. New York: Stein and Day, 1970.

Wimsatt, W. K., Jr., and Monroe C. Beardsley. *The Verbal Icon: Studies in the Meaning of Poetry*. Lexington: University of Kentucky Press, 1954.

Winnicott, D. W. *Playing and Reality*. London: Tavistock, 1971.

Withim, Philip. "The Psychodynamics of Literature." *Psychoanalytic Review* 56 (1969–70).

Woolf, Virginia. *To the Lighthouse*. New York: Harcourt, Brace, 1927.

Wright, Louis B. *Middle-Class Culture in Elizabethan England*. Ithaca: Cornell University Press, 1958.

Zolkovskij, A. K., and J. K. Sceglov. "Structural Poetics Is a Generative Poetics." In *Soviet Semiotics*. Edited and translated by Daniel P. Lucid. Baltimore: Johns Hopkins University Press, 1977.

index

Adam Bede: Arthur Donnithorne, 32, 47
Ambassadors, The, 168, 176
Ariès, Philippe, 42–43, 54
Austen, Jane: attitude toward control, 59, 96–97, 173, 190–91 n. 11, 191 n. 3; compared to Dickens, 123, 141; compared to Fielding and Richardson, 95–96; compared to modernists, 169, 173; concept of character in, 63–64, 170; form in, 84, 145; object-characters in, 51–52, 58; point of view in, 71, 95–96, 175, 176; protagonists in, 38, 62. *See also Emma; Mansfield Park; Northanger Abbey; Pride and Prejudice*

Bayley, John, 99
Beowulf, 35, 37, 38
Bersani, Leo, 7, 173, 193 n. 9
Bleak House, 51, 151–52, 167; Ada, 145; Allan Woodcourt, 155; Caddy Jellyby, 155, 160; Esther Summerson, 150, 155; Grandfather Smallweed, 154; Jarndyce, 143; Jo, 144; Krook, 147; Mrs. Snagsby, 131; Prince Turveydrop, 155; Richard Carstone, 47, 145
Bradley, A. C., 3
Brontë, Charlotte: *Jane Eyre*, 30, 31
Brontë, Emily, 101; *Wuthering Heights*, 46, 47, 62, 122
Bunyan, John: *Pilgrim's Progress*, 66

Calvin, John, 49
Canterbury Tales. *See* Chaucer, Geoffrey
Cervantes, Miguel: *Don Quixote*, 45, 48, 50, 56–57, 62, 79, 94
Character: concept of, 64–66
—kinds of: conscious, 100–102; externally determined, 178; "flat," 99–101, 121–22, 127; with inner conflict, 62–64, 81, 98; negative object-, 20–21, 30–32 (rebellious, 31–32; repressive, 31); object-, 20–22; positive object-, 20, 28–30 (auxiliary, 20, 29–30; goal-, 20, 28–29);

203

204   Index

"round," 99–101, 121–22; simple plot-function, 13–14, 16, 121; subject-, 17–19, 33–35 (negative, 61, 76; positive, 61, 76); type-, 65; unresolved, 121–26
—in novel, 60–64, 66–69, 71–74, 81, 83, 91–93, 99
Chaucer, Geoffrey: *Canterbury Tales*, 54, 66
Children: language of, 14–16, 18; stories of, 24, 25–26
Chomsky, Noam. *See* Linguistic theory
Clarissa
—Anna Howe, 33, 76–77, 79, 81, 85, 96
—Clarissa: compared to Elizabeth Bennet, 103ff.; compared to romance heroine, 48, 55; conflict in, 60–61, 66–68, 71, 74–80; defensive, 34; rebelliousness in, 35, 37, 42, 87; response to, 82; self-control of, 49, 65, 87; unresolved, 122, 126
—compared to *Pride and Prejudice*, 103ff.
—as compromise formation, 53, 56–57, 59
—epistolary form, 80
—Harlowe family, 31, 42
—Lovelace: conflict in, 66, 81; as negative protagonist, 61, 85; as rebellious villain, 32, 34, 38, 47, 71, 87, 123
—as modification of romance, 41–42, 44, 45, 55–57
—Morden, 84
—negative object-characters, 32–33, 42–43, 45–47, 57, 87
—progressive form, 57
—Solmes, 31, 113, 125
Coleridge, Samuel Taylor, 69
Compromise formations, 53–54; absence of, in romance characterization, 73; in novel, 54–59, 71–72, 85–86, 169, 189 n. 14; in novel characterization, 60–62, 72–74, 75–81, 102, 104, 107
Conrad, Joseph, 176, 177. *See also Heart of Darkness*; *Nostromo*; *Youth*
Crews, Frederick, 8
Cromwell, Oliver, 49, 53
Culler, Jonathan, 4

Daiches, David, 99
Daniel Deronda, 165, 166
David Copperfield
—Agnes Wickfield, 143, 144; motherlike, 147, 152; representing submission, 29, 47, 157
—Annie Strong, 29, 157
—Barkis, 129, 138, 140
—Betsey Trotwood, 30, 130–31, 143, 147, 159
—climax in, 147
—Creakle, 132, 143
—David Copperfield, 35, 144, 150, 153; relation of, to other characters, 156–57, 159
—and Dicken's autobiography, 161–62
—Dr. Strong, 153
—Dora, 147, 150, 156
—Emily, 145, 156, 157
—Jack Maldon, 150
—Jip, 137
—kinds of character in, 91
—Micawber: conflict in, 130, 133, 135, 137, 139–40; fatherlike, 46, 141–42, 147, 161–62; as intermediate character, 148, 157; relation of, to protagonist, 150, 159–60
—Miss Mowcher, 140
—Miss Murdstone, 129
—Mr. Dick, 130–32, 157
—Mr. Peggotty, 30, 156
—Mr. Wickfield, 156, 159
—Mrs. Micawber, 137
—Murdstone, 31, 141, 143, 147, 154
—Peggotty, 130, 132–33
—point of view, 151
—Rosa Dartle, 131, 134, 135, 136
—Steerforth, 47, 145; rebellious, 32, 147, 150; relation of, to protagonist, 52, 153, 156, 157
—sublimating control, 51, 52
—Traddles, 139, 156
—Uriah Heep: conflict in, 130, 136; rebellious, 139, 144, 153, 159; relation of, to protagonist, 150, 156
Defoe, Daniel, 45, 50, 56–57, 65; *Moll Flanders*, 45, 56; *Robinson Crusoe*, 45, 56
Dialogue in the novel, 86, 106–7
Dickens, Charles, 47, 71; characterization in, 121–63, 176, 192 n. 2; com-

pared with Austen, 110; compared with Fielding and Richardson, 97; object-characters in, 66, 67, 84, 88, 91; subject-characters in, 34, 63. *See also Bleak House; David Copperfield; Dombey and Son; Great Expectations; Hard Times; Little Dorrit; Martin Chuzzlewit; Old Curiosity Shop; Oliver Twist; Our Mutual Friend; Pickwick Papers; Tale of Two Cities*

Doctor Faustus. See Marlowe, Christopher

Dombey and Son, 52, 148
—Bagstock, 134
—Bunsby, 138
—Captain Cuttle, 130, 139–40, 141–42
—Carker: conflict in, 131, 134; as rebellious villain, 33, 144, 145, 153
—Dombey: conflict in, 128, 138; as repressive villain, 33, 46, 141; transformation of, 146, 148
—Edith, 145
—Florence Dombey, 142, 148, 150, 152, 161
—Game Chicken, 143
—Mr. Toots, 125; conflict in, 129–30, 131, 132, 136, 137; relation of, to form, 142–43, 154, 158
—Mrs. Chick, 135
—Paul Dombey, 144
—Susan Nipper, 137
—Walter Gay, 143, 152

Don Quixote. See Cervantes, Miguel

Dostoevsky, Fyodor, 101

Eliot, George: form in, 84, 120; inside view of characters in, 170–71, 174; point of view in, 175–76; sympathy with characters in, 47, 58. *See also Adam Bede; Daniel Deronda; Middlemarch; Mill on the Floss*

Emma, 29

Evans, Mary Ann. *See* Eliot, George

Fairy tales, 35; "Cinderella," 20, 21; "Little Red Riding Hood," 16

Fielding, Henry, 58, 84; compared with Austen, 95–96, 97, 111–12, 116–17, 119; compared with Dickens, 126, 151; compared with Richardson, 89–93; point of view in, 38, 93, 175–76; response to, 109; unresolved characters, 121–22, 179. *See also Jonathan Wild; Joseph Andrews; Tom Jones*

Form in the novel: in modernism, 177–79; progressive, 57, 71–72; in relation to character, 84, 87–89; as search for ideal control, 51, 55. *See also* Plot

Forster, E. M., 58, 99–101, 121, 127, 173; *Howards End*, 178, 179; *Passage to India*, 30, 168

French novel, 54

Freud, Sigmund, 168. *See also* Freudian theory

Freudian theory, 9–10, 15; and Austen, 97; and Dickens, 133, 156, 161–62; ego and superego, 24, 28, 29–30, 34, 40–41, 52, 53, 69, 168–69; limits of, 8, 10; Oedipus complex in narrative, 24ff., 36, 43, 49, 97, 156, 161–62; and response, 7–9; in relation to structuralism, 5–7. *See also* Lacan, Jacques; Klein, Melanie; Sublimation

Frye, Northrop, 2, 186 n. 10; on desire in narrative, 6, 15, 21; on displacement of narrative, 3, 10, 11, 40; on kinds of narrative, 26, 48, 94, 167

Girard, René, 6–7, 186 n. 10, 193 n. 8

Grand Cyrus, The, 40

Great Expectations, 62, 145, 151; Estella, 48; Miss Havisham, 141, 146, 154; Pip, 153; Wemmick, 130, 133

Greimas, Algirdas Julien, 2, 14

Hard Times, 52; Gradgrind, 141; Louisa Gradgrind, 136

Hardy, Thomas, 167, 174–75; *Mayor of Casterbridge*, 174; *Tess of the D'Urbervilles*, 166

Harvey, W. J., 3, 99, 122

Hazlitt, William, 62

Heart of Darkness, 167, 172, 175; Kurtz, 32, 172, 178

206   Index

Heart of Midlothian. See Scott, Walter
Hill, Christopher, 50
Holland, Norman, 7, 8–9, 82
Howards End. See Forster, E. M.

Iser, Wolfgang, 7–8, 9

James, Henry, 120, 164, 168, 171, 177–78. *See also Ambassadors, The; Portrait of a Lady*
Jane Eyre. See Brontë, Charlotte
Jonathan Wild, 35
Joseph Andrews, 93; Joseph Andrews, 96; Lady Booby, 92, 125; Parson Adams, 92, 122, 125; Parson Trulliber, 122
Joyce, James, 164, 168, 175. *See also Portrait of the Artist as a Young Man*

Keats, John, 69–70, 125
Kermode, Frank, 11, 37, 55
Klein, Melanie, 6, 26–28

Lacan, Jacques, 7, 24–25
Lawrence, D. H., 168, 171–72, 174; *Women in Love*, 171–72, 174
Levin, Harry, 11, 58
Levine, George, 11, 188 n. 14
Linguistic theory and narrative, 3, 14–17, 23. *See also* Structuralist theory of narrative
Little Dorrit: Chivery, 128; Flintwinch, 132, 136; Flora Finching, 128, 135, 137, 148; Frederick Dorrit, 142; Merdle, 146; Miss Wade, 127; Mr. Dorrit, 142, 146; Mrs. Clennam, 129, 131–32, 134, 136, 141, 146, 154; Pancks, 132, 135
Locke, John, 65
Lukács, Georg, 89

Macbeth, 45
Mansfield Park, 33; Mrs. Norris, 31, 97
Marlowe, Christopher: *Doctor Faustus*, 44–45, 50, 65, 73
Martin Chuzzlewit: Anthony Chuzzlewit, 142; Bailey, 145; Chuffey, 142; Martin Chuzzlewit, 153; Mrs. Gamp, 66–67, 88, 135, 138, 140, 145, 148, 158, 162; Pecksniff, 154
Mayor of Casterbridge. See Hardy, Thomas
Meredith, George, 175
Middlemarch, 173
—Bulstrode, 126, 176
—Caleb Garth, 30
—Casaubon, 46, 126; inside view of, 170, 176, 179; negative goal-character, 31, 48, 166
—Celia, 33
—concept of character in, 177
—Dorothea: compared to Clarissa, 52, 66; conscious character, 176; limited by society, 58, 168; self-control, 52, 62–63
—Farebrother, 29, 30
—Fred Vincy, 48, 165
—fulfillment limited in, 58, 167, 168
—Lydgate, 29, 63, 165, 176
—point of view in, 175–76, 179
—romance and realism in, 165, 166
—Rosamond Vincy, 32, 33, 48, 166
—Will Ladislaw, 48, 52, 166
Mill on the Floss, 62; Maggie Tulliver, 33, 47, 62; Mr. Tulliver, 46
Milton, John: *Paradise Lost*, 50; Satan, 45
Moll Flanders. See Defoe, Daniel
Music: compared to character, 70

Names in fiction, 16, 19, 129
Narrative: compared to lyric, 22; sublimating, defined, 25–26. *See also* Children, stories of; Fairy tales; Novel; Rogue tale; Romance
Northanger Abbey, 63, 115
Nostromo, 166, 167; Captain Mitchell, 126; Charles Gould, 179; Mrs. Gould, 168; Nostromo, 35, 174, 177
Novel: modernist, 164–82; rise of, 11, 41–42, 50; two kinds of, 89–91, 99. *See also* Character; Compromise formations; Form; Point of view; Plot; Romance; Sublimation

Old Curiosity Shop: Dick Swiveller, 91, 140, 159–60
—Kit Nubbles, 134, 136
—Marchioness, 159–60
—Nell, 91, 150, 160; represents heart, 144, 159; virtuous submission of, 34, 37, 152–53, 161
—Quilp, 125, 129, 159; as rebellious villain, 32, 34, 37, 143, 144, 153
—Sally Brass, 159–60
Oliver Twist, 142; Fagin, 142, 154
Ortega y Gasset, José, 89
Orwell, George, 156
Othello, 35; Desdemona, 35; Iago, 32, 45; Othello, 35
Our Mutual Friend, 149; Boffin, 30; Podsnap, 154; Wegg, 129
Overbury, Sir Thomas, 64, 65–66

Pamela, 45, 87
Paradise Lost. *See* Milton, John
Paris, Bernard J., 3, 9
Passage to India. *See* Forster, E. M.
Piaget, Jean, 15
Pickwick Papers: Pickwick, 30; Sam Weller, 122, 125, 148, 154
Pilgrim's Progress. *See* Bunyan, John
Plot: and conscious character, 110–16; in modernist novel, 167; in novel, 57–58; in relation to character, 85–87, 88, 91; in sublimating narrative, 26–27, 35–37; and unresolved character, 141–51, 152–57, 160. *See also* Form
Point of view, 19–20, 35, 86, 90, 93–96; and conscious character, 117–19; in modernist novel, 175–77, 179; and unresolved character, 151–52
Portrait of a Lady, 51, 84, 166, 168, 177; Henrietta Stackpole, 126; Isabel Archer, 173; Madame Merle, 177
Portrait of the Artist as a Young Man: Stephen Dedalus, 168, 174
Pride and Prejudice, 30, 33, 64
—Bingley, 104, 117
—Charlotte Lucas, 113, 115–16
—Collins, 31, 126; represents extreme submission, 108, 113, 125; and social control, 115, 117
—Darcy, 108–9, 116; represents control, 47, 113, 114, 115; represents society, 96, 102, 104, 117
—Elizabeth Bennet: compared with Clarissa, 104ff.; compared with modernist protagonists, 173; learns restraint, 33, 66, 95, 101–19; resists control, 35, 47, 96, 104–5
—Gardiners, 115
—Jane Bennet, 102, 108, 109, 113–17; compared to Elizabeth, 103ff.
—Lady Catherine de Bourgh, 108, 113, 115, 117
—Lydia Bennet, 33, 106, 113, 116–17, 125
—Miss Bingley, 115
—Mr. Bennet, 46
—Mrs. Bennet, 46, 97, 106, 107, 113, 115
—Wickham, 115, 116; as diminished villain, 106, 112, 113; as negative goal-character, 31, 110; as rebellious villain, 47, 104, 108, 113, 114, 117
Propp, Vladimir, 2, 13, 14

Reader response, 7–10; to characterization, 67–69, 81–82; to conscious character, 109–10; to form, 88–89; to modernist fiction, 169–72, 174–80; to object-character, 21; primary and secondary, 8–9, 12, 164; to subject-character, 17–19; to unresolved character, 124–25
Realism, 11, 58, 121; "realistic" character, 99, 190 n. 3
Richardson, Samuel, 42, 80; characterization in, 74–80, 123; character's relation to form in, 84–88; compared with Austen, 95–96, 97, 112, 116, 119; compared with Dickens, 124–25, 126, 149, 151, 158; compared with Fielding, 89–93; compared with modernists, 169–70; point of view in, 70–71, 90; suspension of restraint in, 68–71, 83. *See also Clarissa*; *Pamela*
Robinson Crusoe. *See* Defoe, Daniel
Rogue tale, 24, 26, 50
Romance, 35, 48; baroque, 40–41, 44, 47, 53, 85; characterization in, 72–73; desire in, 24–25; naïve, 26; novel

as displacement of, 11, 41–42, 44, 45–48, 52–59, 61–62, 63, 71–72, 74, 115, 117, 165
Romantic poetry, 50, 69–70

Scholes, Robert, and Robert Kellogg, 89, 99
Scott, Walter, 91, 121, 179; *Heart of Midlothian*, 46
Shakespeare, William, 1, 62, 74, 121. *See also Macbeth*; *Othello*
Shelley, Percy Bysshe, 70
Sidney, Sir Philip, 73
Social influence: on concept of character, 64–65; on literature, 10, 23–24, 39–40; on modernist fiction, 166–67; on Renaissance literature, 50; on the rise of the novel, 11, 40–45
Steig, Michael, 133
Steiner, George, 3
Sterne, Laurence: *Tristram Shandy*, 47, 88; Uncle Toby, 125; Walter Shandy, 46
Structuralist theory of narrative, 2–5, 13–16, 184 n. 3, 185–86 n. 1
Style: in relation to structure, 80; in Richardson's characterization, 74–75
Sublimation: in Dickens, 141–42, 146, 147–48, 156, 157, 160–61, 162–63; modified in the novel, 41ff., 51, 52, 54, 55–56, 58, 61, 70, 85, 89, 163, 165–67, 169, 175; in narrative, 25–30, 31–34, 35–37; in romance, 40

Tale of Two Cities, 147
Tess of the D'Urbervilles. *See* Hardy, Thomas
Thackeray, William Makepeace, 94, 175. *See also Vanity Fair*
Todorov, Tzvetan, 2, 13, 14, 15–16
Tom Jones, 30, 32, 34, 51, 93; Allworthy, 30, 34, 46, 96; Blifil, 32, 33, 34; Tom Jones, 29, 30, 32, 34, 91, 129; Sophia Western, 29, 32, 47
To the Lighthouse. *See* Woolf, Virginia
Tristram Shandy. *See* Sterne, Laurence

Vanity Fair: Amelia, 48, 63; Becky Sharp, 35, 63, 94; Jos Sedley, 125

Watt, Ian, 11, 44
Winnicott, D. W., 18
Women in Love. *See* Lawrence, D. H.
Woolf, Virginia, 168, 173, 180–81; *To the Lightouse*, 180–81
Wordsworth, William, 70
Wright, Louis B., 49
Wuthering Heights. *See* Brontë, Emily

Youth, 175

LIBRARY OF DAVIDSON COLLEGE

Books on regular loan may be checked out for **two weeks**. Books must be presented at the Circulation Desk in order to be renewed.

A fine is charged after date due.

Special books are subject to special regulations at the discretion of the library staff.

MAR. 10.1986
4-10-89 FW
JAN 1 3 1993

DEC. -9.1989